LEG

Through The Eyes of the Warrior

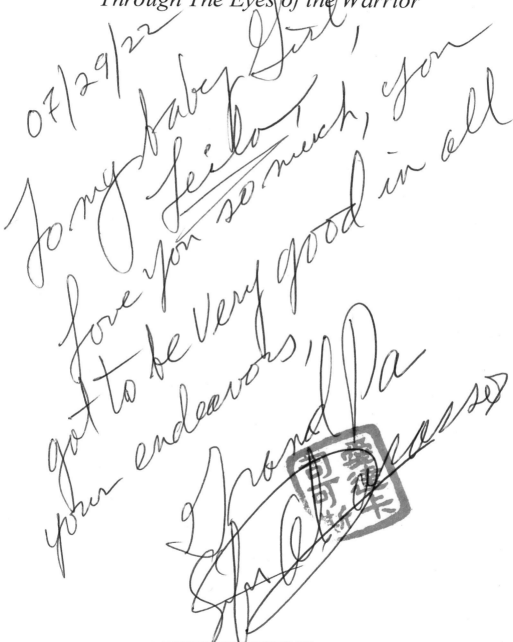

07/29/22

To my Baby Girl,

I feel I love you so much, you got to be very good in all your endeavors,

Grand Pa

LEGACY

Through The Eyes of the Warrior

Al Dacascos

Library of Congress Cataloging-in-Publication Data
Al Dacascos, 1942-
LEGACY: Through the Eyes of the Warrior

ISBN – 978-1-937884-17-8

1. Martial Arts. 2. Self-Help. 3. Philosophy. I. Title

Kaizen Quest Publishing

Acknowledgements

Foremost, I want to acknowledge and thank everyone who helped to make this book a reality with their time, skills, and encouragement. Our 'ohana are the reasons we live. To all my biological 'ohana and hana'i 'ohana, I say Mahalo nui loa kakou!

I greatly appreciate everyone at Kaizen Quest Publishing and Dr. Bohdi Sanders for all the work and professional courtesies extended to me. I also want to thank Dr. Karyn Spencer, who initially started this project with me, and gave me her blessings to continue on without her when her health prevented her from continuing.

I want to thank all of my children, my sons Craig, Mark and Benjamin, and my daughters, Vanessa, Jaclyn, Nikki, Christie, and Jadyn who all continue to inspire me to finish my life for them and their children having to hold in their hands the book and life of their father and grandpa.

I want to thank my best friends Al Dela Cruz, Ron Lew, Birgit Preu, and my favorite cousin, Justine Malalis Dacoscos Gronwald to whom I am indebted for helping me jog my mind and recall some long-lost events which were buried deep in my mind.

And a special thank you to my girlfriend, Toni Amaranto, who has relentlessly endured my writer's brain-dead moments and encouraged me to push on when I felt like putting my head in the sand. Also, I want to thank my pastor, Norman Nakanishi, who has been my confident for so many years. He knew many secrets never shared with anyone else but him, and now shared with all who would like to read them.

I also want to thank my men's Bible study group from Grace Bible Church. We have shared many of our less than happy moments together. Your encouragement is priceless. I must say that when I get into my less than human modes, I thank God for being there and helping me through my walk through the wilderness of confusion and the many challenges and curveballs that life throws at us.

I also want to thank those who came against me during my many travels. It seems comical for me to be acknowledging and thanking those that have been on the opposite end of the spectrum, but without them, this book would not be the truest account of my life.

Again I say, Mahalo nui loa kakou!

Endorsements for LEGACY

I have known Master Al Dacascos, and have been his friend, for over 50 years. I am so proud of what he has accomplished and achieved in his remarkable life.

In the early years, when we both were competing, there were always a few qualities, which Al possessed, that I admired. First, he was the only Kung Fu stylist who competed in open competition and who was highly successful. He was both stylish and possessed great skills, along with a lot of athletic talent. He was courageous and a complete martial artist, both as a fighter and a kata competitor.

What he has accomplished, and what he has contributed to the martial arts, more than compensates for what he has received. He has always been, not only a shining example to others, but has motivated and inspired thousands of people around the world with his skills and his character.

He has shown tremendous scope in his creativity and his imagination as a competitor, teacher, innovator, and practitioner, for over half a century.

The story of his life, with all its joys and frustrations, is a testament to his courage, persistence, and drive to succeed and leave a positive legacy behind. His life is an amazing example of the human spirit, dedication, passion, and excitement, not only to find oneself, but to continually grow and improve, and to be of service to his family, community, and country.

I highly recommend this book for its unbelievable story, and also for its life lessons. It is filled with wonderful examples of love and courage, mixed with life's tragedies and disappointments. There is something for everyone to enjoy in this great book.

I am so proud and blessed to call Al, not only a friend, but a martial arts warrior-brother.

Mike Stone
Shodan Shorin-Ryu Karate

Mike Stone finished his career undefeated in competition. He is a national, international and world karate champion and a two-time inductee in the Black Belt Hall of Fame. He was the Fighter of the Year in 1971 and the Instructor of the Year in1994. Today, he is an actor, producer, writer, and director of martial arts movies.

Endorsements for LEGACY

I've known Sifu Al Dacascos since 1967. I met Al through Mel Lee, who was his student and my friend, at his home in San Leandro. He had peaked my interest as I was learning Kung Fu from Sifu Paul Eng (Ngok Noy Ng). Sifu Al invited me to drop by his school and see what Kajukenbo was all about. After I asked permission from Sifu Paul, I attended one of his classes.

I expected to see a demonstration, but Sifu Al had a different agenda. He was interested in seeing how I fought. He asked me, "Do you spar?"

I replied, "What is spar?"

So, I ended up sparring with his brown belt, Mel Abero. I was quite surprised, and pleased, that I defended myself fairly well. And that was the beginning of his and Malia's journey to learn Kung fu from Paul Eng and then later from Sifu Wong Jack Man, as well as being introduced to Raymond Wong and Kam Yuen. We have become close friends in the 50+ years since then. I enjoy traveling with him to Germany and his yearly WHKD gatherings.

To write of one's life, with all the unforeseen chaos, the hardships, the endless challenges, as well as the love, family, friends and of course, his passion for the martial arts is itself, a daunting task.

To tell it like it is – the good, the bad and the ugly, as well as the heartfelt experiences, takes a lot of courage. Sifu Al has written it all and has openly shared his life. Sifu Al's life has touched many, many people in many ways. You will definitely be moved when reading this book.

The stories of his life are told from his gut. There is no "pulling punches" in this book! This is a tell-all book! Of course, I wouldn't expect anything less from Sifu Al. Enjoy his journey. I have and I still am. This is a great book!

Ron Lew

Ron Lew is Senior Grand Master in Cacoy Canete's Doce Pares System. He is also the founder and a grandmaster in Tibetan Wave Whip System. Ron also founded of the Tibetan Arts – Martial Arts and Healing Center. He also serves as a senior advisor to the Wun Hop Kuen Do International Association.

Endorsements for LEGACY

It has been a blessing for me to have had the opportunity to get to know Sifu Al Dacascos, both as a martial artist and a friend. From the very first time that I met Sifu Al in person, I knew that I was talking to a master. He has a grasp on both the martial arts and life in general that very few people in the world have. I was instantly impressed by the scope of his knowledge and by the heartfelt way that he teaches the martial arts, martial arts philosophy, and his philosophy of life.

I can say, without any doubt whatsoever, that Sifu Al is the greatest martial arts teacher I have ever trained with. Many teachers know their art, that is to be expected, but Sifu Al Dacascos not only knows his art, but he knows exactly how to teach it. He is not only a master martial artist, but he is a master teacher and a master philosopher. This is a combination that I have found to be very rare.

In *LEGACY*, Sifu Al has given you a rare gift, an inside look into his life from his childhood up until today. This is truly a book that will touch your heart. It is one of those rare books that will hold your attention all the way through, even if you are not a martial artist.

As you read this book, you will find that it will take you on an emotional journey. You will laugh, cry, smile, and be engrossed in the amazing life of one of the pioneers of the martial arts world. This is an inspirational story of success and perseverance.

I found his life to be both highly entertaining and gripping. *Legacy* is definitely a page turner that you will not want to put down! This is an inspirational story that will bring tears to your eyes and motivate you to push through all of the challenges in your life.

I am honored to call Sifu Al Dacascos one of my best friends. His wisdom has been gained through both the challenges and successes of a life lived to the fullest, and he freely shares his wisdom with us in this amazing book. This is a book that everyone should read!

Bohdi Sanders, Ph.D.

Dr. Sanders is the award-winning, bestselling author of *Modern Bushido: Living a Life of Excellence*, *Men of the Code*, and *Warrior Wisdom 365*. He is also the CEO of Kaizen Quest Publishing and is a 5th degree black belt in Shotokan Karate. Bohdi has been a martial artist for over 32 years.

Endorsements for LEGACY

Sifu Al Dacascos is one of my idols. I just recently returned from the Philippines where I was doing a movie with his son Mark. Sifu Al choreographed all of my fight scenes.

When he showed me the moves with the Escrima sticks, I was blown away with his remarkable speed, power and effectiveness. He is easily the fastest martial artist that I have ever worked with. Sifu Al Dacascos is simply amazing.

This book is a must read for everyone, martial artist and those who have never even considered getting into the martial arts. It is motivational and inspirational. I highly endorse it. *LEGACY* should be in every martial artist's library!

Cynthia Rothrock

Cynthia Rothrock was the undefeated World Karate Champion in both forms and weapons competitions from 1981 to 1985. She is one of a very small number of individuals to be inducted into both the Black Belt Hall of Fame and Inside Kung Fu Hall of Fame. She is also a well-known actress in martial arts movies.

Endorsements for LEGACY

Al Dacascos is one of the most respected martial artists in the world. He and his family have helped spread the spirit of the arts to many generations of practitioners worldwide. I am honored to have worked with him, and his son Mark, on Mark's movie, *Showdown in Manila.*

They embody the best character traits which the study of the martial arts encourages and strengthens. I am confident that *LEGACY* will teach and inspire others to accomplish their life goals.

We can all benefit by learning about and understanding Sifu Al's struggles and successes! Thank you, Grandmaster Dacascos, for taking your time to help others by writing this amazing book.

Don "The Dragon" Wilson

Don "The Dragon" Wilson is unquestionably, the greatest kickboxing champion of all time. He is the only kick-boxer to win 11 world titles in three weight divisions (light-heavyweight, super-light-heavyweight, and cruiserweight) and six sanctioning organizations (WKA, STAR, KCIK , ISKA, PKD, AND IKF). Along the way, he defeated 11 other world champions, 12 number one contenders, and 15 champions on 4 continents. He is also an actor and has appeared in several martial arts movies.

Endorsements for LEGACY

One of the giants in martial arts, Grandmaster Al Dacascos has written his memoirs. He is undoubtedly one of the most complex and awesome fighters of our time, with a logic and talent second to none.

His book, *LEGACY: Through the Eyes of a Warrior*, is a much awaited, first person account of his life. It covers the gamut – his failed marriages, the loves of his life, his bout with depression, which almost took his life, and the highs and lows of this gentle, yet fierce warrior, who rose to the top of his game.

This book celebrates the life of one of Kajukenbo's finest and the founder of Wun Hop Kuen Do, the Hawaiian legend known as Grandmaster Al Dacascos!

This is a book that should grace the library of every serious martial artist. I highly recommend this book.

GM Frank E. Sanchez

Professor Sanchez is the founder of the San Jitsu System which is Guam's first internationally recognized martial art style. He holds black belts in Judo, Jiu-Jitsu, and Karate, and a Red Sash in Jing Jow Pai Kung-Fu.He is also World Head of Family Sokeship Council. Grandmaster Sanchez has been featured in many martial arts magazines including Black Belt, Inside Kung-Fu, Kung Fu Illustrated, Taekwondo Times, and many others.

Endorsements for LEGACY

GM Dacascos is a pioneer, an innovator, and a martial arts legend. I have known Al for 40 years. I first met Al during the golden age of martial arts in America, the 1960's. The only way that I can describe him is to say that he is a martial technician and a philosopher of the highest caliber.

He has been a source of inspiration and motivation for millions of devotees globally. I am proud to call him my friend and brother. Sifu Al Dacascos is a prime example of unlimited human potential. His book is an integral part of martial arts history and should be included in every martial arts library. Whether you are a martial artist or not, you will find this book inspirational.

Ron Van Clief

Ron Van Clief is a 5-time world Karate and Kung Fu champion and a 15-time All American Champion. He is a 10th degree red belt in the Chinese Goju System and is the author of 8 books. He has also worked in over 300 movies as a member of the Screen Actors Guild. He is also a retired police officer, a retired marine, and served in Viet Nam.

Endorsements for LEGACY

There is a beauty in humility and an even greater beauty in brokenness, for God is closest to those who are broken. Al Dacascos' story embodies such a journey.

While he has known the glory of extraordinary mountain tops, it is his honesty about navigating the deepest valleys that connects his journey to our own. Read on, and as you do, be open to absorb fresh hope for tomorrow and the promise of redemption from He who truly holds our future.

Norman Nakanishi

Norman Nakanishi is the founding Pastor at Grace Bible Church.

Endorsements for LEGACY

Al Dacascos has been one of my most admired and respected martial artist friends for almost fifty years, and although I believe I can say that we are now long-time trusted friends, I am still flattered whenever he spends time with me. I first met him at one of Ed Parker's Long Beach International Championships in the 60s, although I had heard of him for years prior to that.

He was best known as an outstanding competitor in forms, winning almost every event he entered with his impressive mastery of complex forms. Later, he would attend my events and usually win them in both form and free-fighting competition. I was surprised when I finally discovered how well he could compete in free-fighting, and I was always proud to include his well-known name among my tournament's winners. He had astoundingly polished talent and reflexes!

We have never lived close to one another; the closest being when he was living in Denver and I was living in Albuquerque. My first "bonding" with him was in Denver, and he might not even remember, when after one of his tournaments we went to his house. During the visit we had a great time discussing local martial arts and lots of laughs by punching out candle flames.

In 2008 he accepted my invitation to come to Mexico City to present at one of our yearly seminars. He was joined by Bill Wallace. There were several hundred in attendance at the seminar from all over Mexico. As part of the weekend event, the two presented a very well-received seminar to a large group of martial arts practitioners.

Although basically a Kajukenbo seminar, we were invited to present a seminar for a Karate group. On our arrival they formed two long lines, one line facing the other, perfectly white almost glistening uniforms and military attitudes, leaving a long passageway in the center through which we made our entrance. It was extremely impressive. Al muttered under his breath as we walked up that entryway, "my God!" This hit me as hysterical, and in this serious moment I laughed almost uncontrollably as we marched up to the front. I'm still embarrassed and humiliated about this – thanks to Al.

Sifu Al is one of the few TRUE living Grand Masters. Far too many of us in Kajukenbo have the title of "Grand Master," but less than "a handful" are authentically verifiable Grand Masters deserving of the title. Nevertheless, rather than use the esteemed title of Senior Grandmaster, he prefers to only be called *Sifu,* or teacher. He is the "teacher's teacher", and possesses seemingly limitless historical and technical information and technique, spanning the entire history of Kajukenbo and more. Not only this, but his wisdom and counsel are often sought when there is a need.

He has generously shared his techniques and knowledge with me and my students both in the U.S. and in Mexico. He not only remembers almost everything he has ever learned, but as an innovator, he has developed his own branch of Kajukenbo.

Sifu Dacascos has competed in tournaments all over the world, his Wun Hop Kuen Do system is taught in many countries. He designed the most common internationally used Kajukenbo logo; his picture has graced the cover of innumerable martial arts magazines and has been featured in many movies.

His students include countless champions; his German team is outstanding, and he is constantly working for his continued development and the development of Kajukenbo. He has most likely accomplished more for Kajukenbo than anyone else. Furthermore, he continues to evolve as a technician, not resting on his laurels. At his seminars one might learn knife techniques, at the next seminar gun defense, then escrima, then sticky hands; teaching each art with complete mastery... and the list goes on.

I am proud to be a part of this book about my friend, Al Dacascos, Kajukenbo's "International Icon."

Sam Allred, S.G.M.

Sam is the founder of Jukensa Kajukenbo Mexico and is also the author of seven books. He is a member of the Black Belt Hall of Fame and is also listed in *Who's Who in the Martial Arts*.

Foreword

We were in Hamburg, Germany, in the St. Pauli District, in 1980. The air was thick, warm, and smelled of sweat. The sound of heavy breathing and grunts filled the room. Then, all of a sudden, SMACK! A round-kick hit me in the stomach. My t-shirt stuck to my skin. I was 16 years-old, and one of 30 athletic men and women who were enduring body-toughening drills in my father's advanced fighting class. In pairs, we held our hands behind our backs, alternating between throwing a kick at our partner's stomach and receiving one. It stung, and it hurt, but I loved it.

A tall, well-built stranger in his mid-30's, dressed in jeans and a green bomber jacket, swaggered into the middle of our training room and stood there. The other students and I stopped practicing and wondered what the heck this guy wanted. We sensed danger!

My father, calm, with his smile and aloha spirit, walked toward the man and asked him how he could help him. The man looked my father up and down and then asked if he was Sifu Al Dacascos. My father said he was.

The man, now with a grin on his face, said loud enough for everyone to hear, "I want to challenge you." This man was either completely bonkers or one lethal fighting machine. Possibly both! And it made me very nervous.

Over the last decade, my father had proven himself in the ring, and on the street, as an exceptional fighter, and a lot of martial artists all over the world knew of him. He told his students that there were always people out there who were faster, stronger, and smarter. That's why we needed to train hard.

This stranger obviously felt he had a chance to take my father down in a street fight. What if he was the one, the guy that my father told us about – faster, stronger, smarter? What if he injured my father, or even worse, killed him?

I wanted to fight this man first. I probably couldn't beat him, but at least I felt I could soften him up a bit and help protect my teacher and father. It was the right thing to do. Isn't that what we see in all the Kung Fu movies? Students always fight first.

"Sifu, please let me fight him," shouted several other senior students, before I could even open my mouth. I joined in and asked to be allowed to fight this stranger.

My father thanked us, but told us to sit down on the floor, against the walls and give them some room. We sat and no one said a word. The man and my father stood a few paces away from each other. My heart was beating so hard that I could hear it in my head. Adrenalin pumping through my veins, the students and I were mesmerized by the situation. It was a Kung Fu movie in real life, a challenge between some lone, macho, bad-ass stranger, and our teacher, my father, Sifu Al Dacascos.

The fight was epic! And what I learned from it was life-changing. This was just one of the many intense moments I experienced with my father.

I love him with all of my heart. He was my first hero and my first martial arts teacher. He is the best example of what I want, and don't want, to be. Read *LEGACY: Through the Eyes of the Warrior* and experience the roots of his tree and discover the journey that took my father from a young Hawaiian boy to an internationally known martial arts master.

Mark Dacascos

Introduction

When I look back on my life, I realize how blessed I am to be alive. I have wondered, time and time again, how in the world I survived the last seventy something years, but I now know that it was only by the grace of almighty God that I am still here to tell my story, and quite a story it is. Some people watch movies for entertainment, and some people's lives are an adventure movie in and of themselves.

I have wanted to put all of my many experiences, both good and bad, down in writing, for many years, but somehow, I never got around to it. But I now realize the truism of the often heard maxim that everything happens as it should. I have spent many years in meditation and reflection, and I now know that this is finally the right time to publish my memoirs.

Dozens and dozens of articles and stories have been written about me. People have read and believed many different things about me, some true and many untrue. My face has graced the cover of over 100 magazines and many think that they know me, but only a handful of people really know the whole story or who I really am.

At 73 years young, and after surviving many amazing experiences and many dangerous struggles, I am finally ready to tell my story. It is time. It is time to set the record straight about the numerous misconceptions that so many people have about my life. It is time to share my triumphs and my disappointments. It is time to share the truth about my life, both in my martial arts journey and in my personal life. It is time to share how God literally saved my life and has given me a peace that eluded me for most of my life.

My son, Mark, wisely told me that he believes this book will purge my soul and bring me serenity on a spiritual level, something that has eluded me through the years. And I believe he is right. In writing this autobiography, I have fondly remembered people and events that I haven't thought about in years. I have relived the pain, the love, and the triumphs of a life lived to the fullest, but not always to contentment. This process has almost been like mentally watching the movie of my life – the love and heartbreaks, joy and sadness, trials and victories, trust and betrayals, and finally, salvation and peace.

Maya Angelo stated, "There is no greater agony than bearing an untold story inside you." As I have worked to write this book, I have found that this is where my agony lies. I would love for my memoirs to say that I have been totally victorious in life, a wise Sifu who led a perfect life, but that is not the truth. The truth is that I am not a perfect man. I was not a perfect husband, father, son, or leader. As painful as it is for me to admit that, I want this book to be a factual account of my life. Therefore, I will include the good, the bad, and the ugly. This book is not meant to demean or point a finger at anyone in my life; it is merely a recounting of the events of my life, to the best of my recollection. It is my life laid open for all to see.

I remember when I was in middle school in Hawaii. Back then I wanted to become a fighter pilot so I could leave our little island and travel the world over. Well, I didn't become a fighter pilot, but I did become a fighter, and a very successful fighter. I am known as one of the great martial arts fighters, and fought with many of the greats such as Joe Lewis, Chuck Norris, and Bill Wallace, just to name a few.

I have had the honor of knowing many great martial artists such as Bruce Lee, who was a friend of mine and an inseparable part of my story. In addition, I have developed friendships with many other martial arts masters who are not as notable. Their names are not recognized by most, but they are just as great. They are the unsung heroes of the martial arts world.

I also have been blessed to travel the world and see many amazing places and meet a great number of wonderful people along the way. But now I have come full circle, back to my roots, and live near the home where I grew up in the Palama Settlement area of the island of O'ahu. I have lived in many places around the world, but Hawaii is my home. My roots are here and so are the roots of my family.

I still travel frequently and do seminars all over the world, as well as share my testimony about how God literally saved my life one dark night when I was at my lowest point. I maintain close associations with my schools in Germany and elsewhere around the world. It warms my heart to see the students who have immerged from my humble beginning to be a part of my martial arts lineage. I consider my students and teachers as a part of my "ohana," my family.

I developed my own expression of martial arts known as Wun Hop Kuen Do. Wun Hop Kuen Do was developed from the Kajukenbo system and it is important for me to share the reasons I felt led to create Wun Hop Kuen Do and why my life took such a path.

Martial arts have been my life. I think that God gives each of us a special gift and that gift is what we were meant to do. And it is our job to do our best to perfect this gift during our time on this earth. I have strived to perfect my skills and my art. Over the years, I have been honored to be the recipient of many martial arts awards, and I have been inducted into many martial arts halls of fame including:

Black Belt magazine
Inside Kung-fu Magazine
The Soke Council of Grand Masters
The Living Legends Martial Arts Hall of Fame
Mike Stone's Golden Fist Award (the Oscar's of the martial arts)

In addition, I have been featured on the covers of many magazines including:

Black Belt Magazine
Inside Kung-fu Magazine
Professional Karate Magazine
Official Karate Magazine
Judo
Kempo/Kempo
Kajukenbo and more

I have had writers of martial arts magazines and books refer to me as, "Mozart in Motion" and "The Vince Lombardi of Martial Arts." I have been more than humbled by such titles. The world sees me as one of the great martial artists, but those who know me best realize that I have been a guarded man – tormented, conflicted, complex, and challenged.

My history includes tales of street fights, the Karate Wars, the Chinese gang wars of the Bay Area, and the internal political struggles within the martial arts that defined my destiny. I have also included survival strategies that I have learned from my experiences, some sage advice for all of those who read my story, and finally my journey both away from and back to my Lord and Savior Jesus Christ.

I have found that every person needs to learn how to survive in dangerous times and in adverse situations. Adversity introduces you to the person that you truly are. It is easy to be magnanimous in victory, but it is in defeat where we learn the most about ourselves. I have learned the truth in the quote by Tim Duncan, "Good, better, best; never let it rest; until the good gets better and the better gets best!"

When all is said and done, this book will embody my life. I will include many entertaining stories, all true to the best of my recollection. You will get to join me in my journey as I put down on paper the memories of my life as a martial artist, a husband, and a father. I will recount everything from my humble beginnings in Hawaii to the pinnacle of success in the martial arts, from my many loves, to my heartbreaking failures.

I am not writing this as some great "master," but as simply a man, a human being who lived a life, a life with some extraordinary moments and some heartbreaks. In fact, I don't like it when people call me a "grandmaster." In my opinion, the one true master is Jesus, and I would never want to put myself on the same level as my Lord and Savior.

I have been a son, a brother, a husband, a student, a father, a teacher, and a friend. I grew up in a very special historical time in the Hawaiian Islands and started from a very humble beginning. Yet, I somehow managed to rise to the pinnacle of success as one of the most exceptional competitors during the heyday of sports karate in the 1960's and 1970's. Conversely, I was tormented internally by this gift, my passion, and my lifestyle, so much so, that my despair reached the point of my own attempted suicide.

My passions and my stubbornness have been my yin and yang, my light and my darkness, and perhaps the reason that I am still alive today. Being passionate about your calling in life, and disciplined enough to follow your dreams, will bring you both great joy and sorrow. But ultimately, you only have two choices – be passionate about your life or simply walk through life half asleep. I have always preferred to live a passionate life.

Do I have regrets? Absolutely! I have had regrets, disappointments, and the thrill of the "glory days." But in the end, I am simply a man, a man who has been fortunate enough to live a full life, surrounded by friends and family. I have been a man who has reached the top of his profession and also a man who has found the real meaning of life.

Out of all that I have achieved in life, my proudest achievements are my children and my grandchildren. I feel overwhelming love for each and every one of them! As the great John Wooden taught, "The greatest profession in the world is parenting." My family, along with God, holds a special place in my heart!

I, in no way, want to be disrespectful to my parents or any member of my family in writing this book. However, because I want this autobiography to be a true account of my life, I will be revealing many personal stories from my past, including some painful events from my personal family history. I will go into detail on some of these events, and others, for obvious reasons, I will only reveal portions.

I came from a very loving family, albeit very unique. My parents gave all they could to my family. At times I didn't understand this, but now, in the wisdom that comes with age, I can see how all the pieces of the crazy jigsaw puzzle of my life fit together. Oh how I love the Hawaii of my childhood – the simple times and sweet memories.

All in all, I am revealing an unedited life. The events which I write about in this book are all true to the best of my memory. Because of the sensitive nature of some of the events, some names have been changed. I cannot possibly mention or pay homage to every student, teacher, and person who influenced my life in one book, but you can be sure that I remember each and every one.

It is my hope that, by being so open about both the struggles and the successes in my life, I will enable young people, especially in Hawaii, to believe in their own aspirations. I want to motivate and inspire people through my personal story. I want to get across to you that every person has a dark side and a light side, we are all humans. I want to encourage you to follow your bliss, wherever it might lead. Finally, I want everyone to see how God loves you, even when you are at your lowest point.

I am a better man than I was when I was twenty, or even last year, or last week. I have made mistakes, but I have learned from those mistakes. It has been said that a wise man learns from his mistakes, but a wiser man learns from the mistakes of other wise men. I have learned much from both my mistakes and my successes. Each day, I hope to be a better man than I was the day before. I hope that you will also learn from my successes, my mistakes, and my life as a whole.

Some of it's magic, some of it is tragic,
but I've had a good life anyway.
Jimmy Buffett

Mahalo nui loa kakou!
Sifu Al

The Circle of Influence

Observation precedes wisdom.
Only he who can at first see
can at last understand.
Chinese Proverb

Before I get into the story of my life, I think that it is important for you to understand that everyone has a circle of influence. This fact will help you comprehend where someone is coming from. It will help you understand the demise or destiny of an individual.

By going in a reverse order, essentially, retracing someone's steps back through his life, you are able to see his character development, how his habits formed, where his values and beliefs come from, why he developed as he did, and why someone thinks like he does. It is the circle of influence which has made him.

In life, you are influenced by many different factors. From these factors, your circle of influence is formed. You must be aware of your influences and how they have directed your life or set you on a certain path. If you are not careful, your circle of influence will spin out of control and take you down a path that you really don't want to travel.

The good news is that you can control your circle of influence. Make the choice to create a positive life and environment. When you do this, you change your destiny. Moderate to drastic changes of your destiny may occur when sudden trauma or shock occurs after 16 years of age. Death to loved ones, divorce, moving to unfamiliar environments, accidents, or a sudden change of environment are just a few examples.

You are about to read the story of my life, with insights into my own circle of influence. You will have insight into the people and things which have molded my life into what it has been, and what it is today. Everyone has a circle of life; you are about to get an inside view of the people, places, and events which have formed my circle of influence up until today.

Sifu Al Dacascos

The Circle of Influence

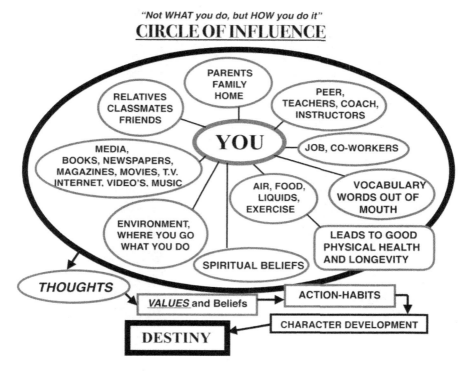

"Not WHAT you do, but HOW you do it"

CIRCLE OF INFLUENCE

PARENTS FAMILY HOME

RELATIVES CLASSMATES FRIENDS

PEER, TEACHERS, COACH, INSTRUCTORS

YOU

MEDIA, BOOKS, NEWSPAPERS, MAGAZINES, MOVIES, T.V. INTERNET, VIDEO'S, MUSIC

JOB, CO-WORKERS

AIR, FOOD, LIQUIDS, EXERCISE

VOCABULARY WORDS OUT OF MOUTH

ENVIRONMENT, WHERE YOU GO WHAT YOU DO

LEADS TO GOOD PHYSICAL HEALTH AND LONGEVITY

SPIRITUAL BELIEFS

THOUGHTS

VALUES and Beliefs

ACTION-HABITS

CHARACTER DEVELOPMENT

DESTINY

In life, you are influenced by many different factors. From these factors in **YOUR CIRCLE of INFLUENCE,** come thoughts, values, beliefs, actions, habits, character development, and in the end, you will become your own destiny. Be aware of how you are influenced. You can control **YOUR CIRCLE OF INFLUENCE.** Make the choice in your life to create a positive life and environment.

MODERATE TO DRASTIC CHANGE OF DESTINY MAY OCCUR WHEN SUDDEN TRAUMA OR SCHOCK OCCURS AFTER 16YEARS OF AGE. DEATH TO LOVE ONES, DIVORCE, MOVING TO UNFAMILIAR ENVIRONMENT, ACCIDENTS OR SUDDEN CHARGE OF EVENTS IN FAMILY, TO THE NEIGHBORHOOD, CITY, STATE, COUNTRY OR WORLD ARE JUST A FEW.

" *Observation precedes Wisdom. Only he who can at first see can at least understand"* -Chinese Proverb"
"*He heeds discipline shows the way of life, but whoever ignores correction leads others astray"* - Proverbs 10:17

He who heeds discipline shows the way of life,
but whoever ignores correction leads others astray.
Proverbs 10:17

LEGACY

Al Dacascos

Chapter 1

The Early Years

A journey of 1000 miles begins with a single step.
Lao Tzu

I was born into a turbulent time in history, the fall of 1942, the Year of the Horse, in Hilo, Hawaii. At that time, Hawaii was still a territory and not yet a state. My parents, Nancy Candida Salba and Benjamin Jose Dacoscos, were not wealthy people, but they worked hard to get by. 1942 was not a good year for Japanese Americans, as many of them would eventually end up in internment camps during World War II.

Two years before the war started, my mother had given birth to my older brother, whom I would never have the opportunity to meet, but who I would later be named after. She gave birth to Albert Sunday, but Albert died two weeks later of pneumonia. So when I was born, my mother gave me his name, Albert.

I guess during the war, Albert must have been a very popular name, as many boys during this era were named Albert. To this day, when I hear someone named Albert, I know that he must be an older guy, born somewhere around the 1940's.

I always hated that name. Growing up, there was a comedy team called Abbott and Costello. My mom had a very heavy Filipino accent and when she got angry and started to talk fast, she didn't pronounce my name correctly – it always came out sounding like Abbott.

Unfortunately for me, that mistake in pronunciation caught on in the neighborhood and the other kids constantly teased me, calling me Abbott and laughing. Maybe that was my first nudge toward an interest in the martial arts, because I got into a lot of fights about *"Who's on First."* This continued until I finally learned to spell and realized that my name was Albert, and not Abbott.

But that was simply the way it was growing up in the territory of Hawaii in the 1940's. The Pidgin English, around Hawaii at that time, was so heavy that sometimes people made no sense at all; we simply had to learn to read body language and the tonality of the voice to figure out what someone was trying to say.

I never liked the name Albert, even after I stopped being called

Abbott, so I shortened it to Al. From that point on, I decided that my name would be Al, and later, in the mid 1960's, I ended up changing my last name as well. This was not due to a dislike of my last name, but rather it was because most people seemed to get confused when it came to my last name.

Once I started becoming successful in the martial arts world, misprints and mispronunciations of my name became rampant. Several martial arts magazines on the East Coast of the United States listed my names as Al Damascus, Al Dekoskis, Al De Costa, Al Decascos, and even mistook me for another black belt fighter at the time, Al Valasco.

Both Black Belt magazine and Inside Kung-Fu magazine called me Al Dacascos, and from that point on, the name stuck. I became Al Dacascos. My original family name is now heard only in Hawaii, where some individuals call me by my birth name even today, but I still don't like it.

Martial arts are ingrained in every part of me, even my name. In some early Spanish military manuals from the 1500's regarding military warfare, particularly warfare with swords and lances, the term for helmets, as in military armor, was "cascos." The plural of it would be "des cascos." As the Spanish colonization of the Philippines expanded, and the language was absorbed, it's most likely that the Visayan tongue pronounced it "Da Coscos."

By changing it back to "Cascos," I have simply gone back to my original roots. Turns out, my family bloodline may have been connected to the martial arts for hundreds of years before my grandfather, who emigrated from the Visayan Islands, in the Philippines, to Hawaii 110 years ago.

History shows that some of my family members were highly skilled pirates around the seas and straights of the Philippine Islands. I guess this also explains some of the fighting skills, and love for blades that my family has.

In addition to martial arts, the Visayan culture also has a long history of music. Music is in my blood, just like martial arts. My father was a big band musician in Hawaii during the 1940's. He played in a band called the Fil-Am Band and prior to his passing on May 12, 1957, he was well known in Hawaii.

My mother served as a Red Cross nurse during World War II, and after that, she held a job as a dress designer and seamstress until her passing in 2002.

My first introduction to the Filipino martial arts came while I was staying with my grandparents in the sugarcane camp on Kaua'i,

Hawaii. Sugarcane plantation workers were segregated into ethnic groups in the camps. Each culture had their own camp. My grandfather's camp was called Camp Seven, where the majority of a certain group of Filipinos from a specific island in the Philippines were placed together.

While staying with my grandfather, I would watch Grandpa and his crew practicing the Filipino fighting arts in the morning before work. I found this style of Filipino fighting very interesting as I watched the click-clack of Bolo knives as my grandfather, Ernestacio Salba, practiced in the early morning hours with all the best eskrimados before heading out to the sugarcane fields.

One early morning, while watching my grandfather practice his martial art, Eskrima, I also discovered match sticks. I was amazed when I discovered that I could make fire simply by striking the matches against any rough surface, and as boys will do, I enjoyed my new found skill immensely. But it wasn't long before my infatuation with matches got me into big trouble.

I was watching the men practice one morning from the bedroom in the camp, when I lit a match and accidentally caught the bed sheets on fire. The smoke filled up the bedroom and my grandpa came rushing into the house with his band of brothers. They put out the fire before things got out of hand, and then, for the first time, I felt the sting of an unbending rattan stick.

I discovered firsthand how fast a rattan stick could move and exactly what it felt like all over my body. Of course, it was not full contact, but it was more than enough to let me know that he could do some serious damage with that stick, if he so desired. From that day on, I never lit a match near a bed again! Pain has a funny way of making you remember a well-taught lesson. Unfortunately for me, this would not be the only lesson I needed to cure my overactive imagination and abundance of mischievousness.

But, being the boy that I was, I could not resist getting into mischief. At night, my friends and I would go around the camps causing mayhem. I fondly remember sneaking up to an old Filipino man's house with rackety screen doors on it. We would take dried chicken feet and scratch the screen door with them, just to hear the screams from inside of the house.

The people in the camps were very superstitious of the urban legend of the Stone Man that lived in the cane fields among a mountain of piled up, gigantic rocks. The Stone Man supposedly came out at night and terrorized the population of the camp.

However, as with everything in this life, our karma comes back to us. We were sleeping at my grandparents' house one night when my brother, Ben, started screaming and woke up the entire house. When questioned about what happened, he said that he saw a tall man at the window, looking inside the house. He described the man as having glowing red eyes.

None of us slept a wink for the rest of that night. The next morning, Grandpa told us that one of us kids must have done something wrong in the camp, and that the Stone Man was looking for us. That ended our Stone Man pranks around the camps for good!

Grandpa Salba died soon after that in 1948. I was six years old. Although I was still very young at the time, memories of this man and his skill with a knife and rattan stick never faded from my mind. His casket was brought into the house and placed in the parlor, what we now call the living room. Now I understand the term funeral parlor, just another way of saying funeral home.

As tradition would have it, Grandpa's shoes were put into the coffin, but not on his feet. The Filipinos believe his spirit would be walking around the house that evening and that it would be better if he walked around without shoes so that he would not scare the kids.

Although my grandpa was gone, the camps still held some intrigue for me. The Japanese and the Chinese both had their own camps at that time. Most of the bosses in the fields were Portuguese. They lived in better camps with nicer homes, but everyone got along fairly well, despite the segregation.

The Portuguese brought their musical instruments like the ukulele and the guitar with them to Hawaii around 1878, which are now both recognized and integrated as a part of the Hawaiian culture and music scene. I can still remember hearing that very distinct music throughout the camps at the end of the work day.

Neighborhood friends and I would venture off to visit the camps often. When we visited the Japanese camps, we watched them practice the art of Judo and Jujitsu. When we visited the Chinese camps, we watched them practice Kung Fu. We watched and learned, and the more we watched, the greater our interest became.

Most of the time, I ran around barefoot or in beach "slippas." Hawaii was not densely populated then, as it is now. There were lots of empty fields filled with tall elephant grass. I don't know if that is really what that grass is called, but that is what the kids called it.

We would go out and play war in the fields, using large cardboard boxes to make our camps. In 1950 the Korean War started. Between the camps, we would get empty cans that were open at one end, punch a hole at the other end, and run a long string to another can being held by a friend. These were our walkie-talkies.

We used some of the cans, especially the taller ones, to tape to the bottom of our feet, so we could be six inches taller and have an advantage over our enemy. One day, while playing army, I yelled out like I was shot. We always did that when we were playing, so no one thought anything about it, and my friends ignored me.

But this time I was really bleeding. I had stepped on an empty can that didn't have the top totally removed and cut the inside of my right ankle, leaving a gash three inches long. This was my official badge of honor, my war scar.

We would run and play far from home, without any fear of real danger. Of course we were young and adventurous, and we did find our share of troubles. But those were good days. We could go hiking up the edge of the rivers and the water was clear, clean and drinkable.

If we got hungry, we would pick mountain apples, mangoes, or papayas and eat our fill. We would suck honey from hibiscus flowers. And, if we were really desperate, or especially daring, we would shoplift candy cigarettes from the grocery store and go play gangsters.

At times, we would take advantage of the food and offerings left at the headstones of the Buddhist and Shinto cemeteries, making our own picnic at our favorite waterfall swimming hole about a half mile away.

We didn't have much, but we made do with what we had, and we had fun. We made our own slingshots using the "Y" from guava trees, rubber bands, and horse shoe nails. Then we would go "hunt" birds and cats. Sometimes, we would roll up paper in the shape of horse shoe nails and shoot them at unsuspecting passersby, running away as fast as we could when they figured out what just jumped up and bit them on the leg or back.

Those were the good days. During that time, kids went outside and played, using their imaginations to create games and to find adventure on their own. Today, most kids are stuck inside all day and their playtime consists of some kind of electronics. As I look back on those days, I feel a sense of loss for today's kids.

At the age of 10, we moved back to the island of O'ahu and my official martial arts training began. My father got me involved in Judo at the Young Buddhist Association in the Nuuanu Hongwanji Boys Club. I loved Judo!

My instructor was Tsutao "Rubber Man" Higami. Much has been written about this famous instructor, and I was extremely lucky to have had such a great instructor right from the start. Higami taught Judo to schoolboys, as well as some of his postwar students who had returned, eager to continue their training. Some of his postwar Judo students included Victor "Sunny" Gascon, Roy Suenaka, Walter Godin, Tony Lasit, Toney Troche, and Bobby Lowe, the first Kyokushin Karate champion of the famous master Mas Oyama. All of us eventually went on to become well-known teachers of assorted martial arts. And it all started from these humble beginnings.

Although my first introduction into the martial arts world was the Filipino arts, I never gave my whole heart to them. The grass looked greener on the other side of the fence, so I dove headfirst into the Japanese art of Judo. I already had a love for the Filipino arts, but at that time, Filipinos were looked down upon and were always teased. Still, I learned much from the Filipino fighting arts and those arts set me on the path that would become my purpose in life.

People would say, "Bok bok all the time pull da knife!" In the language of Palau, the term for Filipino is "Chad ra oles," which literally means, "people of the knife." The Filipino's reputation for carrying knives and using them in fights was well-known. They were, and still are, feared fighters with blunt impact, or edged weapons, and my skills in both arts would serve me well in my later years. I feel blessed that I come from that background.

As I mentioned, my father was a musician. He also was a music teacher at two high schools in 1952 and 1953, and had a music shop in the small town of Waihiwa. Waihiwa was a town that was frequented by military men since it was near the army base called Schofield Barracks, famed home of the 25th Infantry Division which was nicknamed Tropic Lightening and Electric Strawberry.

I witnessed many fights between locals and the military personnel during this time period. These fights convinced me that I really needed to be prepared to fight and survive if I wanted to live to see the age of 25. There was plenty of motivation for me to continue my martial arts studies and that is exactly what I did.

At this point, I was twelve years old, and old enough to start finding a little work and making some pocket change of my own. In the big city of Honolulu, Dad and his brothers owned a dance hall called King's ballroom, a.k.a. King's Taxi Dance Hall.

The ballroom was named after the street on which it was located, King Street. It was situated right across from the train and bus depot in the red-light district at the entrance of Chinatown. That should tell you plenty about what the neighborhood was like.

During wartime, and the postwar era, taxi dancing was a favorite pastime of many military men. A taxi dance is where the dancers, usually young women, called taxi dancers, are paid to dance with the patrons, usually males.

This type of business started in the late 1920's and flourished in America during the 1920's and 1930's. Most of the taxi dance halls disappeared by the 1960's. They are now called hostess clubs and are a lot cleaner than they were during the days following World War II.

I mention this because it had a profound impact on me growing up. My cousin, Ray Jr., a.k.a., Junior Boy and I spent a lot of time cleaning up the dimly lit stairways and corners of King's Ballroom Taxi Dance Hall. Because the place was kind of dark and sleazy, we didn't like touching the trash with our hands, so we would pick up stuff with chopsticks or rolled up newspapers and put them into brown paper bags.

We got paid a penny a piece for everything we picked up, and we were happy to make a quarter or fifty cents during the weekend. That was, until I found out exactly what it was that we were picking up! We got a firsthand education about what grownups really do in the taxi dancing club, and it was gross!

We always thought that we were picking up old balloons and napkins left over from the night before, but I would later learn that what we were really cleaning up was used condoms and women's sanitary pads. Talk about an eye-opening revelation! What was even worse was the fact that we thought that these were balloons. I don't need to tell you how disgusting it really was. It still turns my stomach today to think of some of the trash in the dance hall.

After our enlightenment, I detested cleaning up the dance hall. Forget those pennies; it wasn't worth it! But, we continued to do the job nonetheless, mainly because we had no choice. Junior Boy and I would sometimes take those "balloons" and fill them up with water and throw them out of the third story window aiming at the sailors below. That was great fun, that is, until the day my uncle Ray caught us throwing them at pedestrians.

He stormed upstairs, grabbed us by the neck and banged our heads together like cymbals in a marching band! I remember the ringing in my ears lasted for days. Just another one of life's lessons growing up on the streets of Honolulu! There are consequences for everything you do; sooner or later what you do will come back to you.

The money wasn't the only reason I started cleaning the dance hall. Another part of the deal was that my uncle and dad would teach Junior

Boy and me boxing. My dad and my uncle taught boxing three times a week and on weekends. They taught both Western boxing and Filipino boxing, also known as Filipino Dirty Boxing, called Panatukan or Pangamot.

Since I mentioned the importance of boxing, I feel it necessary to spend a few minutes giving you a brief history of boxing in Hawaii. The islands, both the Hawaiian Island Filipinos and the Philippines had many famous fighters in the ring long before there was Manny Pacquiao. Many of the Filipinos were making a name for themselves in Western boxing.

An interesting fact that many people are unaware of is that there were Filipino World Boxing Champions dating back to the 1920's. There were! Poncho Villa Francisco Guilledo, Ceferina Garcia, Dado Marino, Gabriel "Flash" Elorde, and Joseph Bernard Docusen were some of the greats. Odds are, you have never heard of most of these great fighters.

The Filipino Cajun Docusen lost a decision to the legendary Sugar Ray Robinson in a welterweight title match in 1948. Guilledo and Elorde were so great that they were both inducted into the hall of fame. The Hawaiian Mongoose, Eileen Minooka Olszewski, former world champion, Andy Ganigan, Jesus Salud, and Brian Viloria all had a major influence in the world of boxing. With my training in boxing, and the influence of these men, my circle of influence was beginning to tighten. As your circle of influence becomes more specific, the person that you are destined to be is revealed.

Filipinos have been in the sport of boxing since the early 1900's and have actually helped to revolutionize what is known as Western boxing. Panantukan is a boxing component of Filipino fighting arts and is well-known in the Visayas (one of the three principal geographical divisions of the major islands of the Philippines) as Pangemot.

Panantukan consists of upper body strike techniques such as punches, elbows, head butts, and shoulder strikes. It also includes low-line kicks and knee strikes to the legs, shins, and groin. Some schools group this kicking aspect into the art of Panantukan, which relies on kicking and only uses arms in a defensive manner.

Some Western instructors teach Panantukan or Pangamot as a separate martial art, like the Korean art of Tae Kwon Do. But in the Philippines, it is accepted as part of Eskrima. Pangamot emphasizes speed in striking, with the intent of overwhelming the adversary with a flurry of attacks and indefinite combinations of different strikes, strung together continuously to make a very successful defense. And let me tell you, it is a *very* successful defensive art!

Pangamot is said to be performed on half beats, or in between the major strikes of the combination, so as to disorient and overwhelm an opponent, thus increasing the opportunity for a more devastating attack. An example of this could be performing a swift slap or eye strike after throwing a jab, with the same hand in a standard jab-cross-hook combination. The eye strike both disrupts the opponent's defense and masks the incoming cross.

Additionally, low-line kicks are often executed between boxing combinations to further injure and disorient the opponent. This is my personal expression of my fighting art of Kajukenbo, Wun Hop Kuen Do *buzz saw*.

It has a reputation and name of *Dirty Street Fighting* or *Mean Martial Arts*, aka MMA. Common targets include the biceps, triceps, eyes, nose, jaw, temple, groin, ribs, spine, and the back of the neck. As such, parries and deflections are preferred over blocks. I will discuss this in even more detail in my upcoming book, *The Kajukenbo Bible* (working title). I don't want to digress too much from my life story, so I will continue.

When I was twelve, we lived in the Kalihi district, which was like the ghetto area near Palama Settlement. Both would play an important part in my martial arts life later on. Life was very different at that time. Punishment back then was not like it is today.

For example, my cousin, who was a year older than me, got into trouble and was quickly punished by his dad. He had Junior Boy strip, wearing only his t-shirt, and then he had to sit on the concrete steps in the front of his house, with only an ice cream scoop covering his private parts. Now that punishment would be considered cruel and unusual, but times were very different back then.

My father was a bit more lenient with me. He simply whipped me with the television cord for an incident that happened with one of my childhood friends, Diana. She and I had an argument about avocados. I told her that if she would put the skin of an avocado in the ground and water it, it would grow into a tree in a few days.

She watered that old, rotting avocado skin for days, but what she didn't know was that I had secretly replaced the skin with an avocado bulb that my dad was preparing to plant outside in our small garden. Diana was so excited when she saw that bulb begin to sprout. She believed without a doubt that avocados do grow from the avocado skin.

Well, when my dad found out about what I had done, I was truly sorry. I was whipped with the television cord for lying and for taking my dad's avocado seed. Diana dug up the seed, discovered what I had done, and threw the seed at me, hitting me right in the head, not once, but twice! I guess this was another lesson in karma or the law of reciprocity.

I recall another time when my sister and I got into trouble. We were punished by being forced to kneel down on raw rice and hold our arms straight out to the side of us, hands up, with a book resting on each hand. Dropping our hand even an inch would get us another minute added to our punishment.

Five minutes of that felt like a whole afternoon. It was so painful that we had indentations on our knees and pain that lasted for hours afterwards. My shoulders and upper body felt like I had been lifting weights hard for hours.

If these types of punishments were done in today's society, my dad would have been in jail for child abuse. But this was typical Filipino discipline, at least as far as we knew. We simply thought that this was normal, and it was in our culture.

Discipline was very important to my family, and I learned discipline from an early age, and in many ways. When I was in kindergarten, my family put me into a private Catholic school on the island of Kaua'i. I was to learn many things in Catholic school, among them were more harsh discipline and a love for performing.

My first year in school, I was in the Christmas play. All the lights, music, make-up, costumes, and excitement really had me excited. I got to sing! Imagine me singing and playing what I felt to be the most important part of the show. I was all decked out and the center of attention, with the spotlight on me, I was the best Christmas tree ever.

But this wasn't to be the last time that I would be the center of attention at the Catholic school. I did everything from putting tacks and frogs on the teacher's chair to drawing a nude picture of a girl in class and passing it around the room. My friends and I were always getting detention for playing pranks on other students or on the nuns themselves.

Another time, I drew a nude picture of a girl, but this time I put her name on it and passed it around to the other boys in the room. I had to face 8 nuns, all wearing their black robes and white habits. They obviously wanted to make an example of me and gave me a whole week of detention, where I cleaned the hallways every day after school. A whole week! That feels like forever to a twelve year old boy.

But I wasn't rattled; I responded by putting a frog on the teacher's chair a week later. It was not a live frog, but a frog like you would see in a flower vase, with tons of pins on the base to hold the flower in the vase upright.

Well, sister nun sat on it and sprang up like she had just sat on a hot stove, screaming to high Heaven! Needless to say, she was having none of that. I ended up pulling weeds around the playground for another solid week!

I definitely got in my share of trouble during my school years! My parents had struggled to afford to put us in private school, so I was determined to get our money's worth – in every way. The nuns were like my dad when it came to discipline; they were strict disciplinarians!

And the fact that I had to dress up in blue trousers, a white short-sleeve shirt with a black tie and black shoes every day, didn't help me stay out of trouble; in fact, it added to my trouble. The problem was that I had to walk passed all of my old school mates to get to my new school, and they thought that I was a snob for going to the private school and dressing so nice.

My old school had a lot of Japanese students, and many of them were very good at their cultural art – Judo. I got my nice clothes dirty and bloody many times. The ironic thing was that I didn't like in those fancy clothes anymore than my ex-friends liked me wearing them, but in Catholic school, I had no choice in the matter. Wearing nice clothes never stopped me from fighting back.

With the fights that I was getting into, my dad made sure that I accelerated my training in Judo with Mr. Rubberman Higami, instead of teaching me his Filipino fighting arts. He wanted me to learn Judo so I could defend myself against the Japanese bullies on their level, using my Judo and my boxing skills.

I had a strong spirit and the mindset that even if I got beat up one day, you can bet that I was there waiting the next day to try to even the score. And I would do this until I either won or the bullies gave up! I was a very stubborn boy. I didn't let things like that go, and this attitude would serve me well in the years to come.

But we weren't always fighting. We loved it when the city would clean up the inside edge of Kapalama Canal whenever the weeds got too tall and out of control. City workers would cut, pile, and burn the weeds, and my buddies and I would sit on the concrete walls, inhaling the smoke from that spiraled up from the piles of burning grass, and for some reason it made us feel very good and relaxed.

Later I would come to recognize that smell as pakalolo, better known as cannabis or marijuana. We were accidentally getting high and never even knew what that meant. All we knew is that it smelled good and it made us feel nice and relaxed. Now, the canals are "weed" free and don't even resemble what they were in the past. Boy, am I glad my dad never found out about that!

My dad did all he could to take care of our family. When I was twelve years old, dad decided to run for the House of Representatives in the fifth district in Honolulu. This was to be dad's big chance to break out of our financial troubles and finally find some relief from the stress of trying to make ends meet.

My dad was fairly well-known and had a great chance to win. He printed up 1,000 8 ½ by 11 posters for my sister and me to handout in town. We were going around putting them in mailboxes, on windshields, and handing them out on street corners.

It felt like we had passed out thousands of these posters, but at the end of the day, we still had a large stack of posters left, and I was afraid to go back home with that many left over posters; I didn't want my dad to think that we didn't do our job. So on the way back home, we dropped them in a trash bin. I was always thinking ahead, at least most of the time.

Just two weeks before the election, my dad decided that we should go on one last hunting trip before the election. A few weeks earlier, we had taken my custom-built 22 caliber rifle out with my uncle and a few friends to hunt for wild boar. I was the only one on the trip who carried a gun. The other men hunted with dogs and traditional long spears and daggers. The dogs slowed the boar down and the men would move in and stab it with their spears.

On that same trip, my dad and I took a break and were sitting on an old rock. All of a sudden, my dad realized that it was not a rock at all, but rather an old Japanese bomb from World War II that had never exploded. We very carefully moved away from the bomb, and thanked our lucky stars that it didn't explode! It was probably from a plane crash or something from the attack on Pearl Harbor.

Anyway, we decided to take one last hunting trip before the election, and it would turn out to be a trip that would cost my dad and my family dearly. The events of this hunting trip would change my dad's fate forever.

We took a boat trip to the Island of Molokai from O'ahu, in one of those deep sea fishing boats, rigged with all of the poles and lines. The trip across the Molokai Channel took us almost a full day in itself. We caught a marlin, a barracuda, and even took some of the left over parts from the wild boar, that we killed on our last hunting trip, to use as chub to attract sharks so that we could shoot them.

There were several men on this trip, and they were drinking beer and eating barbecue in an early celebration of my father's expected win in his bid for the House of Representatives. Everyone was having a great time, that is, everybody but me. I spent most of the time sea sick and throwing up over the side of the boat.

When we reached the island, we set up camp on the shore. Our plans were to have a nice campfire, dinner and to get to bed early so we would be ready for the hunt the next morning. But things didn't quite go as planned.

One of the crew talked my dad, my uncle, and the other men into going spotlighting for deer. This part of Molokai was full of spotted deer and we could see them feeding nearby. My dad wasn't up for it, but he went along anyway, not wanting to be a stick in the mud. In case you don't know what spotlighting is, it is taking flashlights and hunting deer at night, which is illegal. When you put the light on the deer, they freeze and just stand there. That is probably where we get the phrase, "like a deer in the headlights."

We had gone less than 30 yards when I heard, BANG! BANG! The men had shot two deer. We were thinking that we were going to have fresh venison for dinner, that is, until we saw a pickup truck with red flashing lights on it, coming our way. It was park rangers!

Three guys drug the deer to the beach and tried to hide them by burying them in the sand, and everyone took off running to the camp. When they reached the camp, they tried to put out the campfire so it wouldn't draw the rangers' attention. A couple of rifles were thrown into the ocean, others were hid in the brush, and the men tried to get rid of all of the evidence they could. Dad and I were tucked into the shrubs when we heard rangers talking and then we saw two more ranger trucks heading our way.

What we didn't know was that these rangers had been watching us with binoculars, from a high vantage point, since late that afternoon. They knew exactly how many of us there were and the exact location of our campsite. Although we had permits for the morning hunt, we didn't have the right to be poaching at night.

Within an hour, everyone was arrested with the exception of my dad and me, but it wasn't long until we were found and my dad was arrested as well. My dad, who had only two weeks to go before the big election, was now in handcuffs and heading to jail with the others.

I made out better. I was taken to spend the night with the sergeant and his family. It was like a vacation for me, as their home was very nice, much nicer than any home that I had been in before. They made me feel very comfortable. I had a nice, warm bed to sleep in and was served breakfast on the beach lawn the next morning. I was living the good life, just for a moment, while my dad was in a crowded jail cell.

On Monday morning, the court released my dad and we flew back to Honolulu, but the word had already gotten out. When we landed at the airport, the press was waiting for us to interview my dad about being involved in deer poaching.

Although my dad did not even shoot one of the deer, we were all implicated and Dad had to pay a stiff fine. But what hurt more than the fine was the fact that this incident cost my dad the election. He now had a criminal record and everyone knew it. Eventually, his record was expunged, but this hunting trip ended his political career. When we look at the things politicians get away with today, this seems like a minor thing, but things were different back then. Politicians were held to a higher standard during those times.

Dad's frustration and depression was very evident in our home after this incident. He was easily angered and blamed himself for allowing this to happen. He punished himself, thinking that he was weak for giving in to the peer pressure. This incident haunted him for the rest of his days.

I remember once after he lost the election, I did something to anger him and Dad lost his temper. That didn't happen often, but this was one of those rare times. He took a long broom stick and started smashing all of my model airplanes that were hanging from my bedroom ceiling. This should have been a wakeup call for me to straighten up, but it wasn't. I was still too young to think about how my dad was feeling, and I was more defiant than ever. Unfortunately, things were about to get even worse!

One day after school, my sister and I wanted to get some dates from the palm tree that grew in an empty lot near our home. The lot was being cleaned up by gardeners, and they had trimmed many of the shrubs under and around the tree. I climbed high up into the tree to get the dates, and I ended up falling from the tree and landed right on top of a newly trimmed shrub.

A sharp branch on that shrub went right through my groin area, piercing my scrotum like a spear and exiting through my right side, just below my navel. Here I was stuck helplessly like a shish kabob! I felt like a piece of meat, marinating to be served, as I could not move and did not know what to do. Terror started to grip my mind and that is never a good thing, but this time it was warranted.

My sister ran home and got my dad. To make a long story short, I was rushed to the hospital and straight to surgery. In the recovery room, I overheard the doctor tell my parents that there was a possibility that I would be sterile because of this accident. But as you probably know, that wasn't the case. Those in the Dacoscos clan took full advantage of this situation, teasing me by calling me, "Wan hung looow," which means, "one hung low."

Money was tight during the months after my dad lost the election. Mom and dad seemed to argue a lot, mostly because there was not enough money to make ends meet. Although we didn't have much money, my dad always seemed to have enough to lend to his friends when they needed to borrow money. Dad would lend them money, knowing that we had to pinch every penny. I didn't understand Dad doing this back then, but today I understand the value of generosity.

Being well-known, my dad did not want others to realize that we were not wealthy like his younger brother was. Dad would give the shirt off his back to his friends, but at times, his frustrations over our financial situation were taken out on our family. His drinking worsened as well. All in all, Dad was a very loving, caring father. No one is perfect. He did his best to provide for us.

My mom used to make Hawaiian shell earrings to help make ends meet. We would go with her and help her sell them at the flea markets on Saturday mornings. It made Mom happy that we went with her and helped her at the market. Sometimes we would even chip in and help her make her earrings.

The smell of the glue would make us light-headed, but we didn't know that it was bad for us. My younger brother, Ben, actually became addicted to sniffing glue after this. I would often find him hiding under the bed sheets, sniffing away.

Although money was tight for us, my family was very generous. At times, when our house was already full with five people crammed into two bedrooms, we found ourselves bringing in another family of six, who had no place to sleep but in their car. Dad invited them to stay with us for a couple of months, until they could get on their feet and get their own apartment. Imagine having seven kids and four adults in a two bedroom apartment! They eventually moved on, but it was still a struggle.

I remember coming home from school one day, and Dad was cooking dinner for us. I had never seen chicken stew like he was cooking before, but it tasted good. I was still hungry and wanted more, but there was not enough for second helpings. After dinner, I went to the backyard to feed my pet rabbit, but it was nowhere to be found. Later, I found out where he was – Roger Rabbit was dinner that night.

My thirteenth year was very eventful, to say the least. It was also the year of my first date. Two of my cousins and I went on a triple date. My date was Katherine Kim, a girl that I had my first crush on. She had the nicest hazel blue colored eyes and being half Korean, half Portuguese, she was very beautiful.

We all went to an afternoon matinee to see a western with Roy Rogers and Dale Evans, now that is a romantic movie for a first date! The tickets were 10 cents apiece. During the movie, I was brave enough to put my arm around her. I wanted to demonstrate my romantic skills. I was very daring and started to caress what I thought were her breasts, but I later found out differently when she asked me why I was rubbing her elbow. I guess that was less embarrassing than if she had asked me why I was rubbing her breast.

After the movie, I wanted to impress Katherine, so we all went to a nice restaurant. Six of us sat in one booth. I had never even ordered for myself before, much less for someone else. And I was getting very nervous as I read the menu, seeing as I only had $1.50 left in my pocket.

Everyone started to order, and each person ordered a burger, fries, and a shake, including my date. I was sweating bullets because it was adding up, so I ordered a glass of water and a bowl of chicken noodle soup. Everyone busted out laughing, but I remained cool and simply said that I loved chicken noodle soup. No one ever knew that I didn't have enough money to buy what I really wanted.

I was always a little envious and jealous of my cousin, Ray, who constantly had better things than I did. He was always showing off and making me feel bad. His parents lived in a very nice, big house in the better part of Kalihi. Junior Boy was my favorite cousin, but we always ended up competing against each other, and that was one competition that I could never win.

This envy, and our endless competition, finally got the best of us. I had gone out of my way to get even with him for a couple of things that he did and that really harmed our special friendship. We weren't as close as we had been, and for the next couple of years, we became fighting cousins. But in the end, family ties won out over any competition or jealousy that I may have had, and our friendship was rekindled.

In February, 1957, Dad had to be rushed to the Queens Hospital with liver pain. He had to have emergency exploratory surgery. He stayed at the hospital for several days, and we all thought that everything would be fine, that is, until I saw Mom in her bedroom crying.

Dad was not home yet; his brother was giving him a ride home from the hospital. Mom called Arlene, my sister, and me into her bedroom and told us that the surgery did not go well. There was nothing else they could do for Dad. Dad had yellow jaundice and cancer of the liver. He was given six months to live.

But Dad did not let that get him down. He didn't simply lie around the house waiting to die. My dad was determined to help my mom look for a house with the money that he knew we would get after his death. He wanted us to finally have a house of our own, one that he could never afford to give us with the money that he earned as a musician.

In the early years, our family lived with Grandpa and Grandma on Kaua'i. During that time, we learned how to survive living off the land. While at times, we didn't have enough to eat; we always had enough to survive.

Most of the Filipinos brought edible plants with them when they migrated to Hawaii from the Philippine Islands, over 100 years before. They did this so that they would be sure to have a food source that they could plant when they arrived in Hawaii. We learned how to recognize these plants while living with my grandparents. Knowing that these plants now grew wild, after spreading for decades on parts of the island, we knew we would be okay.

On Friday, May 11, 1957, Dad started to have hallucinations. He was doing some repairs in the bathroom when he lost his balance and fell to the floor. Dad was rushed to the hospital with Mom by his side. My mom was very afraid as she was only 35 years old at the time. The thought that she was on the verge of being a single parent with five children was terrifying to her.

I was in the Civil Air Patrol Drum and Bugle Corps Marching Band at the time. We had a full dress rehearsal on Saturday morning, to get ready for the Memorial Day Parade. My best friend and I walked to the hospital after practice to see my dad and to find out when he would be coming home. I asked the receptionist what room Benjamin Dacoscos was in, thinking I would just go up and visit him. Without missing a beat, she said, "He is in the basement."

"Why the basement?" I asked.

She simply replied, "That is where you will find the morgue."

That is how I found out that my dad had died. I was stunned and unable to stand, so I just sat down and cried. Dad was 50 years old.

After I regained my composure, I walked all the way back home. Normally, I would have taken the bus, as it was a long five miles to our house. But this time I preferred to walk the five miles back home. I walked with my bugle in my black case, thrown over my shoulder. I felt a huge burden as I made that dark walk home, knowing that now I was the man of the house, and my life would now change forever. I was only 15 years old.

When I reached our home, it was already overcrowded with neighbors who had brought food to help us through our time of grieving and to pay their respects to my dad. This vigil lasted late into the night. While we dealt with the death of my father, the other side of the Dacoscos family had an eerie fear setting in. Our family was very superstitious.

They believed that death always comes in threes. They also believed that whistling was a way of calling demons into the house and that sweeping the house at night was only opening the doors for evil to come in. But their superstitions were proven false; death only came to my father that night.

In August of 1957, we received a $25,000 settlement from my father's life insurance policy, and we moved into our new house in Kalihi Valley. Mom paid $19,000 for the three bedroom house, which didn't leave us much. Looking back, that was pretty amazing because that same house today would cost over $500,000!

I continued to get into more fights throughout my middle school years. My eldest half-sister, Angie, was married to a guy named Manny Dela Cruz. He was a high ranking black belt in Shotokan Karate, and eventually became a Shotokan instructor. He was once a Kajukenbo student, but switched over to Shotokan Karate, making him versed in more than one style of martial arts.

I knew a little bit about Karate and Judo, but only enough to help me hold my own with the Japanese students in my school and to get into trouble. I bragged once too often about my brother-in-law and that led to me being challenged by a guy named Joseph Durante, who I later found out was a brown belt in Judo and a respected tournament competitor in Hawaii.

He and I got into a fight and he threw me to the ground and put me into an arm bar. I was pretty good in Judo, but not at the level that he was as a seasoned tournament competitor. That taught me a valuable lesson about bragging – bragging rarely leads to anything good. There is always someone better.

A week later I got into another fight with a guy who was a couple of inches taller than me, George Fraites. The nuns broke up the fight. After graduation, I never saw George again, but I found out 45 years later that he had retired as the chief of police of Kaua'i. It was probably a good thing that I never saw him again, or he might have arrested me! As for Joseph Durante, the hot shot Judo brown belt became a taxi driver in Waikiki. I find it fascinating to look back and see how our lives took such different paths.

The next year, the money that we received from my dad's passing began to run out, and I had to transfer back to the public school. To make things even worse, I had to enroll in a school in the rough part of the Valley where gangs were always fighting each other. I finished that year averaging about one fight per week. As it turned out, moving to that rough school was preparation for my path in life. There is nothing like real life experience.

I loved to fight, and since there were no weapons involved, I figured that I was not going to die. My fighting skills continued to improve as I got ready to enter high school. But I knew that the fights that I would see in this rough high school would be much different than what I had experienced as a young middle school boy.

I also knew that it was time for me to get even more serious about learning how to defend myself. I also knew that one day I might be fighting for more than my pride – I might be fighting for my life!

Dad, Mom and me at nine months old in June of 1943

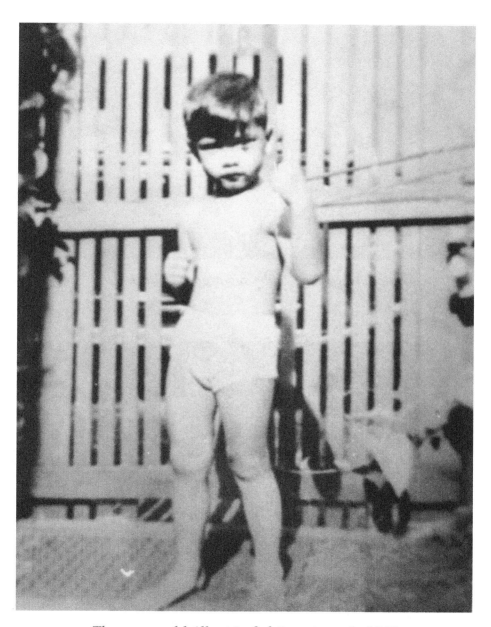

Three year old Albert in fighting stance in 1945

Filipinos working in the sugar cane fields in 1930's

One of the Japanese cemeteries in Hawaii

Dad's Band Fil-Am Band in 1932

*My first Judo instructor, Rubberman **Higami***

ELECT...

BENJAMIN J. (BENNY)

DACOSCOS
(DEMOCRAT)

for

REPRESENTATIVE
5th DISTRICT

Dad's poster for the House of Representatives in 1955

My dad as Charlie Chaplin during his entertainment years

King's Ballroom in 1951

Chapter 2

Getting Serious About Martial Arts

Talent is God given. Be humble.
Fame is man-given. Be grateful.
Conceit is self-given. Be careful.
John Wooden

On June 27, 1959, 93% of the voters from the major islands voted in favor of statehood. Hawaii had officially become the 50th state on August 21, 1959. There were huge celebrations throughout the islands. You could hear politics being discussed basically everywhere you went, but all of this political stuff was new to me. My main concern now was if the United States got into another war, I would get drafted.

The year of 1959 would hold many changes for me, and it would also be a very transitional period in my life. Shortly after my dad was buried, many men started trying to court my mother. She was only 35 years old and was still very beautiful, but I was not interested in any man coming around and trying to take the place of my father.

She dated a couple of men, but liked one in particular. This guy was in the navy and wanted to move us all to the Philippines. Had that happened, my life would have turned out very differently. But she decided on a different suitor, Nash Verano. He had a nice house and a good job, and eventually, would become my stepfather, adding two other step-brothers to my family, Ronald and Nash, Jr., and my younger half sister Christine.

I took my dad's death hard and during this time, I started hanging around with the wrong crowd. My testosterone level was exploding. My voice was deepening, and big trouble was lurking just on the horizon.

It was at this time that I made my first 22 caliber zip gun. Turns out, that was not a very smart idea. Imagine that! My homemade gun blew up in my hand, nearly taking off one of my fingers, while I tested my gun in a vacant lot. Zip guns are made for one reason and one reason only – to kill another man. That should tell you where my head was during this period of my life.

This was my first year in high school. I was driving around illegally, that is, whenever I could sneak away with my stepfather's car. Late at night, my friends and I would roll the car down the hill from my driveway before starting it, so we wouldn't wake up my parents. We didn't have the key, so we used aluminum foil from a stick of gum to hotwire the car. Then we would joy ride around the city all night.

We knew that if we returned the car low on gas, my stepfather would find out that something was going on. So we used a short water hose and five gallon gas cans to siphon gas from other cars around the neighborhood to refill my stepfather's car. I wonder if he appreciated always having a full tank of gas in the mornings.

As I mentioned, my high school was fairly rough. There were fights almost every day. This fact helped fuel my continued interest in the martial arts. One day in class, I met Richard Whaley and was introduced to Ti kan justsu kai, an off shoot of Kyokushin kai, the Karate taught by the famous Karate master from Japan, Mas Oyama.

Richard was only a blue belt at the time, but he was a good instructor and taught me as much as he knew in our backyard. He also joined the same ROTC unit as I was in, thus began our friendship.

During one of our practice sessions, Sid Asuncion, who had heard that we were practicing some Kai-i exercises, came by to watch us. That was a meeting that changed my life forever. After watching us do our techniques, he intervened and destroyed the techniques that we were so proud of.

I was really interested at that point! He had some really big, black knuckles and we listened to him because he was much older than us and obviously knew what he was doing. We were just a couple of high school punks trying to act tough. He was the real deal!

The following week, he picked me up and drove me to his club out in the sugarcane fields in a town called Waipahu, and that is how I became the student of the famous Sid Asuncion. His assistant was Al Dela Cruz, to this day, still one of my best friends, a whopping 57 years later! Al was a green belt at the time and was instructed to teach the beginner's class that I was now in.

Sid's classes were very brutal! Someone was always getting hurt and seeing blood in class was the norm. At one time, I was so bruised that I could hardly walk. Our practice was so brutal and intense that I was getting new cuts before my old wounds even had time to heal.

Soon the day came when I was so bruised and cut up that I decided I wasn't going to go to class anymore. Bad move! Sid came to my house, came into my room, and dragged me out of the closet that I was hiding in. He told me that if I ever did that again, he was going to kick

my butt. I was not too happy about that, but now, I thank him for it. He made me who I am today.

After that, I trained harder and better, and I could both take the pain and dish it out. I became physically stronger and mentally tougher. With Sid, I learned not only how to damage the human body, but also how to develop speed. I was now forever hooked on martial arts. My circle of influence just became much smaller.

As the year wound down and New Year's Eve approached, Sid got into a serious confrontation with someone who had mistaken him for someone else. In that confrontation, this guy pulled a blade and took a slice at Sid, barely cutting his shirt open. Sid threw a vicious punch into this guy's head and instantly killed him. Sid had the biggest, calloused, black knuckle on his index finger and getting hit by it was almost like getting hit by a jackhammer.

Now my martial arts instructor was picked up and taken to jail for murder, but he was soon released after the facts of the incident were revealed. It was ruled purely self-defense. Sid was one of those guys who lived what he taught and had the experiences to back up his teachings. There are not many martial artists like Sid today.

Al Dela Cruz, his assistant instructor, was teaching class about a week after Sid was released from jail. He was in a horse stance when Sid came into the class drunk. Traditionally, the instructor would move around the class while we were in a horse stance and throw a punch to our chests to toughen us up. As the instructor punched, we would let out a loud kiai, or spirit yell.

We knew that Sid had just been in jail a few days earlier for killing a man, and now he was standing in front of us, not completely sober, getting ready to punch us. We were really scared, as we knew what one punch from Sid Asuncion could do!

It would have been fine if he was sober, but being under the influence of alcohol, we were scared. In the end, we survived the night and learned how to control our fear, as well as how to take a punch from a man who really knew how to throw a punch.

Sid was a one-of-a-kind instructor. He was accustomed to going over to his friend's farm before the calves were slaughtered for the supermarkets, and practicing punching the calves in the head to drop them. I once went with him and he gave me the opportunity to try it.

They held the calf, and I prepared myself to do that one killing blow. I came down as hard as I could on the calf's forehead, but I could only buckle him to one knee. The calf got back up as if I didn't hurt it at all. I froze and didn't know what to do, but Sid immediately stepped in and put the calf down with one vicious punch. And let me tell you, he had one vicious punch!

The lesson that I learned from this was that once you make a commitment to really use your martial arts, you must be totally committed, as if your life depends on it, because one day it might. There is no halfway; you must commit yourself to your goal 100%. In whatever you do, commit yourself to it all the way.

As I mentioned, I became very good friends with Al Dela Cruz, in fact, we became the best of friends. Al became the first person to be promoted by Sid to the rank of black belt in his Kempo Karate style which would later be called Kenkabo. I was the second black belt under Sid Asuncion.

This was my first black belt. I was so honored that my mother presented it to me during my graduation two years later. Things were much different back then. I was one of the very few students that earned a black belt, and almost no one earned their black belt in that short period of time.

In addition to my excellent training, I was getting a lot of firsthand experience with street fighting as well. There was a restaurant in the Wailani Inn, outside of Waipahu, that we would go to after training. The advance class would go there for Saimin, the Hawaiian version of ramen noodles. We would eat, drink beer, and talk martial arts into the night. This was a rowdy place where many fights started.

Our uniforms at the time were white pants and a red t-shirt. Some of us, who could not afford the white karate gi, would have to improvise. I was one of the lucky few who did not have the money to buy real Karate pants.

During that period, many sailors came to Waikiki to drink and party. They would get drunk and then make their way back to the base at Pearl Harbor. Well, as luck would have it, the sailors wore nice, white pants. Those of us who could not afford a pair of gi pants would wait outside of the bars for drunken sailors to come out.

It wasn't hard to get a pair of white pants from one of these guys; a couple of good punches and they went down. And when they woke up, they were missing a pair of white pants. I have often wondered what these guys thought when they woke up wearing everything but their pants.

When I look back on that today, I am not proud of what I did. I don't include that in my book to brag about it or to make myself look cool or tough, but that was life at that time. I did many things that I would not do today.

We were all a very rough and tumble bunch of guys, and we did what we thought we had to do to get by. Eventually, I could afford my own white Karate gi, which I later dyed black, and it became my first Kajukenbo uniform.

A couple of years after I started training with Sid Asuncion, I would, once again, meet up with my old nemesis, Michael Ching. We ended up going to the same high school. Walking through the high school hallways to class was like walking through a minefield. We each had our small group of friends who traveled together. In my junior year, the harassment got very intense.

I had a singing group and we were very popular, not only in school, but in the city as well. We even had our own "groupies" who followed us around. Naturally, this made many of the other guys in school jealous. Michael Ching was one of them.

At that time, I was the captain of the ROTC and had my own special drill company. My company was the only one in the state of Hawaii that was capable of challenging any of the top private schools and actually competing on the mainland.

Well, as destiny would have it, Michael Ching was assigned to one of my platoons. He was very insubordinate and didn't like the idea of me giving him orders. One day after drill practice, I took off my rank and we went at it in the back room of the armory.

We didn't get very far when we were interrupted by Sgt. James Lorenzo, the army specialist assigned to Farrington High School as our trainer. Both of us were disciplined, and Sgt. Lorenzo came down especially hard on me because I was a ranking officer. I almost lost my rank, but I managed to get Ching off my team.

Our feud finally came to a head one day, as Ching and two of his buddies waited for me after school. I also had two friends with me and we were headed down to the Saimin stand. Ching was in civilian clothes and was a slick dresser. He was wearing shined, pointed-tip shoes, heavily starched bell-bottom pants, and an aloha shirt. I was wearing my ROTC uniform.

Michael Ching was out for blood! I took my shirt and cap off, and the fight was on. Ching had no idea that I had a few years of martial arts experience under my belt, and that I was a much better martial artist than the last time we fought. This gave me an advantage!

It was a totally one-sided fight; Ching knew he was beaten badly. His two buddies stayed out of it, as did my friends. I had reached my limit with his intimidation and bullying and was determined to end it once and for all, or so I thought.

After the fight, I found out that Ching was planning to ambush me with several of his friends. Michael was a slow learner. I foiled his plans and intercepted him at the place where he thought he was going to ambush me with his friends. I arrived 15 minutes earlier than usual in order to be prepared.

Lucky for Ching, and for me too, the counselor at the school found out about what was about to happen and came and stopped it. If he hadn't done that, I most likely would have lost my place as captain on the drill team. That would have been a disgrace to my family and friends, especially to my Dacoscos relatives that were in high school with me. Years later, I found out that Michael Ching was killed in a gang shootout over some kind of drug issue. It is interesting to see how differently our paths turned out.

My junior year in high school was probably the best year of school for me. The biggest thrill I had was when my singing group, The Tri-Lites, won first place in the state competition at the Civic Auditorium in Honolulu.

For that week, we were celebrities in school. We had our pictures in the local newspapers and the whole nine yards. Our group was even one of the opening acts for Diana Ross and the Supremes during their concert in Hawaii. But it seemed as if every time something good happened to me, I found a way to follow it up by getting into more trouble.

That same year, I got into drag racing, not the legal kind, but street racing. I had a 1949 Chevy two-door coup. It was painted fire engine red, because I painted it that way with spray paint. On both back fenders it had "Tri-Lites" written on it in canary yellow. On the outside it looked passable, but the inside was a different story. The upholstery was torn up and my front driver's seat was held up with a 2 by 4. I bought the car for $50. It was a piece of junk, but it was my piece of junk.

Imagine our group's outfits – white long sleeve dress shirts, canary yellow pants with a purple stripe going down the side, a purple sash, and black and white oxfords. And our car looked like moving billboard.

After graduation, our group lost its two lead singers, who were very important to our group. I tried to get other members, but it was never the same again and so we disbanded. My interest in continuing to try to keep the group together faded when I met the girl who, although I didn't know it at that time, would turn out to be the mother of my first son, Mark.

My interests were also changing. I became more interested in street racing, than singing. Drag racing basically became part of the norm for us. We would meet up at our favorite hamburger drive-in joint, and then head down to either Sandy Beach on the south side of the island or to Campbell's drag racing strip on the southwest side of the island.

My favorite was Sandy Beach. It was much more romantic, especially when the full moon was out. Many drag racers had camp fires on the beach, and we would all party and hang out with our girlfriends after the races.

During the weekends, you would see scores of souped-up cars, some custom-built cars, and some stock cars. The only thing my Chevy had going for it was duel carbs. The paint job and the interior certainly weren't going to win any prizes. Mostly we raced down the strip for a quarter mile.

One Saturday evening, a group of us went to Sandy Beach to meet up for some racing. The quarter mile races were supposed to start at 1:00 a.m. Sunday morning. It was my turn to stand in the center, out front between the two cars, and flag them down the strip. But before I could give them the signal to go, we were raided.

I was standing in the center lane, with the flag in my hand and my hands up in the air, about to drop the flag and signal the cars to take off, when I was cuffed by an undercover cop. Now I was in irons and headed towards the paddy wagon!

The following morning, we were arraigned in court. For some reason, which I never found out, they let us go and we never had to spend any more time in jail. But once again, I found out that karma cannot be cheated.

When we got back to the beach, I saw the hood of my car up and it was obvious that my carburetors had been removed, as well as all four of my tires. My car was sitting on blocks! Oh, and to add insult to injury, all of my 8-track tapes were gone as well.

Some of the other cars were less fortunate. One car even had the transmission taken out. Others had windows smashed and seats removed. That pretty much ended my drag racing career, as well as my driving, at least for a while.

I was still planning on fulfilling my dream of becoming a fighter pilot. The war in Vietnam was just getting heated up and many of our ROTC members had already enlisted in the military to go fight in Southeast Asia. I wanted to go as well, but that was not in the cards.

Even though I was not going into the military, ROTC gave me the added discipline, self-confidence and leadership skills which would be the building blocks that would enable me to run my own organizations in the future.

I was 19 years old when I met Dolly. Dolly was 15 years old. She was in a talent contest and was the only female singer for a group called the Caravans. At the time, I had a group called the Crescents. She was exotic looking and very beautiful with light brown eyes and long black hair. Dolly had a unique background, as she was part Japanese and part Irish. We hit it off almost right away, and within a year, she would become my wife. It seemed that life was starting to fall into place for me.

Her dad, Raymond Lloyd McVey, was a soldier who got wounded on one of the islands in the Pacific during World War II. He was recovering in an army hospital when he met a beautiful Japanese nurse Kiyoko "Jane" Tanabe.

He was from the backwoods of Kentucky and enlisted to join the army after the Japanese attack on Pearl Harbor. He wanted revenge on the Japanese, but he ended up falling in love with the "enemy." Isn't it funny how life throws us curve balls that we never expect?

A few years later, Dolly was born; a product of enemies becoming allies, or in this case, lovers. I guess they both took Jesus' teaching to love your enemies as you love yourself, literally.

This year would also be a turning point in my martial arts life. Al Dela Cruz had already departed from Sid Asuncion to go with one of the co-founders of Kajukenbo, Adriano Emperado, to teach at the Palama Settlement Gym. About six months later, I followed suit.

My departure from Sid must have been devastating for him, as both his first and second black belts had now jumped ship and went to train with someone else. People have asked me why we did that. The truth is that we were hungry for more martial arts knowledge and thought that Sid had taught us everything that he knew.

Emperado was a senior over Sid, so we thought we could advance more with his teachings. In retrospect, most everything that I learned from Sid, I would not appreciate until much later. I realized Sid gave me a rock solid foundation that would serve me well against any attack, from any other style that I encountered. Sid nurtured us well and gave us the foundation that we needed, and I will forever be grateful for that.

Sid was a man who had very good snapping techniques and very fast hands. I emulated his every move, and even did those moves better than he did because my legs were longer. I had better flexibility, but nevertheless, he was the best when it came to speed and snapping power.

The advantage of training with Emperado was that we were now attached to one of the co-founders of Kajukenbo. His teachings also had more of a mental enlightenment rather than just physical training, which was much harder to find. At times, we would just sit and talk. What I would learn from him in five minutes was the equivalent of training for five hours with someone else. It was intense, and his vast knowledge helped me to open up my development and my expression.

With the grace of God, these two men showed me the way. Asuncion was a fast and snappy fighter; Emperado was a power puncher and philosopher. They both had their good sides and their bad sides, like everyone has a dark side and a light side. They were both heavy drinkers, but I was not. Thank God I never fell into that trap.

Along with my martial arts training, I continued performing with my rock group. As I mentioned earlier, even though we were only a high school group, we did have our fair share of groupies, and I took full advantage of my popularity, which ended with my love for Dolly.

My love for Dolly brought about many changes in my life, some of them very unexpected. If you will recall, the doctors told my parents when I was younger that I most likely would be sterile for the rest of my life. Well, I learned that they were wrong! Not only was I not sterile, but I was on the way to starting a new family – Dolly was pregnant.

When Jane, Dolly's mother, found out, she told her husband, a medically discharged World War II veteran. He wanted me to come over for talk at their house. So there I was, nervously sitting across from this man in his army khaki pants and a white t-shirt, cleaning his Colt 45. Dolly was in her bedroom with her mother, anxiously awaiting the outcome.

I could hardly hear anything he was saying because my heart was beating so loudly. I had been in many fights, but this was totally different. My thoughts were running wild, and my mind could not focus.

The only thing that I remember was saying, "Yes sir" over and over again. I did not know how to accept the fact that I was going to be a father, but you can bet that Mr. McVey made sure that I knew I was going to. I was going to be a daddy! Dolly and I got married immediately and started making plans for our family.

Meanwhile, Emperado, Dela Cruz and I were now getting involved with what Emperado called Kajukenbo Tum-pai. I was also studying

Southern style Sil-lum Kung Fu on the side. It would be instrumental in helping me solidify the next pillar of Kajukenbo.

Now at 21 years of age, I was working as a truck driver delivering liquor to bars and stores around the city. I was actually on a delivery when I remember hearing the news that President John F. Kennedy had been shot. I was in shock, as most of the country was, and not paying attention to the speed limit. I turned a corner too fast and dropped a palette of beer onto the street. BAM! Broken bottles everywhere! You can probably guess what happened next – I got fired.

After that, I worked several miscellaneous jobs, from being a chauffeur to managing a steak house. I did what I had to do to provide for my family. The hours and days were long, but very rewarding, and most importantly, I was able to support my family.

Also during this time, my number was called for the draft to go to Vietnam. I wanted to serve, but it was not in the cards. I was eliminated because I was to be a new dad and needed to take care of my family. Being married and having a new child on the way kept me from harm's way. Unfortunately, out of the 12 men from my group of draftees, only three came back alive.

Soon afterwards, Mark was born. I went to the hospital with my friend, Doug Espinda, to see my new son and to check on my beautiful wife. In those days, you couldn't hold your son right away; he had to stay in a room with all of the other babies, so I didn't know exactly which one he was. They were all so wrinkled!

After I made sure my son and my wife were both fine, I decided to let them rest. Doug and I went out to celebrate the birth of my first son. Dolly's parents were both staying with her at the hospital, so I had no worries of her being alone. As I was not a big drinker, it didn't take long until I had more than my fill and was actually drunk. Doug drank more moderately, so he was in charge of driving me home.

We staggered out of the bar, and I saw two military guys by my 1962 sky blue Dodge Fury, complete with tailfins that looked more like rocket fins. One of these guys was actually sitting on it! The other was leaning against it. Well, you can probably guess this did not sit well with me.

As I gruffly told them to get off of my car, one of them actually started to bend the antenna and snidely remarked, "What are you going to do about it."

I could see that there was going to be a confrontation, and I knew that I was in no shape to fight anyone. Nevertheless, I yelled at them to get off of my car. The guy who was sitting on my car jumped off and took a boxers stance, bouncing as if he was Rocky Marciano or something.

Doug had only been studying martial arts for about one month, and he completely froze. I knew that he was not going to be much help. He figured that since I was a black belt that I could take care of it, even if I was drunk. And I was DRUNK! My balance and focus were both off. But I squared off with the boxer anyway.

I avoided a couple of his jabs. Then I decided to throw a front kick to his groin and follow up with a barrage of punches. That would have been an excellent idea for an attack except for one thing – I was DRUNK! I threw a kick, that, in my mind, was lightening fast, but in reality, it was moving in ultra-slow motion. He side-stepped my kick and delivered a right cross straight to my kisser, that sent me flying into the bushes, flat on my back.

I sat up and looked at him, then decided, "I'm not going to stand up and fight. I deserve this for leaving my wife in the hospital with her parents and going out and getting drunk." I just sat there on the curb, thinking what a jackass I was. Doug came and sat next to me, handing me a napkin for my bloody nose. I learned a valuable lesson that night – never drink so much that you are too drunk to defend yourself! You never know what might happen; always be ready.

Two years later, I was still working as an assistant manager for Sizzler Steak House. I just happened to get off two hours early one night and decided to surprise my wife by getting home early. Well, I ended up being the one that was surprised! I caught my wife making out in the front seat of a white Dodge Fury sports sedan in front of our apartment. Dolly was kissing my ex-guitar player from my rock group that I had after graduating from school.

My anger led to a lack of control and a burst of super strength. I reached in through the window and pulled him out of his car. Then I pounded him like I was doing bag work! That unfortunate incident led to me being homeless for three months and sleeping in my car.

Living in a car for three months gives a guy plenty of time to think. I made a decision that would lead to even more big changes in my life. I decided to leave Hawaii and move to Northern California. I was going to go find a place for us to live and get everything all set up, and then Dolly and Mark could join me in a couple of weeks.

There was a small group of four individuals, that when not training or teaching in Palama Settlement with Dela Cruz or Emperado, trained with me at the beach park where I was sleeping in my car. I was still able to continue my training, even while I was exiled from my home.

I had a meeting with Emperado and told him that I was going to be moving to Northern California to start a new life. I wanted his blessings to open up a martial arts school there and follow in the footsteps of other Kajukenbo students who had left a few years earlier.

He gave me his blessings, and I was on my way to a new adventure and a new life, one that would change my life forever. This was the first time that I had ever been to the mainland, so I had no idea about what I would find there, but I was about to find out.

The Tri-Lites 1960
Front row: Mel Abero ansd Mel Caba.
Back row: Al Dacascos, Ray Dacascos and Marshall Eubanks

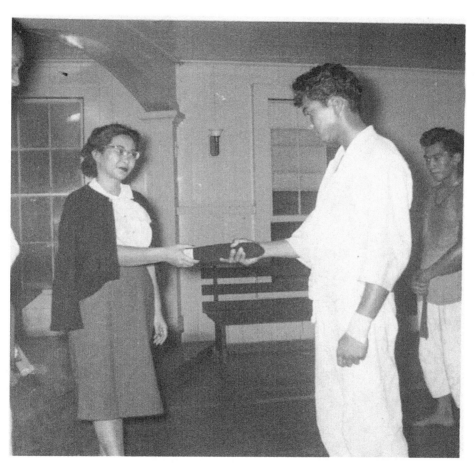

Mom presenting me with my first black belt in 1961

Sid Asuncion's first two Black Belts,
Al Dela Cruz and Al Dacascos, in 1962.
Both Al and I were 20 years old at
the time this photo was taken.

My days as an ROTC officer in 1960

Sid Asuncion and my first wife, Dolly

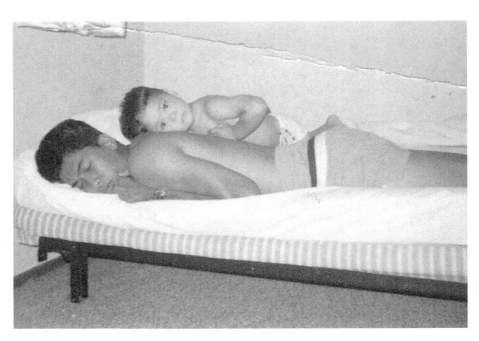

Mark "taking a nap" with me

Chapter 3

Moving to the Mainland

Without ambition one starts nothing.
Without work one finishes nothing.
The prize will not be sent to you. You have to win it.
Ralph Waldo Emerson

I moved to California to try to save my marriage and make a fresh start, but I only ended up accomplishing one of those two things. California was very eye-opening for me, in *many* ways.

The day that I arrived in California, I was slapped in the face by the cold San Francisco weather. I had never been to a place where it was so cold, and for a Hawaiian guy, this was a shock to my system. The wind was freezing cold, there were ice crystals on the grass in the mornings, and I was dressed for Jimmy Buffett weather!

I remember the day after arriving in San Francisco, my brother asked me to go play golf with him. My brother, George, was working as an estimator for a plumbing company at the time and wanted to talk to me about joining his company. Being a plumber wasn't for me; I was focused on one thing and one thing only – teaching martial arts. But I joined George for a round of golf nonetheless, and it was miserable!

George woke me up early that morning. I still hadn't gotten over the freezing cold weather and bone-piercing wind from the night before. I felt like I had been sleeping in a refrigerator the whole night. I had never had so much clothing on in my life! I must have slept in every piece of clothing that I brought with me.

I had t-shirts on t-shirts, pants over pants, and socks over more socks. And here was my brother wanting to go play a round of golf in this Arctic weather. I had never played golf before. My experience with golf consisted of getting paid 10 cents a day to pick up golf balls at the golf range when I was 11 years old; that was it. But off I went, in my new clothes, courtesy of George – thermo underwear, earmuffs, and thick gloves.

To top off the trip, we sped off in a green, two-seater Austin Healey convertible, with the top down, winding through a foggy road to the golf course. The chill factor meant nothing to him, but I can assure you, it meant a lot to me. There was frost on the windshield, and even with the fog lights on, I could barely see twenty feet in front of the car and that was an eerie feeling.

The fog cleared up as we reached the top of the hill, and for the first time, I saw the city of San Francisco. It was beautiful, but *really* cold. Suddenly, I realized that my new life was going to be very different.

I had never had a golf club in my hands, so I simply tried to imitate what my brother did. I didn't finish the first nine holes. My brother eventually got tired of me hitting his golf balls into the ponds, which, by the way, is where the club I was using ended up as well. I got frustrated and threw it right into the pond, and as you might guess, my brother made me go in after it. Luckily, the frigid water was only about a foot deep. I never touched another golf club until 2006!

When Dolly and Mark finally arrived, we stayed with George for about a week before I finally found us a one bedroom apartment. My friend, Mel Abero had urged me to go into Western Electric in San Leandro for a job interview. I was dressed very nice in a dark green suit. I was so eager to find a job that I arrived two hours early and had to wait in my car before the interview started.

By the time I arrived, I was frozen solid and was thinking that I had made a terrible mistake moving away from my beloved Hawaii. I must have looked very awkward to those who saw me, as I was shivering like a plucked duck on an icy pond. My lips were purple, and I could hardly feel my hands. How in Heaven's name was I going to do a good interview when all I could hear was my teeth chattering!

Fortunately, my interviewer took all of that into account and I got the job, starting the next morning. Things were starting to look up. We had our own apartment and now I had a decent job. The first thing I did after the job interview was go to the store and buy lots of thermal underwear!

My first day on the job, I worked with a guy named Earl Cozart. He was a big black guy and had never met anyone from Hawaii before. Earl talked to me like he was talking to a three year old because he wasn't sure whether or not I spoke English. And you know me; I played along pretending I spoke very little English. Whenever he spoke to me, I responded in Pidgin English, and I even threw in some made up Hawaiian words just for the fun of it.

I told him that in Hawaii, we wore a malu wrap around all the time and women wore next to nothing. I also told him that we walked around with spears and wore grass skirts. He was so naïve about Hawaii that he believed every word I said. In the early 1960's, not many guys from the ghettos of Oakland, California knew much about Hawaii at all.

Being a good sport, after about an hour of him trying to teach me my new job, speaking like he was teaching a three year old, I broke down and started laughing and let him in on the joke. After that, we became very good friends and Earl Cozart eventually became one of my first African-American students. Looking back, I know where my sons and daughters got their mischievous side.

On the other side of the conveyer belt was a white guy named Albert Salder. He thought that I was Mexican and had many choice insults for me. We eventually became friends, but not until I kicked his butt for calling me some kind of Mexican name that I had never heard before.

He was an amateur boxer and thought he would wipe up the floor with me. During one of our 15 minute breaks, he started in on me with some of his friends watching. He danced around throwing jabs at me as I stood there with my hands down, simply watching him. I parried his attack and side-stepped all of them. Getting frustrated, he overextended himself with a right cross to my head, and I leaned back and kicked him in the groin; it was all over for him.

That is when one of his friends grabbed me from the rear and put me in a bear hug. I flipped him over on his back and put my knee into his chest, with my left hand to his forehead and my right hand chambered, ready to throw a punch to his face. I couldn't resist; I just had to do it. I said, "Would you like a Hawaiian punch?" Then the rest of them backed off.

He and a couple of his friends came to me later and asked me if I would teach them how to do what I just did to them. After that, I became the talk of the warehouse and was even asked to work in the front office instead of being a selector in the warehouse, but I declined. The thought of wearing a coat and tie every day just didn't feel right to me.

I had done that in Hawaii when I managed the steak house and had no desire to wear a coat and tie to work again. I don't know what it is, but I hate the feeling of being choked all day. Maybe it comes from my grappling days practicing Judo and Jujitsu with all of those choke holds.

After so many guys asked me about teaching them what I knew about fighting, I decided to start a small group with a friend of mine, Melvin Abero, in Fremont, California. I had a nice group of guys from the warehouse learning from me. Within two months, I had more students than I could teach in a two-car garage, so we moved into a dance studio called Cherryland Hall in the Meekland area of Hayward.

Around this same time, another student of mine from Hawaii, Douglas Espinda, moved to the Mainland and started working for Western Electric also. He would eventually become my first black belt on the Mainland.

I decided to show Douglas around the town one night with two of my beginning students, Type Williford and Big Doug. Big Doug was about 6 foot 5, but had the voice of a young girl. We went to a bar that I had never been to before, right across the street from a big night club, thinking we would have a quiet drink and then go to the night club and enjoy some dancing.

We didn't know it, but this bar had a very bad reputation. It was where all the construction guys in the area stopped off before going home for the night. Basically, if you were in the mood for a fight, this was the place to be. It was full of rednecks and had nothing but good ole boy music blasting on the juke box.

We were sitting at the bar, Williford on my right and to the right of him, Big Doug. Doug Espinda was sitting to my left. Having just arrived from Hawaii, Espinda was sporting his dark tan and a blonde streak in his hair from his surfing days. We were minding our own business and sharing martial arts stories.

Big Doug was sitting the furthest away from me, so he had to talk louder for Doug Espinda and me to hear him. Well, his baby voice attracted the attention of a bearded, muscular giant who started mimicking his voice and making fun of him. Big Doug got upset and told the guy to shut up and sit down. Imagine a guy, 6' 5'' with a girly voice, telling another big guy to sit down and shut up. It didn't go over very well.

Things exploded into an old west, free-for-all bar fight. The big redneck smashed a pitcher of beer over Big Doug's head, splitting his forehead down the middle and splattering blood all over the place. Then this guy started to attack Williford. I launched a right side kick and dropped him to the floor, following it up with a barrage of kicks and punches. As he tried to recover, the rest of his friends joined in and attacked us.

There were four of us against the whole bar, ten or more guys! I found myself forced over by the pay phone, so I ripped the phone from the box and used it to crack some heads open. Big Doug was laying semi-conscience on the floor and Williford was basically useless, as he only had one week of training in Kajukenbo. So essentially, it was

Espinda and me against everyone else. We literally had to fight our way out of the bar.

It seemed like forever, but finally we made our way to the parking lot. Big Doug was put into the back of Williford's new 1966 blue Mustang with a white leather interior, which was now red and white from Big Doug's blood dripping all over the place. Getting us all into that little car was not easy to start with, but it was much harder while fighting off attackers.

Getting out of the bar and into the parking lot was just the beginning; we had to fight our way from the parking lot into the car! One guy pulled a saw from out of the back of his truck, and swung it at me, just missing decapitating me by just a few inches. I had to put him down hard. We fought like it was our last minutes on earth, and it very well could have been.

We dropped four or five of them as fast as we could. These guys had no idea what to expect, as they had no knowledge of martial arts, so even though they had the advantage in numbers, we had the advantage in skill.

We drove Big Doug straight to the hospital. In the emergency room, there was only a thin curtain separating one side of the room from the other. None of us needed stitching up except for Big Doug. As we sat quietly, waiting for the doctor to finish, we heard several guys on the other side of the curtain telling the doctor that they were jumped by a gang that consisted of two Mexicans and a bunch of white guys who came into their bar and started a fight with them.

They made it sound like there were 10 of us, when it was actually only Espinda and me fighting with them. During the next 30 minutes, we said nothing, waiting for the time that we could leave. We got out of there as fast as possible, before those guys discovered that we were sitting only a few feet away from them. This made a big impression on my students who had learned firsthand how important it is to take your training seriously because one day it may just save your life. In the end, this is why we train.

I continued to train students at the Cherryland Hall location for about a year. At this time, a San Francisco Chinatown group challenged me, much like Bruce Lee was challenged a couple years earlier by one of these groups. And, like Bruce, I had no intention of letting that challenge stop me.

About eight of these Chinese hoods waited outside for my class to be over. I only had a handful of students that day. These Chinese guys came in and handed me a letter in Chinese. I could not read it and had no idea what it said, but one of my students, Melvin Lee, read it for me. It said they wanted to test my skills and "play."

As I stated, a couple of years before, Bruce Lee had the same kind of encounter with a different group of Chinese and it ended with a fight between him and Professor Wong Jack Man, who would later become my instructor. I knew nothing of this fight at the time.

Their issue with me was different. One of the men recognized a picture of Ming Lum and Emperado and knew that I was teaching the Kajukenbo system when he saw our school flag on the wall and photos of the Emperado brothers. He immediately asked how I was connected to them, and when he found out, they excused themselves and left the training hall.

By that time, I had become so angry at their questioning that I yelled at them, "You came here to fight me; let's do it!" They would have no part of it and left, as my remaining students had assumed an aggressive attitude towards them as well.

I believe that the fact that Ming Lum's reputation of being the unofficial, underground mayor of San Francisco during this time, along with the reputation of Kajukenbo being a no-nonsense, street-oriented, self-defense and a "mean martial art," had a lot to do with persuading them to leave. Kajukenbo is the original MMA.

I had only been in California a short while, and already I was getting into more fights than I was in Hawaii. It seemed as if trouble followed me everywhere I went. At 24 years old, I was starting to wonder if I would actually make it to see my thirties, and now in my seventies, I would love to see my twenties again.

A couple of weeks later, we decided to go dancing, as we had planned on doing the night those construction guys spoiled our plans. As it turned out, that was not the place for us to be either. There were mostly yuppies in the club, and two Hawaiians, who looked like Mexicans or black guys with straight hair, were definitely not welcomed with open arms.

We were dancing and having fun, but as happens on dance floors with fast music, there was a lot of bumping going on. And this bumping led to pushing and shoving, which led to Doug Espinda and me going back to back, fighting again.

This was easier than the rough bar across the street. Most of these guys had no clue how to fight, so it was easy for us to pick and choose who we were going to drop. It wasn't planned, but we were getting a lot of firsthand fighting experience. It taught us what really worked, and what was useless in a real fight with multiple attackers.

One-on-one was easy, but multiple attackers was a completely different set of dynamics. The fight only lasted until the cops showed up and sent us all running back into the club, or in our case, to our car.

When I look back on all the fighting that I did, a lot of it could have, and should have, been avoided. But that is something that most people learn with age. Although I am not proud of getting in so many unnecessary fights, I did learn much from my firsthand experience using my martial arts in the streets.

During the same time period that I was teaching in Cherryland Hall, Eric Lee became one of my students. I don't recall exactly how or when Eric joined our class, but he did make an impression on me. He told me that he had recently emigrated here from China and was looking for a Kung Fu school, and that he had previous training in China. After hearing about my school, and its no-nonsense style of fighting, he decided to check us out.

I could plainly see that Eric had a good foundation. He adapted very well into our fighting system. Many times though, I would have to go outside in the parking lot and pull him into class a good 15 minutes after warm-ups had started. It wasn't that he was lazy or unmotivated, but he and his girlfriend were making out in the parking lot. I had to remind him that the real workout was in class!

Eric excelled in learning the forms that I was teaching. He also loved to do the multi-man defense and attack sequence that we do often. He was short, but explosive and precise in his movements.

The California Karate State Championships, hosted by Ed Parker and Ralph Castro, was one of the biggest tournaments on the West Coast. Eric was just a purple belt when I decided to enter him in his first competition as a brown belt, and he took first place. From that point on, there was no turning back for him; he was hooked!

His fighting was not as good as his forms. Although he had all the right moves, he was usually facing competitors that had a longer reach than he did. Although he enjoyed fighting, his true calling was in the Chinese form competitions. Eventually, he entered into the black belt division and went on to win nationally.

It was at this time that John Corcoran, who was writing for a martial arts magazine, dubbed Eric as "King of Kata." That title stuck with him, and he was well-suited for it. No one could have been more proud of Eric than me! He was the first national champion to come out of the Dacascos School.

The first competition for my school was in 1966 against Charles Gaylord's Kajukenbo School in Fremont, California. At that time, I didn't have any black belts to fight, so I took four of my advanced students, who were still color belts and had them fight as black belts. To my surprise, they did extremely well fighting in a much higher division. This is when we started to get some real recognition.

Charles Gaylord's school was primarily teaching Kempo, and at that time, my school was Kajukenbo Tum-pai. All of our primary forms were Chinese Kung Fu forms or hard style forms taught to me by the Sid Asuncion method, which was – if he hits you, you hit him back harder; if he bleeds you, you break his bones, and so on up the scale.

The way I trained my students was exactly the same way that I was trained back in Hawaii with the Sid Asuncion fight mentality. Although some of my students did not win, those who lost did so on account of excessive contact. Many of them were disqualified or they would have won. Our reputation from that point on was that we were rough fighters.

If I saw that a student had the fighting spirit, I would put him one level higher in the fighting division. We got the same kind of results; most of my fighters were disqualified for excessive contact.

It was not the techniques that I taught, but how I trained my students that caused this issue. I trained them with total commitment and focus, whereas some of the schools in the Bay area had students who simply trained for fun or because their school had black belt students and they wanted to be associated with them.

We averaged two or three tournaments a month, which was great experience for my students. For many of them, it was more of a testosterone release. The males used the tournaments to get their frustrations out. I had much rather they did this than get into dangerous fights with street gangs or in bars.

While most karate schools were focused on the one strike technique, we were practicing snap, speed, and techniques that would flow from one right into the other, like the links on a chainsaw. This kind of barrage of kicks and punches caused a lot of students to get disqualified, but this is exactly the kind of techniques that are used in offensive self-defense.

At the beginning of the Chinese New Year in February 1966, I had asked my wife, Dolly, if she and Mark wanted to come to Chinatown with Doug Espinda, some other students, and me. I am so glad she declined! What happened that day was no place for my wife and child.

Doug and two of my students, Pat Regan and his brother Mike, brought along a friend of theirs so we could all go and observe the

Chinese New Year's parade and celebration in San Francisco's Chinatown. We parked the car a few blocks away from the main street that the parade would be traveling on and walked towards the parade.

Between our car and the parade, we walked through a park that had food, drinks, and carnival rides. On the other side of the park was a Tai Chi school. We were having corn dogs and soft drinks when we noticed a bunch of young Chinese guys, *Hop Sing Tong* fresh off the boat from Hong Kong, throwing firecrackers at two young black men. The black guys seemed to be very scared as they were being surrounded by this Chinese gang.

Two groups of young Chinese gangs already had their own conflict in Chinatown. The local American born Chinese had issues with the new Chinese groups coming in from Hong Kong. Essentially, they were jousting for dominance in the city. The Hong Kong Chinese gang was about 35 feet away from us when I told my guys to hold up, that I thought it looked like trouble brewing.

I wasn't expecting the trouble to have anything to do with us, but I wanted to see how things were going to turn out for the two helpless guys who were being harassed by these punks.

Well, apparently, the Hong Kong gang had a different idea about our involvement. They started looking at my white friends and me, and decided to turn their attention to us instead of the two black guys. They started throwing fire crackers in our direction. Well, at least we got those two guys out of trouble, but now trouble was coming our way.

I told Doug that it looked like the trouble was now our problem. Doug and I went back to back with Pat and Mike, and their friend came closer to us for his own protection. Pat and Mike were students and I knew that they could handle themselves, but I had no idea about their friend.

Firecrackers started popping all around us and above us and more people started to gather. I told my group that it was not a good choice for us to be here in this park, that the safest thing for us to do was to turn the corner and walk up the street to the main drag where there were more people and some police.

As we turned the corner, it looked like we were leading a parade, as more and more people started following us, mostly young Chinese, as they sensed something was about to happen. I could see from the corner of my eyes a guy picking up a five foot long 2 x 2 from a heap of broken wooden crates next to a fish market. Then he attacked and swung at me.

I ducked and with the corn dog in my hand, put the skewer right into his stomach. The corn dog was still on the bamboo stick that was sticking out of him. With that, the rest of his friends began attacking us from every angle. We were now fighting for our lives. This was serious and we knew it!

The guys' friend, who came with us, took off running for his life. Doug, Pat, Mike and I were fighting and deflecting both punches and kicks. Pat had one guy on the curb, stomping on him like he was crushing watermelons. You can bet he was pretty bloodied up!

Pat was an excellent kicker and used his kicks well to ward off a lot of the charging Chinese guys, whom I suspected had some martial arts training as well. Mike was good with his hands, and he held his own too. Doug liked his fast kicks and punches and used them to his advantage. The four of us found ourselves in a very tight, back-to-back spot, fighting off what seemed to be an endless number of Chinese guys who were attacking us. We dropped anyone who looked like an Asian, innocent or not, as we didn't know if they were friend or foe.

We finally fought our way up to the main street, where gongs, symbols, and drums were being played loudly to the oncoming lion and dragon dancers. We were now fighting in, and around, the performers, and eventually we were able to get away and ran up the street, still being chased by a crowd of Chinese. For them, it was easy to spot us in the crowd – two white guys and two Hawaiian guys.

We managed to stop a taxi and barreled in, while the taxi driver was screaming at us to get out of his car the whole time. But when he saw the oncoming crowd of thugs charging at his car, slamming their hands on the trunk, and kicking the doors, he decided to drive instead of argue with us. The whole time he drove, he was yelling at us in broken English. He dropped us off about a quarter mile away, and we threw money at him and hit the road.

We were really glad that this Chinese cabdriver drove away instead of staying there and allowing the gang to surround us. We soon found our way back to the car, and there sat the other guy, leaning on the front bumper, asking why it took us so long to get back to the car. Now, there's a guy that you really want by your side when your life is on the line!

As we drove back to Oakland, laughter eventually gave way to the reality that we could have all ended up dead, well, except for the jackrabbit. The following morning, the San Francisco Chinese newspaper said that several Chinese gang members ended up going to the hospital from fighting with "some unwelcome white gang." I guess they were half right; two out of the four were white.

Soon after this event, I started getting much more involved with the politics within the Kajukenbo schools in Northern California. Five individuals, Charles Gaylord, Joe Halbuna, Alejo Reyes, Tony Ramos, and Gabe Vargas formed the Kajukenbo Association of America. They used the rules and regulations from the Boy Scouts of America as a guiding format. About a month after the formation of the KAA, I entered the scene and would make the fifth member to have migrated to Northern California from Hawaii.

The group found the need to start the association because competing against other schools that were part of the strong, unified Karate organization was very difficult. The Kempo schools of Kajukenbo were not represented correctly. They had to adhere to the rules of Karate, which did not recognize any of the Kajukenbo Kempo techniques or the rules that we used in our own system. Basically, the Kajukenbo students lost in the tournaments because their techniques and training were not the same as Karate.

In order to counter this unfair bias, the Kajukenbo schools organized into their own association in order to have more clout where competitions were concerned. Having an organized system and referees of our own, to balance out the referees from Karate, gave Kajukenbo students a fair chance to win in tournament competition.

Within the structure of the Kajukenbo Association of America, I was having personal problems with my four seniors, Charles Gaylord, Joe Halbuna, Alejo Reyes and Tony Ramos.

Emperado was a man of vision. He had told me that the Chinese systems were becoming more popular. Since he had formed the Ch'uan fa with Dela Cruz and me, it was time for me to teach my four seniors the soft style of the Kajukenbo system.

It was difficult for the seniors, who had come to Northern California before me, to humble themselves and learn these techniques to implement into their hard style Kempo, especially from a junior. All of them were either 8 to 12 years older than me and very set in their ways, as far as the hard style was concerned.

Alejo Reyes told me that he was too big, too heavy and too set in his hard style to be jumping in and doing flying kicks. He would rather stay focused on the hard style Kempo, but that he would have his son's wife come down and learn the Ch'uan from me. Another student of his, Joyce Davis, also came to my classes to learn Ch'uan; she was one of the best form competitors that I had at that time.

Joe Halbuna stayed strictly to his Kajukenbo Kempo. Tony Ramos, although hesitant at the beginning, was perhaps the most open-minded of the four. He made arrangements to drive an hour from Fairfield, California to San Leandro, California after he had finished teaching his classes at 9 p.m., to learn the Kung Fu forms. But he was still going to use his own self-defense techniques and was only interested in the forms.

Charles Gaylord ended up having some of his top students study with other Kung Fu masters in the Bay area and would rename his expression, the Charles Gaylord Ch'uan fa method.

The original Kajukenbo Ch'uan fa style had a written system that was laid down by Emperado, Dela Cruz and myself. When I relocated from the Bay area to Denver, Colorado, a few students from the Gaylord's method, via Gabe Vargas, moved to Denver to study with me. Mike Abbot, Karen Sheperd, Fred King, David Poole, Richard Mananti and Cheryl Mananti were just some of the students to come train with me.

The KAA was looking to have a new patch, logo and emblem made. It was narrowed down to three possibilities. One was presented by Joe Halbuna that was turned down. The other two were a design from Tony Ramos, and my design, that was actually a design for my school of Chinese Kempo-Kung Fu.

Tony Ramos' design had a white background with a person in a white karate uniform, standing on a red world. Although the design was good, it did not represent the new Kajukenbo.

First, it had a white Karate uniformed man standing on a red world which didn't make sense to us because all the Kempo people wore black uniforms. Also, having the person in the white uniform standing on the red world did not go over well. We were still in the Cold War, and some of us connected the red world as a socialist or communist symbol.

When my emblem was presented with its background meaning, it was overwhelmingly voted for and adopted as the new local patch and emblem of Kajukenbo. This was a huge turning point in the mentality of the seniors. And since the Chinese martial arts were on the rise, many schools were adding Kung Fu to their advertising and signs.

Many instructors went from Karate and Kempo uniforms to using Chinese uniforms, even donning sashes instead of belts. Instead of using the term instructors or sensei, they were using sifu or sigung. Everything that was once in English or Japanese, was switching to Chinese terminologies overnight.

Also, 80% of English or Japanese terminology was changing to Chinese. Even the salutation changed. The influence of what I presented, unbeknownst to me at that time, would be the catalyst for the direction of Kajukenbo in the future. This logo and emblem would be the international standard from which all other designs originated.

My training continued to evolve and incorporated different aspects from different styles of Kung Fu. Mel Lee introduced me to Ron Lew, who eventually sponsored me in the San Jose Chinese Kung Fu Club. Paul Ng was teaching Southern Style Kung Fu, but was also learning Northern Style from Professor Wong Jack Man.

I found that very interesting, and I soon became a student as well and learned very quickly, adopting many of the techniques into the Kajukenbo Tum-pai style that I was teaching. Kam Yuen, another one of Paul Ng's students, would eventually be hired to teach David Carradine, star of the popular television show, *Kung Fu*, directed by David Chow. This television series became very popular and caused the interest in martial arts to greatly increase in the United States.

Things were really taking off for me, so much so, that our location in Cherryland Hall was getting too small for the number of students that I was getting. We relocated to a storefront on the main drag in San Leandro, California.

After several months of hard work and lots of renovations, it began to look like a martial arts school instead of a furniture store, which it had been before we moved in. I put a new façade up with a red pagoda against a black wall as the entrance to our school. It looked very sharp. Above the door was a sign which read, School of Chinese Kempo Kung Fu. The sign was in yellow and drew lots of attention to our school.

One day I was working in the school, balancing myself on the edge of an eight foot high wall, finishing the trim around a dressing room. I had my hammer in my hand and a nail ready to pound into a wood panel, when Anthony and Mary Lou Ribeiro walked into my training hall.

I had not been expecting anyone to come in because my sign on the outside said that we were closed. I had the door open because I was bringing in supplies. They just wandered in; hoping that someone would be there that could help them. This ended up being a chance meeting that would change my life for years to come.

Tony and Mary spent the weekend visiting Karate and Tae Kwon Do schools, but really didn't know one martial art from another. In fact, they thought they were walking into a cooking school because my sign said, School of Chinese Kempo. They thought it had something to do with Chinese cooking, but were stopping in to ask if I knew of any martial arts schools nearby. Tony was looking for a school where his wife could learn self-defense, as that is what he was giving her for her 25th birthday.

After learning what they wanted, I stepped down and gave them a quick demonstration and some information. Mary Lou signed up and started class the following Monday. She had good coordination from her time spent in sports and water skiing, and her drive and determination was very strong.

After a couple of weeks of instruction from both my wife and me, Dolly and Mary Lou became very good friends with Dolly. Back then, only two out of every 10 students were females, so she was definitely in the minority. But in my school, women were expected to train just as hard as men. Their friendship blossomed to the point that our families shared time together, enjoyed dinners together, and our sons played together.

About six months later, Mary Lou came in one day and asked if we could talk in private in my office after class that night. I had no idea what she wanted, but said that would be fine. Dolly and I had just moved into a house up the road, but previously we were living in a spare room in the school. Dolly had already gone home to put Mark to bed, so we had complete privacy for whatever Mary Lou wanted to discuss.

In my office, Mary Lou seemed very nervous, and I could see in her eyes that she was very troubled. I had thought that maybe she was getting ready to tell me that she was going to quit since classes were starting to get much harder. This was about the time in class when students started dropping out because the contact was much harder. But that was not what was on her mind; what she said was much worse than that, and left me shaking with anger and disgust. To this day, that conversation still sickens me.

I knew that Dolly had asked Mary Lou to babysit Mark sometimes, which I had no problem with at all, but I was about to have a big problem with it. Turns out, Dolly was asking Mary Lou to babysit almost every morning, as soon as I left for work at Western Electric. Mary Lou told me that this had been going on for over two months. She paused, as if she did not want to continue the conversation.

Now I was getting concerned. I didn't want a student mixed up in any of my marital problems, but Mary Lou had become more than a student, she was our friend. I appreciated her honesty, but the information that she shared next knocked me to my knees. I just couldn't believe it!

It turned out that Dolly had been seeing the guy who owned the motorcycle shop next door, who was also the owner of our building where we rented. She saw this guy for a few hours each morning while Mary Lou kept Mark. There was a heated affair going on between my wife and my landlord, and not only that, but she had started using pakalolo, marijuana, as well!

Mary Lou was having marital troubles too, something that I would not become aware of until a couple of months later. And of course, Mary Lou did not feel comfortable with what was happening, and she also did not have the time to babysit every morning just so Dolly could see her lover.

At first I thought that we could work through this, after all, this was not the first time that Dolly had cheated on me. That was why we moved to California to start with, to try to save our marriage. But the fights and arguments got worse, and actually became so heated that I had to move back into the room in the school. I filed for divorce because it had become obvious that it wasn't going to work out.

During the course of the next six months, Mary Lou and I spent more time together, not romantically, but in training. She was working hard to become the number one fighter in women's martial arts. After training, she was also my shoulder to cry on, and she helped me get over the pain and disappointment of dealing with a broken marriage.

The divorce with Dolly didn't take long, but during the course of the divorce, I found out that Dolly was also having an affair with the president of the Kajukenbo system. This shocked me even more! I never thought a man that I respected, and considered my friend, would deliberately hurt me like that.

As time passed, I would find out that she had several other affairs that I did not know about. My friend, Al Dela Cruz, who was a Honolulu Police Office working undercover, provided me with some information that completely made me sick to my stomach, but some things are better left unsaid.

Needless to say, this was a very hard time for me. I went through the five phases of grief: denial, anger, bargaining, depression, and acceptance. This would not be the only time in my life that I would have to learn to live with these same emotions; my future would be one wild rollercoaster ride.

Dolly and I have not talked in 50 years, with the exception of seeing her at her father and mother's funerals, and at the premier for Mark's movie, *Only the Brave*, about a Japanese American in WWII, not to be confuse with another movie of his called, *Only the Strong*, about a group of juveniles in Miami and the Brazilian fighting art of Capoeira.

I continued to teach classes and Mary Lou continued to be one of my top students. This is how Mary Lou summed up training with me in the following way:

I entered into Al's world at the age of 24. His role in my life was to be my martial arts teacher, to teach me self-defense and all that I was told was in his program. I was excited from the moment I set foot into the training room. It was so foreign to me. I noticed bags and hanging weapons to the side, and other types of training equipment that I had never seen before. My blood was pumping from fear and excitement. I had no clue what I was going to learn. I was totally unprepared for what I was about to begin. I had just walked into the world of the unknown.

His school was made up mostly of guys. Women were few and far between. I was soon to find out why. It was plain to see; it was a man's world and no place for the weaker sex. I said to myself, "Okay guys, you're not going to run this female out. I'm here to stay." I was already involved in waterskiing and snow skiing. My legs and arms were strong. No push over here!

As my teacher, I would soon find out that Al was a terror to deal with. I don't think that gentleness, understanding, and patience were in the Hawaiian dictionary. He was young, impressive, demanding, and talented. He was just plain mesmerizing. Anyone who saw him perform was left speechless. His following was huge; everyone wanted to train with him.

Al was new to the mainland from Hawaii, the new kid on the block so to speak. His style was different and exciting. It was not really contemporary, but at the same time not traditional.

I was soon to find out that there were such things as Karate tournaments. Of course, Al put me into them. Ready or not, here I go, was kind of how it went. It was fun and exciting. As I looked around and saw all the competition, I realized that this was where Al should be to really promote his style. He put his students into the competition but not himself.

His students were great, but we did not do justice to his style. I felt he should be in the ring. So, as bold as I was, I told him so. We had formed a strong student-teacher relationship. He saw I had potential and pushed me hard. We had respect for one another.

He realized I was for real and wanted me to be the best. He listened to what I had to say and agreed to enter into the next tournament. It was wild. No one had ever seen anything like him. They didn't know how to fight him, and he was so fast, officials couldn't catch all that he would throw out. He was a blur.

Me playing my ukulele

My school of Chinese Kempo-Gung Fu in San Leandro, CA

Me with Ron Lew, Mel Lee and Dennis Futamase in 1967

My Kung Fu pose in 1965

Bringing home the trophies in 1967
Kneeling left to right: Mike Regan, Bill Owens
Back row left to right: Doug Espinda, Dolly Dacascos, Pat Regan

Sifu Paul Ng on Jan. 08, 1942
Sifu Ng passed away on January 8, 2015 at the age of 73.
Ironically, he died in the same day he was born.

Professor Wong Jack Man in the 1960's

Chapter 4

My Tournament Career Begins

The will to win, the desire to succeed, the urge
to reach your full potential...these are the keys
that will unlock the door to personal excellence.
Confucius

I had not entered into any competitions myself; I was simply content to be a trainer, a coach, and a budding martial arts entrepreneur. I had no interest in competing at that time. Mary Lou encouraged me to get into the competitive side of things because I had no advanced students or black belts to represent my school.

My top black belt, Doug Espinda, had come into the school one night, all worked up and in a panic. He told me that he just found out he had gotten his girlfriend pregnant and that he did not know what to do. I advised him that he now had to be a man and take the responsibility of being a husband and a father. He would not return to the martial arts until several years later, and by that time, I had moved to Colorado.

Mel Abero, my very first student in California, and the one responsible for me opening up my first group, was now expecting his second child. He had to lay off his training to get a second job. Pat and Mike Regan had decided to enlist in the Marine Corps, and Ted Sotelo had gotten upset with me concerning another student's ranking. At this time, all of my original students were no longer training with me and I had no advanced students to compete in the tournaments.

The first tournament I entered was the South Bay Karate Championships in Los Angeles. This is where I made a major change in my fighting style. Mary Lou and I had already won first place in form competition. I had already fought in the lightweight division and took first place, and now I was facing the heavyweight champion for the grand championship.

This championship fight would alter my competition tournament fighting style forever. I had no problem breezing through the competition in the lightweight division, but this heavyweight guy was exceptionally good. He and I went toe-to-toe for the grand championship title. Not only was he fast, but he was also powerful and outweighed me by a good 40 pounds. A big fighter that is also fast can be a lethal combination.

I came out in a typical Kempo pose – left lead forward and hands high like a boxer. He came out in his typical high Tang Soo Do stance and attacked me with a quick right side kick that caught me in the side of the left ribs before I could drop my hand to block it. This kick cracked a rib or two and sent me over the table into the judges. I knew that I couldn't take another shot like that to my ribs!

It hurt so bad that when I came back out, I switched sides, putting myself into a right forward lead, but letting my hand drop so that my arm would be protecting my ribs from his devastating side kick.

My left hand would come up, open palm facing outwards, protecting the right side of my face. This allowed me to launch a fast back fist and attack with my own offensive side kick to take the lead in the match.

My left punch was useless in this match because every time I extended the counterpunch it hurt. I fought primarily with my right lead forward, scoring with right roundhouse kicks to his groin, sidekicks to his ribs, and my back fist to his head, winning the championship. From that point on, I fought with my strong side forward, even though, by birth, I was left-handed.

My second tournament was in Oakland, California, where I fought Gabe Vargas from Charles Gaylord's school. I won and went on to fight a Tae Kwon Do fighter. He expected me to only do ground techniques, and only expected back fist punches and roundhouse kicks.

Instead, during the opening match, as soon as he took his fighting stance, I launched with a jumping, spinning, back kick and caught him squarely in the chest. I think this surprised me more than it did him! My kick sent him flying backwards and made a definite point – I was not just a floor fighter, but could go airborne if I wanted to.

I outscored him with kicking techniques and went on to fight my third match, which, if I won, would have brought me into the grand championship. But I was facing a very smart fighter who had been watching my previous fights.

His name was Smiling Rick Alemany. He went point for point with me until he was a point ahead just before the time ran out. Rick and I would face each other five more times during my fighting career in the San Francisco Bay Area. We would take turns winning first place trophies during each Karate championship.

He was a counterpuncher and remained one of my very best friends. We would be teammates on the Kajukenbo team and win 1st place at the Northern Pacific Nationals a couple of years later. As I racked up wins and grand championships in the area, my reputation, as well as Mary Lou's, grew fast.

My greatest competitor and friend, Phil Cornan, from the Alejo Reyes' school in Valejo, California was shot dead by his girlfriend before he reached his prime. His very quick footwork and explosive kicks and punches, made me work very hard to pass him in our division. Phil, like Rick Alemany, and I, would also trade off taking first place or the grand championships for several years, until his untimely death.

There was a time that if anyone had any desire to get to the grand championship via the light weight division, they had to pass through all three of us first. Both of them would have had no problems going higher in the national rankings had they had the opportunity to compete in more national matches, like I did.

I have often been asked how I was able to become a top 10 fighter in the late 1960's and early 1970's, as a Kung Fu stylist. But, to tell the truth, it wasn't all that difficult. At that time, Kung Fu fighters were rare. Other stylists were very curious about what we did.

First, I want to be very clear about one big misconception that many people have about me as a Kung Fu fighter. In the 1960's, hardly anyone on the Mainland, outside of the Chinese community, knew much about the Chinese fighting arts. That lack of knowledge gave me an edge. In addition, I had a background in Judo, Jujitsu, boxing, and Kajukenbo Kempo before I ever got involved with Kung Fu.

If I had nothing but Kung Fu training, the road to the top would have been much harder and longer for me. I was competing as a Kung Fu stylist in forms or kata competitions and fighting as a Kempo stylist. Eventually, my combination of Kajukenbo Kempo and Kung Fu led me to a hybrid style all my own, which I called Wun Hop Kuen Do, via way of Tum-pai and Ch'uan fa, which means combined fist arts. Wun Hop Kuen Do is still going strong today in both the United States and in Europe.

There were a few Kung Fu stylists competing in San Francisco and in Los Angeles, but they primarily competed in forms and weapons. Those who did dare to fight rarely made it to the finals. One reason for this was that they had to compete using Karate rules.

I fought Michael Sandos for the first time in Albuquerque, New Mexico at Sam Allred's Thunderbird Karate Championships. The following are his thoughts from that day:

I was paired off in a sparring competition with Sifu Al when he was a 4ᵗʰ degree black belt out of California, via Hawaii, and I was a young 3ʳᵈ degree black belt under the Kaju style of Dr. Robert Rapue.

He fought and beat me by using the ring against me. I was so impressed with how he had beaten me and the other four black belts from my school, who were previously paired up against him, that I would never leave his side from that point on.

This Division had 32 fighters. By the time the elimination was over with, Sifu Al was the only one left to take on the middleweight and heavyweight winners of their divisions. Sifu Al fought them all and ended up with the Grand Championship after defeating the Heavyweight champ, Russel Perron, from Denver.

What was even more fantastic was the fact that he did a Kung Fu demonstration of an impressive Kung Fu form, did the breakdown of self-defense from that form, and ended the demonstration defending against an eight man attack. He had the crowd on their feet.

In the evening, after the tournament, we all went to dinner and a young black belt was sitting next to him in the restaurant and I came and grabbed him and told him to sit somewhere else that this was my seat. Sifu Al had changed my life that night. I wanted to go everywhere with him and learn everything I could from him. Sifu Al had it all – speed, timing, power, agility, knowledge, and the experience to teach me what I needed to do and where I needed to go.

Boung Yu, at that time, was a 6ᵗʰ degree black belt in Tae Kwon Do and had only been in the country for about a year. He was 36 years old at the time and was probably the oldest person on the tournament circuit. The first time that I fought him was in Sacramento, California. He was wearing his white, traditional Tae Kwon Do uniform, a towel covering his shoulders, presumably to block his name, and a straw hat to cover his face.

He was warming up and doing some very intimidating flying jump kicks. I have to say, it was impressive! He had already used a form of mental warfare by psychologically putting fear into some of the other fighters' minds. We were both in the lightweight division. He fought his first round and had beaten his opponent impressively. Now, he was paired off with me in the second elimination round.

I watched him eliminate the first fighter and knew how great his kicking techniques were, so when I lined up to fight him, I decided on a different approach. At the sound of the bell, I lunged forward and struck him with a punch to the head. Immediately, he did a jumping, spinning, back kick to where he *thought* I would be, but as he landed, I was on the floor waiting for him. I threw a sidekick straight to his groin.

He wasn't wearing a groin cup on that day, and it was obvious after that kick; he was hurting! He was now two points behind me. It was do-or-die time for him. Boung Yu never expected to be behind in this match. As the referee restarted the match, I could see him cursing under his breath. I knew then that he had lost control. He lunged at me immediately when the referee said, "Start!"

Again, I wasn't where he expected me to be; I was off to his right side and countered with a reverse punch that caught him in the kidney. He was out of the match and embarrassed that he had lost like this in front of his students, who were all expecting him to take the grand championship. After all, he was a great 6th degree champion from Korea.

A couple of months later, we met again at another Northern California tournament. We were paired off to fight each other in the third round. Arrogantly, he came across the line before the referee started the fight, lightly put his finger on my chest, and said, "I am going to kill you."

I looked at him and smiled. Then I said, "Your name is Boung Yu, is that correct?"

He replied in a heavy Korean accent, "Why you ask?"

I said, "I'm going to bong you!" And when we fought, I did exactly what I said I would.

I had beaten this great champion twice, and I knew without a doubt, that the next time we would meet, he would be coming for blood and revenge!

His opportunity came the following year at Ed Parker's International Karate Championships. Sadly, he won that match by default. I was fired up for the fight as well, and made a little too much contact with a punch to the head. He was given the winning point. I was disqualified, and he went on to fight against Joe Lewis, a fight that he would lose.

We would meet once more in 1973 at the United States National

Black Belt Championship in Albuquerque, New Mexico. Boung Yu badly wanted to win outright and prove that he could actually beat me straight up, without the benefit of a disqualification.

Once again, we were paired up after eliminating and surviving the first few rounds. Again, he came up to me pointed his finger at my chest and said the same thing, "I'm going to kill you this time!"

I smiled and said, "Bong you, let's do it!"

I scored the first two points very fast. Already 2 points ahead of him, I could see the fear on his face that he was going to lose again. He pressed his attack harder and instead of retreating, I lunged forward and hit him in the head. He went down immediately. Again, I was disqualified, and he had won another match by default. So as it stood he won two fights out of five because of my "excessive contact." I guess when someone tells me that they are going to kill me, I hit a little harder.

He was never satisfied, knowing that in reality, he had actually lost to me 5 times. But, when all is said and done, we remain friends, even to this day. After all, when it comes right down to it, tournament competition is just a game of tag.

By this time, my reputation was growing on the West Coast. I was again invited back to Sam Allred's Thunderbird Karate Championships in Albuquerque, New Mexico to defend my grand championship that I had won just eight months earlier.

This time, I fought Louis Delgado, who had just beaten Chuck Norris a few months earlier. He was now rated as one of the top fighters in the United States. This match was supposed to be the highlight of the tournament, and it did not disappoint. I ended up winning the match by two points and retaining my grand championship.

After the grand championship match, came a national championship tournament that was promoted by Leo Fong and Ron Marchini in Stockton, California. At this tournament, all of the top rated fighters from all over the country came to participate. Most people thought that the final fight would match up Boung Yu and Louis Delgado for the grand championship, as both of these fighters had a fierce reputation. But I had a different vision; these people just didn't know it yet.

As it turned out, I had to fight my good friend, Phil Cornan, one of the toughest competitors in California, right off the bat. This was no easy match. He made me work my butt off to advance to the next round.

Boung Yu and Louis Delgado had both beaten all of their opponents to remain alive and advance in the competition. The elimination came down to the four remaining fighters in our divisions. Out of the four, everyone had expected, and wanted to see, Boung Yu and Louis Delgado battle it out. This was being advertised as the "Fight of all Fights," with only one person being crowned the grand champion.

Delgado had beaten his opponent to move to the final fight. And, as luck would have it, Boung Yu would have to beat me in order to move to the final round and fight Delgado. Both Boung Yu and Delgado were anxious to fight each other to prove who was best.

Boung Yu was two points behind and knew that his possible championship was on the line. He tried to attack me with a quick side kick, but ended up getting kicked in the groin instead. With that kick to the groin, I advanced to fight Delgado. It was a 3-0 win! I had killed one giant and now was facing an even bigger one.

The cheering of the crowd, and the jeers that came from Delgado's fans, raised my energy level, and I was determined to end this championship fight in good form. The points between Delgado and me went back and forth, but at the last second, I scored the winning point and won the so-called "Fight of all Fights," and people started calling me *Al the Giant Killer*.

Some martial arts fans in the audience complained to the promoters because they really wanted to see Boung Yu and Louis Delgado fight. So the promoters decided to have them fight an exhibition match at the end of the tournament. They put on a good show, but since nothing was on the line, it was evident that they were just going through the motions; there was no heart involved like you would have seen in a real championship fight.

Mary Lou was still my top student, and like many other tournaments during this time, she took first place in both forms and fighting competitions. It was not unusual for us, as a team, to take home four to six trophies from almost every tournament we competed in. We both took home many grand championship trophies.

During 1967, I had seen Joe Lewis and Chuck Norris on the covers of many martial arts magazines. Their names, along with Skipper Mullins and Mike Stone, were all very big during this time period.

The biggest and most prestigious tournament on the West Coast was Ed Parker's International Karate Championships. If you competed in this tournament, and won, you were going to make a big name for yourself. Because of that fact, this tournament drew competitors from all over the United States. It was usually held in August every year, in Long Beach, California, and its legacy still continues to this day.

Joe Lewis and Chuck Norris were the most well-known competitors during this time. Their fighting style, personalities, and characters were as different as night and day, yin and yang. I had admired both of their fighting styles after having watched them in competitions for several years, even before I got into tournament competition myself. I had a lot of respect for each of them.

Joe Lewis' style was based on the Okinawan style of Karate. He fought from a very low horse stance, and usually with his right hand forward. He had a very fast and deceptive right hand back fist. It was his trademark to skip and throw a right leg side kick as well. His punching techniques were devastating. Joe was very good, and he knew it.

Chuck Norris, on the other hand, was a Korean stylist, Tang Soo Do fighter. He had both excellent kicking and aerial kicking techniques. He was more mild-mannered and a top-notch gentleman. Although I would meet both men at the tournaments and talk to them on several occasions, we kept things at the level of acquaintances.

But, in time, as my reputation grew, I was accepted into the "in group." I would end up staying with them at their place or rooming with them during tournament events.

In 1968, during the International Karate Championships in Long Beach, I walked off with an incredible record of accumulating trophies, which no one has matched to this day. I took first place in forms, the grand championship in forms, second place in fighting, a trophy for the most accumulated points in the tournament, and the best sportsmanship trophy.

I believe that I would have ended up fighting for the grand championship, and taking first place too, if I had not dislocated my left wrist and broken a couple of fingers. That really hampered my performance.

I was fighting Steve Sanders, a.k.a. Steve Muhammad, from the Black Karate Federation out of Los Angeles. He was an excellent right hand, counterpuncher, and I was a great left hand, counterpuncher. As the referee gave us the signal to fight, we both attacked at the same time. Like a mirror image, he and I lunged forward, and at full speed, his right fist collided with my left fist. It was the loudest sound of bones breaking that I had ever heard.

Both of us kiai'ed at the same time, and those kiai's turning to screams of pain before the medics reached the stage. But we didn't let that stop us. We put the match on a short pause, as both of us struggled to get off the floor.

Neither of us had scored a point, but we had both done great damage to each other. After a quick patch up and hand wrap, we continued the fight. We traded points, with Sanders getting the final point on me, just before the bell rang at the end of the match. Steve went on to fight for the Grand Champion but lost in his final match. Joe Lewis ended up as the Grand Champion.

My first forms (kata) win, 1967 International Karate Championship

Malia congratulating me on my Grand Championship in New Mexico

Louis Delgado and Al Dacascos fight for the Championship

Scoring with one of my famous drop kicks

Me with my Porsche in front of Tracy's Karate studio in Denver, CO

Mike Stone's 1972 team in Hawaii
Top row left to right:
Steve Muhammad, Ralph Alegria, Al Dacascos, Cecil Peoples,
John Natividad, Darnell Garcia, Bob Burbidge
Kneeling left to right:
Steve Fisher, Benny Urquidez, Mike Stone, Howard Jackson

On the cover of the U.K. magazine, Fighting Arts

Chapter 5

The Bruce Lee Conflict

Instructors don't make problems for each other;
students do. So don't worry about it.
Bruce Lee

I want to start this chapter by saying that I hold both Bruce Lee and Wong Jack Man in highest regards. I have great respect for them and knew them both personally. Each contributed in their own ways to my martial arts and to making me the person that I am today.

The stories of Bruce Lee and me disliking each other are totally false, and I will give you the truth about what really happened in this chapter. Also, the commonly held beliefs about Bruce Lee and Wong Jack Man are also riddled with falsehoods and misinformation.

For example, I bet that you thought Wong Jack Man wanted to fight Bruce Lee because Bruce was teaching non-Chinese the Chinese arts. This is not true. Wong Jack Man had many non-Chinese students in his school, including my Mary Lou.

Let me go back a bit and cover the Bruce Lee "conflict" from the beginning. I did not know who Bruce Lee was when I first moved to California. All I knew was that I was ready to teach Kajukenbo Tumpai in the San Francisco Bay area, and I wanted to teach it with the Sid Asuncion mentality and attitude.

I have already written about my early days in the Bay area, so I will not repeat all of that information. What I want to do in this chapter is to go back and interject the information about Bruce Lee and clarify some false ideas concerning Bruce Lee, Wong Jack Man, and myself. As with most stories, this one has taken on a life of its own.

I met Ron Lew through one of my students, and Ron would eventually introduce me to Sifu Paul Ng in San Jose. This led me to continue my training in the Chinese arts. During this same time, Ming Lum, a very well-known personality in San Francisco, and another Hawaiian transplant and advisor to Emperado, introduced me to Professor Wong Jack Man, Paul Ng's Northern Style Kung Fu instructor.

A couple of weeks later, I found out that the incident that happened to me at my school, concerning the Chinese martial artists who came to see what I was up to, had also happened to Bruce Lee a few years earlier. But with Bruce, Wong Jack Man was the man who was selected to confront Bruce about his school. Wong Jack Man was also the man who fought Bruce Lee in that now famous fight.

Bruce Lee and James Lee were names that kept popping up in casual conversation after tournaments around the Bay area. This was during the time that I was getting involved with tournament competition myself.

As I have already discussed, I had a couple of Chinese guys come to my training hall and confront me about what I was teaching. Well, one of those guys was carrying a beige-covered book titled, Chinese *Gung Fu: The Philosophical Part of Self-Defense*, written by Bruce Lee. This, along with the fact that these guys had the gaul to question me about my martial arts in my own kwoon, or training hall, peaked my interest.

A few weeks later, my students and I were doing a demonstration in the Oakland Auditorium, and there again were these same two Chinamen, sitting in the front row. One of them, a skinny, handsome young man, sat with his legs and arms crossed, and the other sat smoking a cigarette, something that would be unheard of at a martial arts demonstration today.

They watched our demonstration from beginning to end. When the next martial arts group came up to do their act, they politely left. I was told by a guest at the show that one of the fellows was a Gung Fu teacher, teaching Wing Chun in the Oakland hills. I never heard of that art and was curious to know who this person was.

A couple of weeks later, we were doing another demonstration and that's when the sparks began to fly. After the demonstration was over, Ted, one of my students, got into a verbal confrontation with two of James Lee's students about which style was better. Like all students, they were each proud of their own instructor and style.

Ted and his brother were two of my very best students, and it was obvious that I favored both of them. These two boys must have made impressions on Bruce and James Lee during one of our demonstrations. Their names kept popping up as faces to watch.

In this confrontation between Ted and James Lee's students, the name of Sifu Al was said to be the only person who had knocked Bruce Lee off his "horse." That did not sit well with Bruce's students.

I was supposed to have a friendly meeting with Bruce after the events of the day, but Bruce cancelled it. I guess he was angry with me about what he heard concerning me knocking him off his "horse."

In return, I was upset that Bruce did not want to talk to me and had no idea why he called off our meeting. All I knew was that I felt like I was being blown off and it did not make me happy. After all, I was one of the top competitors during this time.

When I found out about Ted's confrontation with Lee's students, I immediately told Ted to go and straighten this out with James and Bruce Lee. Ted went to James Lee's house and told James that there was a misunderstanding between Bruce and me. Bruce was in another room while James Lee and Ted talked.

Ted was young and eager to learn more as James invited him to show his stuff. Bruce intervened and wanted to see how Ted would block a certain punch that he threw. When Ted parried to the side and countered, Bruce was surprised that Ted moved so well.

Naturally Ted responded that Sifu Al Dacascos trained all students that way. Ted told me that he was not sure at first whether or not it was Bruce because of the thick glasses he was wearing at that time.

I later found out that Ted was referring to Sifu Al Novak as the one who had knocked Bruce off his horse with a punch to Bruce's chest a few months earlier. Those two students never connected the name of Al Novak as the culprit. Ted had heard this from a friend of James Lee, Newt Kamikani, who witnessed the event between Sifu Al Novak and Bruce Lee.

When Ted mentioned this event to those two students, they assumed that he was talking about Sifu Al Dacascos and Bruce Lee. With the loud music of the band blaring, and a boisterous crowd in the background, these two students did not understand what Ted was talking about, and that was where the misunderstanding started.

I went to James Lee's house a few weeks later to clarify this rumor because it was still being spread throughout the area. I had heard that Bruce was in Oakland during a short break from the hit show, *The Green Hornet*.

I introduced myself to James Lee, who was already very familiar with me, and told him that I came to clear up this rumor. James was very hospitable, but told me that Bruce was not there because he had been delayed. But he promised that he would convey the message to Bruce when he came up to Oakland.

I was determined to make sure there were no hostilities between Bruce and me, but I guess the time was not right for me to meet Bruce just yet. Instead, I met Bobby Baker, a student of Bruce and James, and at one time a student of my instructor, Sid Asuncion back in Hawaii.

Bobby Baker was the person holding the pad at the International Karate Championship in Long Beach where Bruce did his famous one inch punch that sent Bobby flying back a few yards. I was surprised and happy to see that Bobby continued his training in the martial arts after serving his time in the Navy and being stationed at Pearl Harbor, Hawai'i. He was very concerned about finding an art similar to what we were teaching back in O'ahu.

I finally met Bruce Lee face to face for the first time at Ed Parker's 1967 International Karate Championships in Long Beach, California. After months of seeing each other from a distance and hearing the rumors that were flying back and forth about the two of us, it was very nice to finally meet him. This would be the first of many more meetings to come and our cordial friendship.

The year before at the 1966 International Karate Championships, I was competing in the tournament in forms. Bruce was sitting in the front row, next to the stage where the final contestants from the Chinese, Korean, and Japanese first place winners were to compete for the grand championship. John Pereira represented the Japanese form, Chuck Norris represented the Korean style, and I represented the Chinese style.

I had torn my left hamstring muscle while warming up for the evening finals, and John Pereira ended up taking the Grand Championship in kata that night. Bruce would later tell me that he was cheering for me. I cannot remember who won the fighting grand championship title, but I think it was Chuck Norris. The pain I had in my thigh was so intense that I really didn't care who won. However, 1967 would be different.

Bruce Lee's name had become bigger than ever. His *Green Hornet* television series was doing well and he was appearing in more martial arts magazines than ever, while giving Gung Fu and Karate exposure never before seen in the United States. Even his tournament appearances were more frequent, and people came to these events just to see, and hopefully meet, Bruce Lee.

Both of us were promoting Gung Fu, only in different ways. He was doing it in the entertainment arena and I was doing it on the national tournament circuit, by performing demonstrations and as a competitor. Many of my performances were in forms and self-defense against multiple opponents, and mostly on the West Coast of the United States.

I also competed in forms under the Chinese Gung Fu banner and fighting as a Kajukenbo Ch'uan fa stylist. My Wun Hop Kuen Do expression had not yet been named; that would come a couple of years later.

Because of my Chinese forms and my own personal way of fighting, the public looked at me as a Gung Fu fighter instead of a Kajukenbo fighter. This drew a lot of interest in the Chinese martial arts communities because there was no Chinese fighter winning in those early tournament years. In fact, most of them were being creamed.

Our School of Chinese Kempo Gung Fu drew a lot of unwanted attention during those days. Our black *jing-mo* uniform, fast lead side back fist, left reverse punch, lead foot side kick, round kicks, drop kicks to the groin, and rapid hand combinations all became our trademark. I am sure that Bruce was curious to see how far I would go in competition as a Chinese Gung Fu fighter against the other stylists.

As the evening came to a close at the 1967 Internationals, Bruce Lee, elegantly dressed in a blue blazer, turtleneck, and white pants, was standing in the hallway to the exit. I had just changed out of my uniform and had come out of the dressing room, when we bumped into each other. I said, "Hi Bruce."

He replied, and from that point our acquaintance had finally begun. I told him that for the last year, there had been many rumors going around in the Oakland Bay area concerning us. He cut me off and told me, "Instructors don't make problems for each other; students do. So don't worry about it."

Those were comforting words for me to hear. It would have been nice to have had that behind us from the beginning, instead of thinking about it for the whole year. Instead of departing, we ended up in the lobby talking for the next hour about techniques and training methods.

Bruce went on to do bigger and better things as his career took him to Hong Kong. As for me, I moved to Denver, Colorado in 1969 and used it as the center point from which to travel to more states to compete.

The next time we would meet would be at a team competition where I fought for the Midwest team going up against a team that Fumio Demura had put together. Bruce Lee was sitting ringside. I was pitted against a sixth degree black belt, Japanese stylist. He was fresh from Japan and eager to see what American fighters could do.

There were other teams there also. There was Tracy's team which was led by Joe Lewis, Chuck Norris led his own team, and there was a team from the East Coast, one team from Texas, and a team from the Chicago Great Lakes area.

When our team came up to fight, we were pitted to fight the Japanese team and I was selected to fight second in a five-man team. It was a total point accumulation type of tournament, and I scored five points to my opponents zero. On one attack, I launched in with a back fist and reverse punch, followed by a spinning kick that sent my opponent flying out of the ring and straight into the lap of Bruce Lee. As the opponent got up and tried to shake off the kick, Bruce smiled and gave me two thumbs up.

My fighting style had changed and I was now using a right lead side forward, right arm hanging, and my left-hand on the side of my face to cover or parry. Again, Bruce and I chatted after the fight, and Bruce asked me why I liked coming out that way. I told him that traditionally, I used to come out with my two hands guarding high but that all changed when I was in a competition against a Korean Tae Kwon Do fighter from Los Angeles.

He had slipped in a sidekick to my ribs that sent me flying into the judges table. That guarded position became another trademark of my Wun Hop Kuen Do (WHKD) tournament fighters and it worked for them too. A year or two later, I would see my posture in Bruce's posters and films. I smiled because I knew where Bruce had probably discovered that stance, but I didn't mind.

I was sitting down watching television with my family on one hot night in July, 1973, when the news flashed across the television screen about Bruce's death. Like the rest of the martial arts world, we were saddened and shocked.

A group of us from Denver, and some of my friends from the Chinese community in San Francisco, flew to Hong Kong and witnessed the post funeral chaos among the news media that claimed they knew the inside story of Bruce's death. Many magazines and newspapers made fortunes on anything surrounding the mystery of Bruce's passing.

A year later, in 1974, Mike Anderson formed a group of elite martial artists to tour several cities in Europe. My wife Malia and I were among the top names in the Kung Fu world at that time. Malia and I had just finished an appearance on Merv Griffin's TV show with Joe Lewis and Howard Jackson. Joe Lewis had mentioned on national TV that Al Dacascos was the "King of Kung Fu" now that Bruce Lee had passed away.

Linda Lee was upset with that comment, but I assured her that I had no prior knowledge about what Joe Lewis was going to say. The relationship between Linda Lee and Malia grew as we spent the next three weeks in Europe together on Mike Anderson's tour.

After our return to America, Linda Lee invited Malia and me for a short stay at her home. She wanted me to review some material that Bruce had in his file cabinet because there was a great interest in having his life's work published through *Black Belt* magazine. Bruce had become a major celebrity in the martial arts world and it seemed that everyone was positioning to capitalize on his name.

I told her I would look at it and then give her my opinion. After seeing it, I told her she had better get people like Dan Inosanto and Bruce's other original students involved. When I asked her why she wanted me to review it, she replied, in confidence, that Bruce had high respect for me. She said that he stated that I was not just talking the talk, but was out there proving it. I was honored that Bruce had acknowledged my fighting skills, as well as my work in the martial arts. When she wrote her book on Bruce, *The Man Only I Knew*, in 1975, she made Bruce's comment about me public.

I returned to Europe a few months later, on contract to teach in Hamburg, Germany, promoting Kung Fu. Linda tracked me down and told me that I needed to fly to Hollywood immediately and audition for a possible movie. Linda said Hollywood had already done a worldwide search in major cities looking for the right person to play Bruce Lee in a movie.

I told her that I was not interested, but she insisted I do it. "Why?" I asked.

Her reply was that none of the others could play the part, but she knew I could mimic Bruce's movements and be convincing. A few days later, I was at her home again, reading the script and readying myself for the screen tests. Those next few days in Hollywood, California, would be the craziest period in my life.

While I stayed at Linda Lee's house, I was given access to all of Bruce's training equipment, books, clothing, and I was even driving around in his right sided, red Mercedes-Benz convertible. I was immersing myself in his life, mind and spirit so I could accurately portray him on film.

Linda offered me all of Bruce's clothing and footwear if I wanted it. I told her that it would be nice, but Bruce was 5' 7'' and 140 pounds, but I was 5' 9'' and weighed 150 pounds. He wore a 7 1/2 and I wore a 9 1/2 shoe. So I declined the offer. Now that I think about it, it would have been worth a lot to somebody who may have wanted it for a museum, but hindsight is always 20/20.

Instead, I accepted four separate pieces of workout gear and training equipment. Regrettably, those items later disappeared in Hamburg, when fans found out it first belonged to Bruce Lee. Likewise, two photographs of Bruce and me, taken after the 1967 Internationals, suddenly grew feet and walked off. I have a strong suspicion about who took them, but cannot find the guy. Lucky for him!

After passing the screen test at United Artists, I was in the Burbank sound studios with Howard Jackson as my counterpart, Robert Clouse, the director of *Enter the Dragon,* told me that I was it. The next thing to do would be to get the William Morris Talent Agency to sign me up.

That was the easy part. What happened in the next couple of days sealed my destiny. Since Mike Anderson, Don Quine and Judy Quine were involved with the Professional Karate Association circuit and promoted me in their *Professional Karate Magazine;* PKA president, Don Quine, felt that he should be my agent and manager.

Linda Lee urged me to stay the course with the William Morris Talent Agency. Now the backstabbing to get me to sign began. I had just come back from having a photo shoot for *Inside Kung Fu* magazine with Curtis Wong. The article was about the announcement of me being chosen for the lead in the Bruce Lee movie.

The political dickering over who should be my agent, my manager, and the fight scene choreographer, did nothing but stall that project. I did not know it at first, but Pat Johnson was selected as my fight choreographer. Had I had known that, I would have agreed because I knew that Pat and I could work well together.

Not knowing that it was Pat, I made my voice heard and highly objected to "this karate guy showing me how a Kung Fu artist should move." Also, I wanted to make sure that they knew I was not the "new Bruce Lee."

They wanted me to change my name so that it sounded more like a Chinese-American name. I wanted to remain Al Dacascos. After months of negotiating and various arguments, things fell apart. And, as history shows, the project was shelved for nearly two decades.

During that time, Linda Lee and her family kept in touch with us in Denver. Linda and her children, Shannon and Brandon, visited us a couple of times to go skiing, and we visited them in California. Brandon and Mark became good friends, and that extended into their adulthood. When the news reached us of Brandon's death, while shooting *The Crow,* we were traumatized.

After Brandon's death, my son, Mark, telephoned me in 1991, and said that he had been called to look at a script and see if he was interested in auditioning for the part of Bruce Lee for a movie called *Dragon*. Mark wanted to know why it had not been done earlier and why I had declined to take the movie role back in 1975. I told Mark there could only be one Bruce Lee. I did not want to change my name and we just could not come to an agreement that suited me.

Mark told me that my answer made a lot of sense, and he also decided to decline the offer. He said that he had another option for a movie on Capoeira called *Only the Strong*, for which he was also asked to audition.

"Take it, Mark," I said. I knew this film would make Mark an original instead of being labeled another Bruce Lee. When the television project for *The Crow: Stairway to Heaven* came out, Mark hesitated and we discussed it as well, before he finally decided to do it. In hindsight, it was a good decision.

He did not want to do a bad job on it, because it was his friend, Brandon Lee's, television project at first. After a long year of doing this series, and a fatality on the set, Mark called it quits and moved on to other projects.

The part of Bruce Lee in *Dragon: The Bruce Lee Story* was eventually played by Jason Scott Lee, a friend of mine. Although I thought that he did a good job with it, the movie did not accurately portray the life of my friend, Bruce Lee. One major falsehood that was included in the movie had to do with the fight between Wong Jack Man and Bruce Lee.

Here is what my friend, Linda Lee, wrote in her book, *Bruce Lee: The Man Only I Knew*:

> *Chinese, particularly in America, have been reluctant to disclose these secrets to Caucasians. It became an unwritten law that the art should be taught only to Chinese. Bruce considered such thinking completely outmoded and when it is argued that white men, if taught the secrets, would use the art to injure Chinese, pointed out that if a white man really wanted to hurt a Chinese, there were plenty of other ways he could do it. After all, he is bigger.*
>
> *However, Bruce soon found that his views were not shared by members of the Chinese community in San Francisco, particularly those in the martial arts circles.*

Several months after he and James Lee had begun teaching, a Kung Fu expert called Wong Jack Man, turned up at Bruce's kwoon on Broadway.

Wong had just recently arrived in San Francisco's Chinatown from Hong Kong and was seeking to establish himself at the time, all his pupils being strictly pure Chinese. Three other Chinese accompanied Wong Jack Man who handed Bruce an ornate scroll announcing a challenge in Chinese. Bruce read the scroll which appears to have been an ultimatum from the San Francisco martial arts community.

Presumably, if Bruce lost the challenge, he was either to close down his Institute or stop teaching Caucasians. At that moment, I was over eight months pregnant with Brandon, our son. I suppose I ought to have been nervous. Yet the truth is that I could not have been calmer. I was not in the least concerned for Bruce; I was absolutely certain that he could take care of himself.

I may even have smiled a little, realizing that none of these men, apparently, had any inkling of how dangerous Bruce could be. The two men came out, bowed formally and then began to fight. Wong adopted a classic stance whereas Bruce, who at the time was still using his Wing Chun style, produced a series of straight punches.

Within a minute, Wong's men were trying to stop the fight as Bruce began to warm to his task. James Lee warned them to let the fight continue. A minute later, with Bruce continuing the attack in earnest, Wong began to backpedal as fast as he could.

For an instant, indeed, the scrap threatened to degenerate into a farce as Wong actually turned and ran! But Bruce pounced on him like a springing leopard and brought him to the floor where he began pounding him into a state of demoralization.

"Is that enough?" shouted Bruce.

"That's enough!" pleaded Wong in desperation.

Still highly incensed, Bruce allowed the man to rise and then threw the whole bunch off the premises. I don't think I've ever seen a more startled or frightened crowd of "paper tigers."

The San Francisco martial arts community never again dared to threaten Bruce directly. But a year later, Al Dacascos, who had opened a martial arts school of his own in San Francisco, and like Bruce, had begun teaching Caucasians, was also threatened in a similar way and had a similar reaction.

The Chinese clans then tried to create bad blood between Bruce and Al, spreading rumors that each was "calling the other down;" indeed, at one stage, they circulated the story that Al claimed he had taught Bruce everything he knew – all this in the hope, apparently, that the two men would lose their tempers and put each other out of business.

Bruce, I may say, was well aware of the machinations were being directed against him and, when Al approached him at an international tournament in Los Angeles and pointed out that he had never "called him down" or uttered anything derogatory about him and that he suspected it as merely some of their own people trying to create bad blood between them because they were both instructing Occidentals. Bruce slapped him on the back and told him to forget it. And the two men shook hands.

As Al Dacascos puts it today, "And that was the last time either of us had any trouble with the Chinese community. In fact, if you go down into San Francisco's Chinatown today, or any other Chinatown, you'll find that Bruce is a great hero. They'll tell you, "Yeah, Bruce is a Chinaman and he's a great Kung Fu man!" And they couldn't be more proud of him!"

There is another version from Ricky Wing, a colleague from within the same system, and Wong Jack Man's protégé. He wrote a book on Wong Jack Man called *"Showdown in Oakland: The Story Behind the Wong Jack Man – Bruce Lee Fight"* in 2011. I found this book to be highly entertaining and very interesting. I highly recommend that you read the book from cover to cover. It puts things in a much different light. This is a small part of what he writes:

It is with some trepidation that I write about this duel between Wong Jack Man (b. 1941) and Bruce Lee (Nov 1940 – July 1973). There are many myths and legends surrounding this fight. One might say that this story is shrouded in myth and layered in controversy. What we are short of is a clear picture based on fact.

This is arguably the most significant fight in Bruce Lee's life because it initiated an immediate and major change in his martial thought. People all over the world have been influenced by Bruce Lee in their approach to martial arts and even life itself. But what happened in Bruce Lee's life to influence his development? For this reason alone, their encounter might be of historical interest.

Upon hearing the talk about what had happened at the Sun Sing Theatre, where Bruce Lee did his Kung Fu demonstration, a group decided that someone should take Lee up on his offer after hearing Lee boasted, during a demonstration at this Chinatown theater, that he could beat any martial artist in San Francisco and had issued an open challenge to "fight anyone who thought he could prove him wrong." The men at the Gee Yau Seah Society believed they were responding to a challenge, not instigating it.

Although Wong Jack Man was not at the Sun Sing Theatre and did not hear the challenge directly, he, being also young and bold, like Lee, but in a different way, heard the talk and offered to take Lee up on his challenge. David Chin (b. 1943), twenty-one years of age and a member of the Gee Yau Seah, and Bill Chen were instrumental in bringing together the participants for the bout. The letter, of course, was addressed to "Lee Siu Lung," as that was Bruce's Cantonese name.

From Wong's point of view, this was a sporting contest; otherwise he would not have offered his hands in the traditional gesture of sportsmanship. He didn't expect Lee to strike him at the outset, nor would he have tried to do this to Lee as Wong would consider this to be an ungentlemanly and dishonorable act. He did not consider this a "no-holds-barred" fight by any means. Wong could never have imagined how the story would change over time, with aspects of it turning into legend as the story passed into popular culture.

Lee maintained that he did not issue a challenge from the stage of the Sun Sing, but clearly, many thought he did.

In my opinion, neither man wanted to see himself as the aggressor; Wong believed he was responding to Lee's challenge, while Lee believed he was responding to Wong's. Lee also mentions that Wong came to his studio in order to "punish" him. It would therefore be natural for Lee to be angry and to feel justified in defending his studio.

For those who would criticize Wong for even attempting to defend himself at all, considering the ongoing and widespread media portrayals of him in words and in the movies, Wong has been extremely reticent and has acted with considerable restraint concerning the matter throughout the years.

At Lee's premature and tragic death in July of 1973, Wong knew the matter was over, and any connection between the two had long since passed. Contrary to what people may think, Wong had no great dislike of Lee, and that essentially, all that had happened between them was essentially a matter of pride and honor between two very young Chinese men. Wong even had flowers sent to Bruce Lee's funeral out of respect for his former adversary.

Ming Lum reminisced about the fight and summed it up in the following way, "The fight didn't have anything to do with teaching other races. It had to do with Bruce Lee's remarks at the theater. That's where the problem began."

I hope that people will not read this and see this as a slight towards anyone. The heights which Bruce Lee achieved are nothing short of amazing, and it is well known that Bruce Lee is the gold standard to which legions of martial artists still aspire.

In retrospect, you cannot fight with a legend. Many people have seen the movie *Dragon*. Remember, this was a fight that occurred over 50 years ago. With Wong Jack Man being as reserved as he is, and without anyone having the fight on video, the fight has regressed into urban legend.

As for Bruce Lee, he is a legend that helped change the way martial arts are perceived and practiced today. That is a fact that will never change. All I can tell you is that I knew both Bruce Lee and Wong Jack Man, and I considered them both my friends and I have the utmost respect for both of them.

My tournament fighting stance in 1971

Throwing a left lunging punch to opponent

My friend, Bruce Lee

Linda Lee's book, Bruce Lee: The Man Only I Knew

Chapter 6

The Rocky Mountain War

*My concern is not whether God is on our side; my greatest
concern is to be on God's side, for God is always right.*
Abraham Lincoln

My divorce with Dolly was finalized and Mary Lou and her husband had also gotten divorced. As we had been close for a couple of years, Mary Lou and I had naturally been drawn to each other, and a romantic relationship had developed. In 1969, Mary Lou and I decided to make a big change in our lives and we moved to Denver, Colorado.

My friend, Gabe Vargas threw us a farewell party that lasted well into the night. The next morning, still kind of out of it from the party, we packed as much as we could get into our forest green 911T Porsche and hit the road to Denver.

We took our time on the drive and kind of turned it into a weeklong vacation, sightseeing and romancing our way through Nevada, Utah, and Wyoming. Finally, after a very long drive, we arrived in Denver.

We were excited to make a fresh start. One of the things that I felt needed to be changed was Mary Lou's name. I figured that since this was a new start for us, and no one really knew us in Colorado, it would be the perfect time to change Mary Lou's name to something that was less common and that stood out more. She was really starting to do well and I wanted her to have a name that set her apart from the crowd.

Mary Lou's name is Malialu in Hawaiian. I thought about it, dropped the "lu" and Mary Lou became Malia. This name would really stand out, and I knew that it was time to establish her as being totally unique.

We also got Malia a new uniform, which I custom made for her, a new competitive form, and a new hair style. Our first Kung Fu uniforms, and even some of our fighting uniforms, I personally designed and sewed myself, thanks to my mother who taught me how to sew. It was a total makeover for Malia, and a completely new start for us both. And all things considered, it was perfect timing.

I didn't just pick Denver, Colorado out of mid-air. I was offered a job teaching martial arts in Dr. Robert Rapue's dojo in Lakewood, a suburb of Denver. Rapue had been impressed with my contacts and the knowledge that I had in the martial arts. We were very excited about this opportunity, but our excitement would not last long.

We arrived in Denver, where we were met by an entourage of Dr. Rapue's students and black belts. They were ecstatic about having a true Kung Fu "master" in their school. But Malia and I had no idea what we were really getting into!

Rapue had offered me the position of running his school, stating that he had business in Mexico and needed someone to run the school for him. We thought that he would be gone for a couple of years before returning to Colorado, but that was not the way it turned out.

When we arrived, we were immediately taken to a tournament, where Dr. Robert Rapue was waiting for me. After a warm welcome from the crowd, we had some time to talk, and he took me to his school. I had never seen a school like this in my life! It was very odd, but beautifully decorated with nude Greek statues and Roman style drapes. He had it decorated in shades of red, black and gold.

The place had really big training halls, one with a waterfall on the inside going to a small built in pond and another hall, similar in design, but slightly smaller in size. There were dry and wet saunas, steam rooms, an ice water pool, and huge dressing rooms with plenty of locker space, and showers that had no limit to the amount of water coming out.

There were many private rooms. His personal office was full of white, marble statues standing on bright red carpet, with green ferns everywhere. I was very impressed to say the least. I had never seen a training hall that looked like this.

Dennis Roe, Rapue's manager, handled the day to day activities and would later become my good friend. Rapue had a wife, Annie, but I found out later that the relationship was only for show; she was a business partner only. The next four years in Denver would not only change my life forever, but would also change the way I looked at life and the martial arts.

After a week of Rapue's wining and dining us, we were convinced that this would be the best place for us to start over and get away from our ex's in Northern California. We thought that Denver would be a great location for us. It was in the center of the U.S. and would be a good base for us to travel to tournaments throughout the country. Besides, I was very frustrated with the martial arts politics that were starting to hamper my personal growth and development.

I had some lose ends to tie up in California, so I returned to wrap up my business. Part of that business was deciding who I was going to put in charge of my school. I turned my school over to one of my brown belts, Bill Owens, and made him a proxy black belt. Bill was a great guy and our friendship would grow over the years, but would abruptly end 32 years later in 1999.

But in the meantime, he was a devoted student who developed many great tournament competitors. He was going through a very nasty divorce at the same time as I was getting my divorce from Dolly. Traumatic events, like a divorce, have a way of bringing people together for mutual support.

Bill was somewhat influenced by the militant attitude of the Black Panther Party which was only a few miles north of my school in San Leandro, California. His admiration for them would cause problems that I would not recognize until many years later when it actually threatened my reputation. Nevertheless, he was there at the right time and place, when I desperately needed someone to take over the school.

Two of my other senior students, Mike and Pat Regan, had joined the marines during the Viet Nam conflict. They were actually two of the first Caucasians in my school to reach the level of black belt.

Pat would become a skilled sniper with dozens of kills under his belt, and Mike would be a very skilled point man for Recon. Both returned with honors after the war, but they weren't appreciated like they should have been by the hippy, psychedelic, marijuana, peace loving, free love generation.

Both Mike and Pat were wounded in action and were involved with multiple hand to hand kills. They later credited their survival to the training they received in the Kajukenbo system of no-nonsense, practical self-defense. But post traumatic stress, which was not recognized at that time, and Agent Orange took tolls on the bodies. This would eventually affect their emotional, mental and physical states with those closest to them, myself included.

Another one of my very skilled students, Ted Sotelo, would have been a great candidate to take over the school as well, and he was one of my favorite students. Sotelo, being a sensitive and passionate guy, got his feelings hurt over the fact that Pat Regan got his black belt before he did. These hurt feelings caused a rift between us that would never heal.

During tournament competition, I liked to give my students the experience of fighting really good fighters, so I would allow many of my advanced students to fight either in the brown belt or black belt division. Ted was one of my students who I allowed to do this. Everyone knew that this was only for tournaments only and that it was not their legitimate belt rank in my school. I made this perfectly clear to everyone.

Pat had received his black belt by default while competing in a Kajukenbo Memorial Tournament in Hawai'i in 1967. Pat and Mike Regan, and Bill Owens, came with me to Hawai'i for this tournament. In reality, Pat was only a green belt, a junior to Ted Sotelo. Mike was a purple belt, as was Bill Owens, but their skill level was better than the students at this tournament. I believed that putting them in a higher division would give them more experience fighting students who were closer to their skill set.

Instead of letting them fight in their own belt division, I made a decision that would haunt me in years to come. I allowed Pat Regan to fight as a black belt in the black belt division, and Mike and Bill to fight in the brown belt division. They all won and took first place.

Pat won first place in lightweight division destroying all those fighters like it was no problem for him at all, and next he was pitted against the winner of the heavyweight division, which was a guy in Kajukenbo, named Benny Medarios. Benny was a legitimate seventh degree Kajukenbo black belt.

In reality, Pat had no business fighting out of his class, but since no one in Hawai'i knew what Pat's real rank was I thought we could get away with it. According to my way of thinking, I wanted them to get the experience of fighting the best fighters in Hawai'i. I knew if they could fight with these guys, they could compete anywhere.

Pat was about 19 or 20 years old. He was long legged and was now paired off with Benny, who was 20 years his senior. In this final match for the Grand Championship Trophy, Pat won all three rounds with his devastating, lightning fast kicks. A haole boy (Hawaiian for white boy), trained by a local, beating a local fighter was nothing short of amazing.

Adriano Emperado, the founder of the Kajukenbo system, came up to me to congratulate me for teaching and doing such a great job coaching Pat. I confessed to Emperado that Pat was only a green belt getting ready to test for his brown belt when we got back to California.

Emperado was amazed at how well Pat did against his seasoned black belt. He said to Pat, you can never go back to fighting in the lower division after today. You are now a black belt.

I tried to explain to Emperado that this would only be for competition and that Pat would still be a green belt, testing for his brown belt before testing for his black belt, which is the normal progression for my students.

But Emperado said "No!" If anyone ever found out that a green belt beat one of my best black belts, and a seventh degree black belt at that, it would be a disgrace to me!" So Pat was made a black belt by default, and I was expected to honor that decision.

After we left the tournament, I told Pat that he would still have to go through testing the way everyone else did. But his ego got the best of him, and the friendship between Ted and Pat diminished as soon as we returned to California from our Hawaiian trip.

Ted left the school and I would not hear from him until a couple of years later when he invited Malia and me to visit his own group that he had started. Ted wanted me to see that he was a better as a fighter than Pat, regardless of rank. With his knowledge, he could train students to be just as good as I could. Yes, he was good; I never doubted that for a second.

It was at this time that I made another mistake which would haunt me years later. So often, we never see the consequences of our actions until years down the road. Ted, unbeknownst to me, had built up a group of over a hundred students training in a large clubhouse in Union City, California. During one of our road trips from Denver to California for a tournament, Ted invited us to come visit his club. I was about to be floored with a big surprise.

We thought that Ted had a small group of people that he was training. As we drove to his clubhouse, the parking lot was so full that he had parking attendants out there directing traffic. When we finally got out of our car, I asked one of the attendants how come there were so many cars here. He replied that there was a, "big-wig celebrity coming to inspect the club."

I didn't think anything about it because I thought this "big-wig celebrity" was going to that adjacent building. Walking closer to the entrance, a couple of individuals came up and stopped us from going in. I could not see what was happening behind the closed doors, but apparently Ted was having all his students line up.

When the door opened, Ted came out and invited us in. I was totally surprised to walk into this large hall with over one hundred students, all neatly standing at attention. Ted said he wanted to surprise me. I thought that he was only working with a handful of students.

To my amazement, after being seated and introduced, his students performed only self-defense techniques. No forms, no tournament style competition exhibitions, just self-defense techniques against blunt and edge weapons, two-on-one, three-on-one, and gang style attacks. Ted trained his students well, and I was very impressed and was honored by the reception that was given to us when we arrived.

What was impressive was that his students only wore red T-shirts and black karate pants, no ranks or belts of any sort. The reason was obvious; he wasn't teaching according to all the requirements that he had learned while directly under me, and therefore, only taught street self-defense.

I made a declaration in front of all his students that from this day forward, Ted Sotelo would be a proxy black belt so that he would have the ability to promote his students according to the requirements of my school and promote them properly. I don't know what happened afterwards except that I was told that his group lasted another six months or so and then disintegrated. His club had dropped to less than 20 students. Maybe his students were only interested in self-defense; I am not sure what really happened.

Every year during the summer in Denver, I held my annual Western U.S. National Championships. Two of Ted's advanced students, Flo Calteverio and Wally Estropia, (both formally my students that were left to Ted when I moved to Denver in 1969), drove from the Bay area to Denver in the summer of 1973.

The purpose of their visit was to discuss Ted's rank. They felt that Ted Sotelo deserved to be officially promoted to a higher black belt rank so that they could also advance. I agreed, and it was there that I prepared and gave them Ted's third-degree Certificate, which would officially make him a Sifu, or teacher, in Kajukenbo Ch'uan fa.

Ted's skill level was very good and even if he did not have all of his requirements to validate the third degree, his attributes exceeded the norm. I knew, without a doubt, that he would have had no problems at all attaining any of my set requirements.

I also promoted Flo and Wally. I presented them with their first degree black belt. They were not tested, but they had all earned it. He was spreading my art of Kajukenbo, the Dacascos method of Ch'uan fa. I was very proud of him at that time, but the future would bring out another side of him.

I learned firsthand that personality and character are like oil and water. Personality is when everyone is looking at you and you are trying your best to impress them; true character is who you are when no one is looking. A person's character is already formed, for the most part, during their pre-teen years. Martial arts training does help to reshape a person's character, but it cannot totally erase a bad character which is deeply ingrained in someone.

Bill Owens, who I had turned my school over to, became a regional and national champion. Bill concentrated on tournament competition, and Ted Sotelo concentrated on street self-defense. Both were very talented in their own areas. Bill developed many champions like Lionell Seals, Tommy Gilbert, Doug Jones. Eric Lee was actually promoted to black belt under the Dacascos banner by way of Bill Owens and the Cascos Academy.

I had not given Bill Owens direct permission to use the name Dacascos, as I had the name under license. Bill had come up with a clever way to connect the school to me; he used "CasCos." He came up with CasCos by taking CA for California, S for students, CO for Colorado, and S for students. Therefore, the name "Cascos" really stood for California students and Colorado students, fusing his California students and the Colorado students as one organization.

It was confusing to many when they heard the Dacascos Academy. In introducing students from his school, he would say this is "Cascos" students and many times people would think that they were Dacascos students.

At this time, I was becoming very well known in the martial arts. My new found fame led to some very interesting experiences. At Ed Parker's International Karate Championships, in Long Beach, California, in 1969, Steve Armstrong, was assisting Ed Parker in lining up all of the lightweight fighters. I was at the head of the line. I had my black uniform on, which had my name, DACASCOS, on the back of it, high above the shoulders.

I had just warmed up and had my towel over my head and shoulders. Behind me were about 20 to 25 other lightweight fighters. Steve Armstrong was getting us ready to be paired off and assigned to certain rings.

I turned around and saw the fighter behind me and never paid any more attention to him. About a minute later, I turned around to speak because I knew I would be paired off with him, but he wasn't there. About five seconds before I turned around, I had taken off my towel and he had noticed my name.

Rather than face me during the first elimination, he decided to go to the end of the line in order to be paired up against someone else. So the next guy lined up right behind me. I chuckled to myself, but then, a few seconds later, he too went to the end of the line.

That went on for about five or six fighters. They moved up behind me, saw my name, and headed to the back of the line. No one wanted to be paired off with me! Finally, Steve Armstrong put a stop to that.

At that time, the fighter who was lined up behind me knew that he had no choice and would have to fight me in the first round. The look on his face told it all.

I could tell that he was already mentally defeated. As we stood on the starting line and bowed, I took my fighting position, but he was still standing in shock, thinking that the match was over for him; which it was. As soon as the bell rang, I immediately launched my attack. This was more of a quick warm-up for me. Within 10 seconds, he was eliminated.

This kind of situation happened to me in several other tournaments throughout my career, where the young upcoming black belts were afraid to face off with me so early in the matches. Of course, those that had already been beaten by me were already looking for a rematch and I usually enjoyed handing them another defeat.

That said, there were a lot of fighters that I admired. One of these fighters was Fred Wren from of St. Louis, Missouri. He and I fought each other back and forth, and we both had great respect for each other's abilities. I really respected Fred for being a true gentleman as well.

Outside of the ring he was the nicest person to be around. But once you bowed and stood opposite of him, he was the whirlwind, as he would soon be nicknamed. It was definitely a name well deserved.

I remember in one tournament in Houston, Texas we roomed together on the 20th floor of the hotel. That night, prior to fighting the next day, we drank a little and smoked some pot to ease our tensions and stress. We knew that we would possibly be fighting each other in this tournament. We felt that we might as well enjoy each other's company that night, before we beat up on each other the next day. And as it turned out, we did just that.

We started laughing and goofing off on the balcony of the hotel room, when one of us had the idea of jumping from one side of the building to the other. This was ludicrous because we were 20 stories high! We were very close to actually attempting this jump. If we had, I know we would have made a big splash in the pool down below, or a big splat on the concrete.

The next morning, prior to breakfast, we just looked at each other and started laughing, knowing that this craziness would never happen again. We did face each other later that day in the tournament, and he beat me.

We wouldn't face each other again until the Mardi Gras Championship in New Orleans, Louisiana. Fred Wren took the heavyweight division and I won the lightweight division. We then had to face each other for the grand championship.

We had fought each other many times before and could read each other's intended attacks. I faked a left roundhouse kick and lunged in with a right ridge hand strike, intended for the left side of his neck. Wrong move, Al!

Fred moved in and blocked with his left hand, catching my right shoulder and dislocating it. I couldn't continue the match and was rushed to the hospital. The pain from my dislocated shoulder was severe!

After the tournament, he stayed with me in the hospital. He was a class act all the way. Not one to allow a little dislocated shoulder to ruin his weekend, he asked me if we could go out drinking after they put me back together. I was on a lot of medications and pain pills, so I said, "Oh heck, why not." We had some great times together.

Meanwhile, in Colorado, Dr. Bob Rapue had prepared a two bedroom apartment for us next door to his school. We would soon move into the place as soon as Malia's four year old, Craig, came to live with us. In the meantime, Rapue had a studio apartment in his school that was elegantly decorated, and he allowed us to stay there for a month.

I was put to work teaching Kajukenbo Kung Fu classes and learning his system of running the business. But soon, Dennis Roe, whom I had mentioned earlier, would tell me the real reason that I was there. The big change in our life was about to take a very dark, sinister turn.

A few weeks later, we were settled into our new apartment. I had befriended Mike DeHart, who was Rapue's top fighter, and who I had beaten at Sam Allred's National Thunderbird Karate Championship. We became close enough that Mike felt comfortable sharing some very private information with me. What he shared stunned me!

It started with casual small talk and then I popped a question about how Bob (Dr. Rapue) could afford all the things that he had in his school? After all, I had never seen a martial arts school that had so many amenities. That was when my world was suddenly turned upside down.

Mike told me that many of Rapue's students worked for him at night in his "midnight express business." I asked, "What is a midnight express business and what does that have to do with the school having so many nice things?"

He explained that "his boys" would go to a suburb that was in development and take all the wood, plumbing, electrical fixtures, basically anything that Rapue put on his list. This is how he built his school. He took whatever he didn't need for the school and sold it to other contractors. In other words, Rapue organized raiding and looting parties.

I found out that he never paid for anything in the school; I mean nothing at all! The carpets, drapes, mirrors, paint, windows, Jacuzzis, and even those nude Greek statues, all came from construction sites and development areas. Everything was stolen! My excitement immediately disappeared as I learned I was working for a crook.

He had all of his inner circle students working for free, or in trade for martial arts lessons. Rapue had a pure, 100% profit business going. Even the beds, electrical fixtures, and appliances, and plush furniture were stolen. They came from model showroom houses. Even the grass and flowering plants were stolen from somebody's front yard!

Little by little, a broader picture was being laid out for me. Dr. Rapue's school, aside from being Alameda Kaju Academy, was also fencing stolen property.

Mike DeHart also shared with me the reason why I was brought to Denver. Those shared secrets lit a fire inside of me; I was boiling mad when I found out that I had been scammed!

The following day, I went to Dennis Roe's office. Dennis was happy to see me and reached out to shake my hand and try to give me a "buddy hug." My hand didn't reach out to greet his, but instead, I immediately grabbed him and jerked him up by his shirt. I lifted him up on to his tiptoes against the wall in his office.

He didn't know what was happening until I told him that I knew what was going on, and I needed to hear it from him now. I let him know that I was going to beat it out of him if he didn't come clean; one way or the other, I was going to hear the truth. I forcefully seated him in one of the chairs in his office and continued with my interrogation. Everything was confirmed to be true, and I even found out more information than I knew when I walked into his office.

My blood had reached the boiling point. I got my samurai sword and walked into Rapue's office, fully ready to go crazy samurai on this scumbag who had completely turned my life upside down.

Rapue was playing classical music from Chopin on his grand, concert style, Steinway piano. He was a fan of Liberace and seemed to fancy himself as some kind of local Liberace. I moved in as if I was going to behead him, but controlled myself and stopped short of giving him the closest shave of his life. It is always better to be self-controlled instead of acting out of passion in the heat of the moment.

After a few more threatening gestures on my part, I listened to what he was saying. He was a smooth and very polished con man. Rapue said that he was set up, framed by his competitors. His school was the biggest in Denver. He was not only the biggest, but was considered the most professional, well-equipped school with the best fighters. He had a staff of professionals working full-time.

His competitors were only part-time schools, teaching out of rented halls or local YMCA's. The only profitable school, besides the Alameda Kaju School, was the school that belonged to the Tracy brothers.

They had a franchise organization of over 500 schools throughout the United States back in 1975, two in Denver and one in Colorado Springs near the Air Force Academy. All of the Tracy Schools in Colorado belonged to Chris Trujillo, with whom I would be in close association within a year.

Rapue told me who his competitors were and pointed out that the Tae Kwon Do, Karate, Judo, and Ju Jitsu organizations were all against him. He stated that they hated him because of his success and because his students wore black uniforms and represented the Chinese form of self-defense. His competitors all wore white uniforms, except for a few renegades that were from the Korean, Okinawan and Japanese systems.

I believed him because I had faced the same situation in the Bay area and in different places in the country where I competed. It was a war of styles, although not as vicious as the pending war between Rapue and I, which was to come in the months ahead. In hindsight, I wonder if Rapue did not know about these things from my past and used them to con me.

His competitors knew something else that I didn't know previously, something even more sinister and sickening. It seemed that I had been lured into an association with the Devil himself!

Malia's son, Craig had come in from Walnut Creek and was now living with us. He was invited to go see "Uncle Bob" in his office, without us knowing. We stopped him when we found out, and things began to get nasty from that point on. Strange things began to happen, and I was about to enter into a long-running war.

During the next week, people entered our apartment without our permission. We began to notice that things were not in order; it was like somebody was looking for something. Some of Rapue's inner circle began to watch our every move; they even tailed us as we ventured out of the apartment. Our private lives were now being monitored. We felt like we were living in a fish bowl, watched constantly by the Rapue Midnight Express.

I now wanted out of this situation very badly. I prepared to find an apartment of our own. I didn't want anything to do with Rapue or his business, and that including living in an apartment that he owned. I needed to get a job quickly because I was going to be out of a teaching position very soon. My income was going to come to a screeching halt. I knew that I could not remain associated with this man.

Wayne and Pat Welsh, who had a school out in Westminster, a suburb outside of Denver, helped us out and gave me a job teaching at their school. Students who were loyal to us helped us find a new apartment near Wayne's school. Without telling Rapue, we moved out, but not before he had his inner circle ransack our apartment. He was still looking for something and even changed the lock on our front door before we were able to move out.

We were able to get in anyway and had our things out in less than 10 minutes, while my small group of friends confronted Rapue's guys and kept them occupied. We didn't have much anyway. All we had was what we could stuff into our Porsche.

The war only grew worse when over 15 of Rapue's black belts and a dozen or so lower ranking students decided that they were going to defect and come with me to the Westminster school. Four of Rapue's top students, Mike DeHart, John Platt, Wayne Welsh, Leonard Endrizzi and Mike Sandos all stayed loyal to me. Mike DeHart was one of Rapue's top fighters in competition, as well as one of Rapue's strong arm guys. An enforcer for Rapue's little organization.

Wayne Welsh had his own school and was glad that I was coming over to teach his students. He was excited about having someone with my reputation in his school. Leonard Endrizzi was a green belt and joined me because he saw my art as being a no-nonsense art, a down-and-dirty, take-care-of-business kind of art, and he was a down-and-dirty, take-care-of-business kind of guy!

Leonard was a family member of the Sicilian Mafia, and had family connections in both Kansas City and San Francisco. I didn't know it at the time, but Leonard would become my dark angel, my protector and bodyguard. God was watching out for me, even though I had gotten myself involved with people in the dark, criminal underworld.

Mike Sandos left Rapue's school after a personal confrontation with him. Sandos challenged Rapue's claims concerning his deadly

Chinese Dim Mak strikes, where only a touch could paralyze or kill you. The martial arts, especially in the 1960's, were new and very mysterious to the western world. Most westerners were so naïve that they were easily deceived when it came to such things.

Rapue instilled fear in his students, making them believe that he had the power to control his chi, or energy, and to use it in a deadly way. He told them that through his mind and concentration he could just point at them or touch them and knock them out.

Many of his students were even to the point that they believed he had powers much like the Darth Vader character from *Star Wars*. They thought that he could elevate them just by pointing at them. He really had them brainwashed! No wonder he could convince so many of them to turn to criminal activities.

It was true that Rapue had some hypnosis skills, but even with that, he needed a willing subject to cooperate with him for his skills to actually work. Apparently, he had many willing subjects, as many of his students were awed by his lavish training hall and his power.

He would have some of his top black belts play along with him at demonstrations. They would fake it all the way to the floor, pretending they were touched from five feet away and knocked down. He had crowds in awe, but not those Chinese Kung Fu masters who knew he was a joke.

But to others, the words Kung Fu and Dim Mak meant a serious and deadly fighting art from the Orient. Mike Sandos had Rapue attempt to apply his chi, Dim Mak, on him; but instead of pointing or touching Mike, he actually drew his hand back in a cocked position and did a full power strike to the side of Mike's neck. Mike absorbed the strike. He was a little bit wobbly, but was able to withstand it. He shook his head and told Rapue, "You're a fake!" And with that, Sandos joined the ranks of those students who followed me.

As if that wasn't enough, Mike had other reasons to be very upset with Rapue. He had allegedly molested Mike's younger brother sexually a few months earlier, and Mike had just found out about this. That was the prime reason for his visit and the ensuing confrontation. Mike left that year and joined the Navy and eventually became a Seal Team member.

After several tours, and getting wounded a couple of times, he returned home in 1973 and was involved with a world class sky diving team performing all over the world. He, and another one of my black belts, Chuck Shields, were a couple of the top performers on the world USA Skydiving Team. While performing a team jump, Chuck's parachute malfunctioned and he crashed to the ground, a tragic loss to our organization; literally another one of students bit the dirt.

Mike Sandos eventually moved back to Utah, but not before coming back to Denver and helping me run my school on 38th and Tennyson for a while. Several months later, and with the war with Rapue still going on, he got into a confrontation with Malia about teaching methods and Mike departed for Utah.

I saw Mike again several years later, while on a layover in Salt Lake City. He was repairing a passenger seat on a Western Airlines plane. Mike became very wealthy after developing the first nylon, Velcro, locking wallets that became known as Bear Body Wallets during the mid 70's. He then ventured into the financial world and went on to become one of the top financial advisors in the world.

After moving into a new apartment, we found that we were short on money, even though I was still teaching. Needing cash, I had to look for other work. Mike DeHart and I eventually found a job building a dog racing track in Loveland, Colorado. I worked in sub-freezing weather during the days and as a part time stocker at a super market at night. I knew that neither of these were my calling, but you have to do what you have to do to put food on the table.

Shortly after our move to Denver, I entered one of Allen Steen's tournaments in Dallas. It was a predominantly white uniform, Tae Kwon Do tournament. As usual, I wore black. At that time, the black belt forms division wasn't divided into hard and soft styles, primarily because there were very few Kung Fu competitors.

Imagine a division of nearly 80 Karate and Tae Kwon Do form competitors, all in white uniforms, and me doing my thing in my black "pajamas" with my red sash flying through the air. It was always hard to do well in tournaments where the judges knew little to nothing about Kung Fu. Although I caused quite a commotion, I did place in the finals.

The sparring competition was next, and people were interested in seeing what the Kung Fu stylist could do. I slipped into my all black Kempo uniform and off I went. Realizing that most fighters of that era started with their strong side back, I continued to make my living by doing some things backwards.

I used strategy in everything that I did, using strength against weakness. In other words, when most fighters were standing high in their stances, I was positioning myself in a deep horse stance, my head at or below the waist. If they stood high, I went low. If they went low,

I went high. If they fought with their strong side back, I fought with my strong side forward. I wasn't going to fight their fight.

Whenever possible, in life as well as in martial arts competition, always pit your strength against the other person's weakness, and you will have the advantage. Use a strategy that quickly confuses or surprises your competition and then enact that strategy before they have time to contemplate how to react to it.

The key to my way of fighting didn't involve a lot of combinations or techniques. I basically used the same techniques all the time, but delivered them from different angles. I used primarily four techniques: right back fist, left reverse punch, right side kick, and right roundhouse kick. As you notice, three of these were right side techniques, and I'm left-handed.

I beat some of the best fighters from the South in the lightweight division and ended up in the final fight, fighting a top-rated fighter by the name of Demetrius Havanas, the Golden Greek. That evening we fought for first and second place. That was one of the bloodiest fights I ever fought.

Exchanging super hard blows eventually got us warnings for too much contact, and the referee had to stop the match a few times to wipe the blood off of the floor. We were equal opportunity fighters – the blood came from both of us. He struck first and cut my lip. Then I went after him and bloodied his nose. The match went back and forth until the very last second, when he scored his final point giving him a 5-4 win. Demetrius Havanas had a great fighting future ahead him, but was killed on July 23, 1981 in a horrible airplane accident.

You had to be tough if you were going to fight in Texas. It seemed like every match that afternoon was just as brutal as the one before. But I didn't regret fighting in the tournament; and went back for more the next year.

I had a policy of not teaching any technique to my students unless it was battle proven; so I entered just about every tournament that came around. I wasn't going to teach anything to my students that I hadn't personally tried first. That way I could see if a technique worked under the stress of competition, and not just in the training hall or in theory.

It is dangerous to teach students techniques which don't work. I see this happening throughout the martial arts world today. That is just preparing a student to get hurt or killed on the street, should they ever get into a real life-or-death conflict.

A person fights in a real fight, just as he or she trains on the training floor. I remember when I was still in Hawaii, and I had to defend myself in a street fight. I had been practicing martial arts for a couple of years already and learned to control my kicks and punches when delivering my techniques in training.

My opponent hit me from my blind side by first offering to shake my hand. When I extended my hand to shake his, he nailed me; just by my natural reaction, I delivered a double jump kick to his head. But, by habit, I controlled the technique and it didn't even touch him! Suddenly, I was fighting for my survival. My martial arts techniques had failed me, so I picked up a chair, smashed it over his head, and actually knocked the guy out.

From that time on, all my training and teaching was conducted at full speed and full contact, with safety gear of course. Because of this, the dropout rate at my school was high, but we had only one thing in mind – to develop an attitude and fighting style that, no matter who the opponent was, and no matter what he knew about combat, he was in trouble if he dared to attack one of us. It is better to teach students the harsh reality of fighting instead of giving them false confidence. False confidence can get you killed in the street.

It was just around this time that I had the honor of fighting Chuck Norris in the final fight of his martial arts career. When the invitation came for me to fight Chuck Norris, I was very excited. I had no idea that this was Chuck's last fight and that this fight was to be featured in *Black Belt* magazine. Just the thought of being on the same card as Chuck Norris was a great honor for me.

The funny thing about this fight was that I was not the guy who was initially selected to fight Chuck; it was a case of mistaken identity. A few months earlier, Chuck fought on the East Coast against a fighter named Al Velasco. I later found out that Chuck actually lost that fight, and he wanted to have a rematch, but this time on the West Coast in Los Angeles.

For some reason, the names got mixed up. To some, Al Velasco sounded very much like Al Dacascos. Al Velasco was supposed to be put on the East Coast team, but instead, I was chosen and put on the East Coast team. I hardly knew anyone on the East Coast team. The only guys on the team that I really knew were Victor Moore, who, if I remember correctly, was disqualified for getting overly excited and throwing a chair at one of the referees.

At Joe Lewis' urging, America's first kickboxing bout was promoted as an adjunct fight to the 1st Professional Karate Team Championships. It was to be a landmark point fighting event, in Long Beach, CA. Lewis defeated Greg Baines by 2nd round knockout to become the inaugural U.S. Heavyweight Kickboxing Champion and establish the new sport.

Lewis also fought successfully as a member of the winning team, making him the first martial arts fighter in history to win, in one tournament, dual titles in full contact kickboxing and point fighting. It would take over 15 years before any other fighter would duplicate Lewis' impressive feat.

The team championship marked a historic turning point in American sport Karate for three reasons. First, it was Chuck Norris' last fight before retiring with a reported record of 65-5. Secondly, it was the first and only time that five of the greatest early fighters, Chuck Norris, Joe Lewis, Mike Stone, Bob Wall, and Skipper Mullins, would fight on one team, the West Coast Team. And it was one of only three losses in the career of my friend, Mike Stone.

Mike pulled a muscle in his shoulder and was unable to continue against his opponent, Victor Moore. The West Coast Team defeated the East Coast Team by a cumulative score of 377-330. The East Coast Team consisted of Chuck Loven, who fought Joe Lewis, Walt Mattson who fought against Skipper Mullins, Victor Moore who fought against Mike Stone, Billy Watson who fought Bob Wall, and me fighting Chuck Norris.

I had competed against Chuck Norris a couple of years before, but in forms competition. Chuck Norris had won the overall Korean style form competition, John Perera had won the overall Japanese style form competition, and I took the overall Chinese style competition.

All three of us were pitted against each other for the grand championship form competition in the 1968 International Karate Championship. We were given about 15 minutes to warm up prior to the finals. As luck would have it, I pulled my left hamstring while doing a split during warm-ups. The pain was so intense that I could hardly get off the floor.

One of my students helped me wrap my left thigh to keep the muscle in place. It was extremely painful, but the show had to go on. John Pereira went 1st and did his form. I was up next. The form I did was called, "Lo Han Kuen," which means the Monk form. The Chinese form was very traditional and actually originated in the Shaolin Temple of China.

Chuck Norris performed last. During my performance, my friend Bruce Lee was sitting in the front row. Bruce and I had talked prior to the finals and met after the competition to continue our conversation on martial arts philosophy and shared tips on our techniques.

I struggled to complete my form. Bruce never took his eyes off my performance. I don't remember who won the grand championship that night, as I was in so much pain that by the end, I did not care; I was just glad to have it over with.

Bruce came up to me and told me I did a good job, he knew I was hurt, but he complimented me on my performance nevertheless. I told him that I appreciated the compliment and that I did my best to represent the Chinese community.

Now back to the fight with Chuck Norris and the team competition in Los Angeles. As I said, this was Chuck's retirement fight. Although I admired Chuck Norris greatly and was aware of his devastating kicking techniques, I wanted to be in the ring with him. It was a great honor.

Chuck and I were billed to go three rounds and each round was to be three minutes long. I can tell you that, by the end of our match, we were exhausted. When the bell rang to start the fight in the first round, Chuck came out of his corner like a bat out of hell and caught me with the spinning back kick that had me bouncing off the ropes.

I came back with a back fist and a flurry of punches to rack up my own points. The first two rounds went back and forth and by the time the third round came, I knew that the match was going to be Chuck's.

I had been warned prior to getting into the ring, that I had to remember that this was Chuck Norris's last competition and that there would be no way that Chuck would lose. The warning fell on deaf ears, and I fought my heart out. But in the end, Chuck won; and he deserved it.

The great thing about that fight, other than fighting the legendary Chuck Norris, was that the fight showed me a couple of my weak spots that I would later correct. In essence, I also won because I learned something useful and improved my skills. Not many people can say that they fought Chuck Norris. I can, and it was an honor that I will always remember.

Since he was now free from competition, Chuck Norris looked to the future and got into the action adventure film industry. This would eventually bring him even more fame and fortune.

Joe Lewis had the same aspirations as Chuck Norris, as both of them were at the top in their class. I knew them both and can tell you that Joe Lewis and Chuck Norris were totally different kinds of guys.

With the talent that Joe had, many within the martial arts community wondered why he was not as successful as Chuck Norris in Hollywood. I got to know Joe on a personal level when we were both recruited into the Tracy's Karate Organization, which at that time was beginning to become the largest Karate franchise in the world. This is where I first met the Tracy brothers, Al and Jim.

During my relationship with the Tracy's organization, Joe Lewis was the head coach for the fighters on the team. I was one of the select few to participate in one of the many seminars in which Joe Lewis was introducing his new fighting principles called the "25 Technical Fighting Principles." I adopted and used these principles in my own way and with my own expression in my Wun Hop Kuen Do style.

These concepts and principles would greatly enhance my fighting ability in street self-defense, as well as tournament competition. I am greatly indebted to Joe Lewis for this. As martial artists, we should never be completely satisfied with our skills. We should always continue to learn and improve ourselves.

I know that Bruce Lee had a direct influence on Joe's fighting style and therefore, indirectly it also affected me. This was all before Bruce Lee died and I was invited to stay at Linda Lee's house and had the opportunity to go through all of Bruce's files and teachings. The puzzle was finally starting to come together. My circle of influence was getting more focused.

I had to be in Southern California for a martial arts event, and Bob Wall, who had fought Bruce Lee in the movie *Enter The Dragon,* picked me up at the airport, and we went to spend some time with Chuck Norris.

That evening I spent the night at Chuck's house and met his family. He is a strong Christian who believes in righteousness and justice, and we spent some time talking about his beliefs. After that, Chuck's celebrity skyrocketed; he became the top dog in martial arts adventure films in the USA. I was impressed and moved by his faith, and felt that, although I believed in God, something was missing from my spiritual life.

I soon moved to Germany and lived there for eight years. During that time, I kept hearing his name and seeing his films posted on marquees in theaters throughout Europe. Chuck was likable and easy to work with in Hollywood. Many of his students would also go on to find a place in the movie industry.

Chuck actually put Malia in a film; she played a Kung Fu teacher doing a form in competition. He has been involved with many worthwhile organizations and has helped many people throughout his journey. There's so much to write about Chuck, but I will end it with this – he set a very good example for all martial artists to follow. He was always learning, always generous, and a true gentleman. I have nothing but respect for Chuck.

The Tracy Brothers had their own schools in Denver with Chris Trujillo running them. I was offered a position and a chance to join them in 1971 after they discovered that I was working at the Loveland dog track. This was an offer which was hard to turn down since working on the dog track in the freezing weather was not to my liking.

They sent me to Baltimore, Maryland to their central training center for two weeks of intensive training. I learned every phase of their studio operations, from teaching and supervising, to marketing and management. It was a boot camp that changed the way I looked at the martial arts business forever. The Tracy System was complete and very well organized.

I took over Chris Trujillo's school in Lakewood, which was managed by Boyd Holbrook who transferred to another one of the Tracy's Karate Schools across town. Tracy's organization was expanding. With names like the heavy weight champion, Joe Lewis, Roger Green, Jay T. Will, and myself, Tracy's was beginning to build a team of top fighters and form competitors. They became one of the largest and oldest martial arts organizations in the country.

I will give you just a little background on the Tracy's Karate Schools and how they changed the path of martial arts in the United States. The Arthur Murray Studios started out in 1912. When Arthur and Kathryn Murray retired in 1964, a group of franchisees purchased the company and infused it with a fresh new spirit and better leadership. Under its new leadership, the Arthur Murray Dance Studios kept pace with the rapidly changing youth culture of the 1960's and still continue to flourish today as the world's largest dance studios.

The Tracy Brothers followed the same concept when they started with their first location in San Jose, California in 1962. In the height of the martial arts craze during the mid 1970's, they had over 300 studios throughout North America. They continue to flourish today with their tradition of teaching no-nonsense Kempo Karate in their time proven private and group class environment.

Ed Parker's Kempo Organization followed a similar path, utilizing many of the Tracy's business practices. After seeing commercial success, Parker began to put professional programs together which changed the atmosphere of martial arts in the United States.

Just after I started working for the Tracy's Organization in 1971,

Ralph Krause, a very prominent Tae Kwon Do instructor in Denver, promoted his third annual Rocky Mountain Karate Championships with special guest, Mr. Sam Allred, *Black Belt's* Man of the Year.

Sam Allred was the first person in Kajukenbo history to be awarded this prestigious title. He was appointed as the head referee for this tournament. I had never been defeated in my hometown of Denver and wasn't going to let anyone dethrone me on this important occasion. I was completely fired up for this one!

The finals brought nearly 3,000 spectators to their feet, watching all divisions, including a new breaking championship. The breaking championship was hilarious. One particular individual had decided to break some boards between two cinderblocks, stacked up at least six inches high.

This guy had one of the biggest afros that I had ever seen. He looked like he would fit in perfectly with the black power movement of the day. He must have used five cans of hairspray to keep that hair in place, which was definitely not a good strategy on this day.

He decided to break the boards with his forehead. He would have had no problem doing this and probably could have won the breaking championship if it weren't for one little problem. At the last minute, he decided to make his breaking feat a little more impressive by putting lighter fluid on the boards and lighting them on fire. I thought it was a bad move; and I was right.

He prepared himself for the break by taking his gi top off and doing a couple breathing exercises. Then, with a loud kiai, he slammed his head straight down on the boards, his forehead smashing through all of the boards. That was impressive, but the most entertaining part was yet to come.

The excessive amount of hairspray that he had on his Afro ignited when it came into contact with the flames! He was jumping around like a frog in a hot frying pan, trying desperately to put out the fire on his flaming fro, while others ran to his aid with wet towels.

Now that was one of the most entertaining demonstrations I had ever seen! I would have definitely given him the grand championship for his engaging performance. But that was not to be. He was rushed to the hospital with serious burns on his head, and a 24 year old, Kin Won Kyon, the youngest fifth degree black belt in Hapkido, won the breaking championship.

His demonstration of the art amazed spectators and competitors alike. With tremendous power and control, he broke seven huge cinderblocks with a head break.

After all the other divisions had been completed, it was time for me to fight for the grand championship. I was slated to fight a heavyweight fighter, Isaac Williams.

Williams tried to overwhelm me with his power, but my experience in fighting heavyweights helped me out. I was able to move laterally and struck him with a reverse punch to the head, giving me the first point. I continued with a front snap kick to his chest for the second point. Williams came right back with a reverse punch and scored his first point.

Isaac Williams was a Tae Kwon Do stylist, and he knew that I had an arsenal of counters against Tae Kwon Do kicks. He was obviously worried about this. This preyed on his mind and he became overly defensive. I sprang forward with a flying back fist, which gave me the final point as time ran out.

The title of the new Rocky Mountain Championship Grand Champion was bestowed on me, and I received a magnificent six foot, grand championship trophy. I actually had to take the trophy apart to put it into my Porsche 911T. With so many of our students winning awards and trophies, I encouraged them to take their trophies home instead of putting them in the school. We simply had no more room to display the amount of trophies that we were winning. It was definitely an impressive showing!

For about a year and a half, together with the help of Chris Trujillo and the Tracy's system, my school flourished, both in the number of students and in our financial success. After being in business for a week, we were able to cash out $495.00!

I was so excited that I rushed to tell Malia after I had signed another student up. We looked at the cash on the desk and threw it up in the air, bathing ourselves in the first of what would be many profitable weeks. Now I know that $495 may not sound like much money to you, but in today's standards, it would be like making $2,500.00. That is $2,500 in one week! Boy, were we excited!

Our name was becoming well known. Malia developed a strong women's group and it dominated the Denver area. I was becoming the guy that everyone wanted to beat in the Rocky Mountain Region. I was consistently being ranked as the top fighter in the rankings for the region, and a top ten fighter in the USA, according to *Black Belt* magazine. *Black Belt* magazine listed the top ten yearly.

I was never defeated in Denver, and I was only defeated once in the state of Colorado, and it was by my team mate, Jim Hawkins, in Fort Collins. Jim and I had been sparring partners, so he knew my moves. I took home the Grand Championships in tournament after tournament in the Rocky Mountain Region. To make things even better, many of my students were taking home the gold and silver medals. We were having great success and I loved it!

I know that, at 29 years old, this would have never happened had I stayed in California and continued to work in a warehouse. Tracy's helped me get my first house up on a hill overlooking the city of Denver. I felt like I had finally made it, but Rapue was still seeking revenge.

Rapue continued to harass my family and me. He never let up. He continued to make things uncomfortable for us. This man hated the fact that I had become successful and was fearful that, because I knew too much about his illegal business, I might cause him problems. He wanted me either out of town or dead!

We had moved from the duplex that we were living in, to a rental house while our permanent house was being built. I went from working on a racetrack to having my own profitable business in a very short period of time. My name and reputation were growing stronger by the day. This drove Rapue crazy. Rapue was not a man to take defeat lying down.

Also, at this time, I was getting flak from other schools in the area that kept losing to my students or me. At times, I even thought the Tae Kwon Do and Karate schools were teaming up with Rapue to go after me, but that was not the case. They were all going after me, but for their own personal reasons.

Rapue came after me because of the number of his students who defected to my school and because I was his biggest threat, knowing what I knew about his personal life and operation. The Tae Kwon Do and Karate schools came after me because we were the top guns, the new kids on the block, and we were cleaning house. When you are on the top of the mountain, it seems like everyone wants to see you fall, but that is the way of the world.

Championship competitions in the Denver area became the events to watch, as our Tracy/Dacascos fighters and teams dominated. We started with one school and soon opened two more locations under the Tracy banner.

Our house on the hill was in the final stages during the late fall months, and we hoped that we could move in before the end of the year.

In the middle of November, on a Thursday night, Tony Ramos had invited us to be the special guests at his North American

Championships in Oakland, California. Malia and I decided to fly out at the last minute, so we made arrangements to have Wayne and Pat Welsh babysit Craig and Mark.

Mark was 5 years old when he came to live with us the year before. Mark was not supposed to have been coming to Denver for good. His visit was to last only two weeks during Christmas, and then he was supposed to go back to Hawai'i before the New Year. But I felt duty bound, as Mark's dad, to change these plans. Sometimes honor requires that you do what's right, not necessarily what's legal.

This was a bold move on my part, as we decided not to send Mark back to live with his grandparents, Ray and Jane McVey. They were good grandparents, but I felt that this was not a good situation for Mark.

I had lost Mark in a custody battle during my divorce, and Dolly was given sole custody of Mark. But Dolly was not in Hawai'i. She was in Wisconsin, at least at this time. She had become an exotic dancer, traveling from state to state with her boyfriend.

I could not allow Mark to be raised this way, so I made the hard decision to put my freedom on the line, defy the courts, and keep Mark with me permanently.

I had not seen Mark for a couple of years and was excited to get to spend time with my son. When Mark got off of the plane with the stewardess and met me at the gate, Mark was hostile and behaving very badly. He had turned into a spoiled brat. His actions and the words that came out of his mouth were like a kid who had been raised in a ghetto environment. I could not believe his undisciplined behavior!

Within days, I found an attorney and discussed my rights and was told that possession was over 90% of the law. Gosh, I had Mark with me, so that gave me a big advantage. With Craig already living with us, we could show that with Malia and me, Mark would be with his biological father and stepmother, and in a much better environment. I thought that we had a great chance to get permanent custody.

Malia and I weren't married at the time, but that obviously did not matter. We already went by Al and Malia Dacascos and had a child in tow. To everyone who knew us, we were a happily married couple. It seemed like the natural thing to do and nothing was going to stop me from doing what was best for my son.

I was not sure if my attorney could get the job done at first. I didn't know what that meant for me, because I was determined to raise my son and give him a good life. The people who referred him to me told me he was very good, but they never told me that he was a pot head and a drug user.

While in his office discussing my options, I was beginning to get high just from sitting there, as he openly smoked his marijuana without any concern at all. He even offered me a hit. Of course, I declined. I guess I should have known better. He was from Boulder, Colorado after all; if you know anything about Colorado, you will know what I mean by that. Suddenly, I was reminded of John Denver's song, which was popular at the time, *Rocky Mountain High.*

Regardless, I had Mark with me. Now I had to wait and see if his grandparents would file kidnapping charges against me. I now know that I made the right decision, as this move alone changed Mark's destiny in life.

Had I sent him back to Hawaii before the New Year, his life could have been one of crime, since his grandparents lived in the Makiki area of Honolulu, known at that time for a lot of youth gang activities.

Mark was a rascal, and still has some of those same, youthful traits even today, but he is now controlled and highly disciplined. Today, he credits his martial arts training over the years to the fact that Malia was his mother.

We made arrangements to have Wayne and Pat Welsh babysit Craig and Mark, and we were set to leave for California on that Friday. When we left that Friday afternoon, only a few of my students knew Malia and I would be gone for that weekend tournament. Our Porsche was parked in the drive way, and not in the enclosed garage attached to the house. Our dog Silver, a German Sheppard and husky mix, was in the house with the door open between the garage and kitchen so that he could go back and forth.

Arrangements were made for Wayne and Pat to pick the boys up from school and take care of them over the weekend. They also checked on Silver to make sure that he was okay. We wanted to give the appearance of being home for security reasons. After all, we knew what kind of enemies we had in Denver; those people were capable of anything, and we knew it.

With the car parked like it was and an automatic system in place to turn lights on and off, it appeared as though someone was home all the time. Everything was in place and we had done as much as possible to secure our home while we were out of town. I had done all I could, but I still had an uneasy feeling in the pit of my stomach.

I did feel better knowing that Leonard Endrizzi would be watching over the school and teaching class for me on Saturday morning. We planned on returning to Denver on Monday in time to pick the boys up from school.

Saturday morning while we were at the tournament and getting ready to fight, I received a call over the intercom system, to come to the front desk for an urgent message. Leonard was on the phone; something serious had happened back in Denver.

Somewhere between 3 a.m. and 4 a.m. Saturday morning, my house was attacked. It appeared to be an assassination attempt on our lives, but luckily for us, we were in California at the time, and the boys were staying with our friends.

The front of the house was cinder blocks and stucco. These criminals had completely shot up the front of our house from the outside! The front door was blown apart. The windows and walls in the master bedroom were riddled with 30-30 caliber holes. Our house looked like a war zone!

We could have easily been killed if we hadn't left town for this tournament in California. No one knew we weren't home except for Leonard, Wayne, and Pat. Silver had been slightly wounded from the pieces of glass flying all over the place. He found refuge by running through the dog door and into the back yard.

Whether this was meant to scare us out of town or kill us is something that the police could not answer, but I knew. I knew what kind of man Rapue was. This was an attempt on our lives that mirrored a mafia hit.

Malia and I wanted to return home immediately because we feared that the boys' lives might be in danger. But we were told that they were well protected. All of my own black belts were now armed and ready for any shootout. There was nothing I could have done from Oakland but to try and do my best in the competition and return home as planned.

A sense of total helplessness and anger preyed on my mind until I was almost crazy with my desire to get the people who did this. The anxiety on the plane ride back was nothing but pure anticipation of war. I was losing my usual self-control and my discipline as a martial artist. My mind was overcome with thoughts of retaliation.

I had let my emotions get in the way. It is never wise to allow your emotions to do the thinking for you. I forgot the critical principle of the *Art of War* – strike at a time and place when your enemy least expects it. I wanted to strike now. I was coming home for blood!

Leonard met us at the airport and filled us in on what was happening. Denver had been hit with a heavy snow storm late Friday evening. When the attack occurred, it was a blizzard outside. The high winds and snow muffled the sounds of the gunshots. Only the neighbor closest to my house, heard the shots and called the police. The Police could not carry on the investigation until Sunday afternoon because of the weather.

When we got home on Monday, the ground was still covered with 6 to 9 inches of snow. It wasn't until Tuesday afternoon that the police came back to recover gun shells and casings. They had to wait until the snow had melted away enough to find some evidence of shoe prints, car treads, and information about which direction the shots originated from.

Leonard had made sure that the front of the house was boarded up with heavy construction plastic to keep the house secure from the weather and animals. With my emotions running wild and my patience with these people almost completely gone, Leonard begged me to be patient and do nothing at this time. A moment of control is better than a lifetime of regrets.

He said that he was going to make sure that whoever was responsible for this would be dealt with. He added that he just wanted me out of the equation so that nothing could be traced back to me personally. I had a pretty good idea what that meant, but I left it at that.

Within a month, two of the individuals who we discovered were responsible for this despicable action had "disappeared" and the third guy had fled town. Later, I was told there were two bodies found rotting in the sewage system under the city. These bodies were later identified as two of the men responsible for the assassination attempt on my family.

I warned all of our black belts and advance students that things could explode into an all out war between the Alameda Kaju School and our Denver based Tracy Schools. This would have been very bad for business, so we tried to keep this as quiet as possible. But we soon found out that everything we said in our school was going straight back to that sleazy criminal, Rapue.

Rapue had placed a spy in our school and we didn't find out about it until we caught him going through the files in my office one afternoon. Dean Bothem was a brown belt that I thought had left Rapue's school to train with me, but in fact, he was nothing but a mole, planted to feed information back to Rapue.

To say that Leonard wasn't nice to him would be an understatement. And by the time Leonard, a big 315 pound mass of walking destruction, got finished "talking" to Bothem, Bothem was more than willing to give us all the information we wanted on the activities that Rapue had bribed him to perform.

Bothem told Leonard that he was ordered to leave the bathroom window unlocked so that someone could climb through it and place an illegal sawed off shotgun behind the water heater. They were going to set me up and have my school closed down.

The window was so small that only a very small person would be able to squeeze through it. Sure enough, we checked behind the water heater and there it was, an illegal, sawed off shotgun, wrapped up in a brown paper bag.

In two of my other schools, these guys had planted bags of cocaine and marijuana taped under our office desks. They even went as far as to plant pipe bombs in small storage boxes and placed them under our training equipment.

Rapue's people were planting illegal items in all of our schools so that they could call the police with anonymous tips and tell them that we were involved with illegal drugs and weapons. With this information in our hands, we immediately called the Lakewood Police and informed them of the situation. They came and removed those items from our schools, and finally, the police launched their own investigation into Rapue's shady dealings.

The schools were now being guarded around the clock. Someone always slept at the school with a rifle or shotgun, just in case any of Rapue's guys tried anything. We had purchased silent alarms in all of the schools, but my black belts elected to stay at the school and guard it because we had a lot of our own valuable training equipment there and couldn't afford to have it stolen.

In the meantime, Leonard had contacted his "family" from Kansas City and asked if they could possibly help him with this situation. These guys from Kansas City did not play around; they meant business!

A plan was made to put explosives on the top of Rapue's school, directly above his office. They planned to blow that part of the school up when Rapue and his thugs gathered there for their secret "business" meetings. Leonard was keeping a time log documenting Rapue's schedule and the times that he held his meetings.

A couple of days before the plan was supposed to be executed, Rapue got arrested for the transportation of illegal firearms across state lines and indecent liberties with minors. The police also found a stash of illegal weapons at Rapue's home, along with a lot of ammunition. There were other charges too, but those were the ones that I remember as being the worst. Rapue never had any idea how lucky he was to have been arrested; it probably saved his life.

A week later, we were all present in court for the hearing. Rapue stated his case. First, he addressed the charges of indecent liberties with minors. He proceeded to address the judge and demonstrate that in the martial arts, you must make contact and touch students' bodies to point out correct targets. He stated that grabbing students' groins and squeezing their chest area were a normal part of training in the martial arts.

He was trying to impress upon the judge that all these techniques were necessary to teach effective self-defense and that anyone, including a minor, had to be subjected to feeling what specific types of pain felt like so that they would know firsthand about their own power to injure or hurt someone.

Jerry Evens, one of Rapue's guys, was sitting across from me. He pointed to me and made a hand gesture indicating that he was going to cut my throat. He then followed that gesture up with his finger pulling an imaginary trigger of a gun. Leonard was aware of Jerry and was watching him from the beginning, even when we were all in the parking lot getting ready to enter the court room.

In those days, there were no security officers to check for weapons. And you can bet that all of Rapue's guys, as well as our group, were packing some kind of weapons. Even other groups, that really had nothing to do with the war between Rapue and us, were there simply to hear the outcome, but they had their own source of protection as well. It seemed that everyone was armed back then in Denver.

The other charges had not yet come up. In all, it took several days to get all of the charges. Rapue was sentenced to serve time in the federal prison, although I don't remember how many years he had to serve.

I knew that his right hand man, Jerry Evens, meant business and that I would have to deal with him sooner or later. Leonard also knew this and told me not to worry about him, that Jerry would not see the New Year. Jerry was found dead in his apartment on New Year's Eve 1972, with a "self-inflicted" gunshot wound to the head. God was still using my dark angel to watch out for me. I shudder to think where my family would have been without God protecting us during this time.

Leonard, when not in class, was a collector and enforcer for his "family" who ran a dry cleaning business as a front to cover for the illegitimate activities going on in the back. He operated whenever and wherever the bosses sent him. He repossessed vehicles and collected money from their loan sharking and protection business. I promise you, he was the ultimate repo man!

In the tournaments, he was our anchor man for team competitions. At one team competition, we had to pull him off an opponent when Leonard was trying to dig his opponent's eyes out. What a bloody mess that was! I asked him why he did it, and he simply replied, "I don't like anyone to call me a fat fart."

Good ole Leonard was not a guy to screw around with, but he was a great guy to have around if you needed a friend to watch your back. And he watched my back for as long as we lived in Denver.

Two other advanced students, who were already Tracy students before I took over, were from Chicago, Raymond Johnson and Roland Jenkins. They were very good friends and immediately became trusted individuals who took up arms with us and guarded the three schools under my wings.

Roland, or Jinks as we called him, was a Vietnam veteran with an attitude. He was always ready for anything; after being in Vietnam, Denver was a cake walk. Ray was just a big ole 6'5" street fighter with a pleasant, yet very confident, smile that told you, "You better walk the other way."

I also had other support at this time. Brothers Mike and Pat Regan, recently honorably discharged from the Marines, heard about what was happening in Denver and came in for support. I have already talked about how tough these guys were. Kenneth Lambert, another one of my students, was a brown belt in the Ed Parker's system of Kempo, and he also found himself in the impending battle of the schools. It was not what he was expecting, but he stepped up and accepted the challenge nonetheless.

Our back-up team was growing as both sides seemed to be stock piling weapons for the imminent fight. We weren't carrying the traditional oriental weapons like swords or spears anymore; things had escalated much further than that. We were all armed with side arms, pistols and rifles in our cars, trucks, and in our coats.

We were in Denver, a western city still reminiscent of the old west at that time. Sure, some of the other students carried nunchucks, shuriken, Japanese throwing stars, and fighting knives. Sometimes these weapons were even openly displayed in plain sight on their belts. This was a big city, cowboy town; you had to be ready to play for keeps here.

Speaking of Ken Lambert, after he joined my club, he was my student for nearly five years and was slowly converting over from a hard style to the soft style I was teaching. He was stiff, too hard, and his stretch was terrible. I jokingly told him maybe it's better you take some ballet lessons.

To my surprise, he did! Of course he didn't like it at first, but with all the beautiful girls in the class, his stretching improved. But then it got out of hand. He thought that I would be happy with his results; in one way I was, in the other, I was not.

What happened next embarrassed me, as well as, stunned the audience and participants at a Karate championship in Denver. Ken, thinking that this would be great, decided to create his own Kung Fu form and enter into competition with it. I did not know about it ahead of time. Halfway through the form that he created, which, up until that point, was pretty impressive, the unthinkable happened. He went into a ballet mode! I am serious!

He started on the tip of his toes, with both hands touching high above his head; he spun around once and looked like he was tiptoeing through the tulips. Spinning around once more, he was ready to do a ballet jumping split with his back arched. He completed his form and stood there, waiting for the judges' score.

The judges looked at each other with a confused expression, biting their lips in a failed attempt to not burst out laughing. They had no clue how to score what they had just seen, or even what it was that they had just witnessed. They knew that Malia and I turned out champions, but this one, this one they didn't know what to think. Was Kenneth doing a skit? Was he doing some kind of spoof on Kung Fu? Was he serious?

You could see people in the audience, who knew me, starting to look at me to see what I would do or how I would react. Many of them were chuckling and giggling. Frankly, I was shocked that he did this without first having the respect to consult Malia and me!

I was red-faced and embarrassed. Ken, thinking that he should get at least a 10 for his innovation, waited for the judges' score to be shown. I immediately left the bleachers and headed straight down to his ring and stripped him of his belt. In a not so hospitable way, I said, "See you later. Don't come back until you know what respect is!" The judges still did not know what to think. I doubt those judges ever saw anything like this again.

Six years later, in 1981, the year I departed Hamburg, Germany to return to United States, Ken Lambert had become very successful and was the vice-president of a large advertising agency from the United States. His European office was in Madrid, Spain. Taking time off from a business trip, he flew to Hamburg, Germany to participate in a tournament that I hosted yearly, called the North European Championships.

At this tournament, he presented me with a beautiful sword that was made in Toledo, Spain. The inscription on the blade read, "To Sifu, Thanks for teaching me the meaning of respect. Your student, Ken."

Wow! What a turnaround he had made. Ken had definitely learned something about discipline and respect. It was then, much more mature and responsible, that he earned his rank back and was allowed back into the system.

My schools had expanded from three to six within those two years, and what seemed like the growth and expansion of a ten year period was accomplished in only a couple of years. However, the speed that it took to get to the top was nothing compared to the speed that everything came crashing down.

No one in our organization was prepared for the oil crisis and during that time, we were forced to downsize. On top of the economy, our war with Rapue was still ongoing with hit and run battles.

Tournaments in which his students and our students competed were sure to include guns in the workout bags and gear bags. Rival groups sitting across the gym from each other could have easily ended up in a gang fight, complete with deadly weapons. No one dared to go out alone. We always had to have four to six others in the group, even to go to the restroom at a tournament.

Everyone knew how volatile the situation was, and that fact kept the tournaments on an even keel. Both sides made sure that their fighters played be the rules, knowing that one loss of temper or silly action could lead to a deadly night. It seemed that we all maintained the peace through mutually assured destruction.

After a while, undercover police were attending every tournament in the area, knowing that there were two rival organizations there that meant business.

As bad as things were between us, we were not the only groups who had these kinds of tensions. Russell Perron's Tae Kwon Do group and their rivals, the United Tae Kwon Do Federation, led by Chuck Sereff, could have ignited their own war at anytime, complicating tensions we already had with Rapue's people.

I recall having all four organizations at one tournament competing against each other. It felt like we were walking on 90 year old dynamite the whole time. You could never tell who might lose control, triggering a blazing gun fight.

For a while, participation in tournaments dropped; it had just become too dangerous. It was getting too stressful to compete in the city. Top competitors from Denver began to travel to other states for competitions. Malia and I were among those who sought competition elsewhere.

Eventually, when security was enforced, the families came back and things, at least on the surface, appeared normal. The Japanese group kept to themselves and only participated in their own sponsored tournaments. They had their own set of competition rules which many of the open stylists avoided.

As bad as things were in the tournaments at that time, there were some very funny things that happened while we were in Denver as well. I remember at one tournament, I was in the bathroom relieving myself, and some guy walked in and started using the urinal on the right side of me.

Both of us were relieving ourselves prior to lining up and being paired off for the fighting segment of the tournament. I was in a black uniform and so was he.

On the back of my fighting jacket, I had my name printed in large letters – DACASCOS. We were both standing there doing our business, and somehow he noticed the name on the back of my gi. I have no idea how the guy read the back of my gi while standing next to me at the urinals, but he did.

He was surprised that he was standing next to me, as if well-known fighters are somehow above having bodily functions. He was obviously a little star struck because he was standing next to me. So without thinking, he introduced himself and stuck his right hand out to shake mine while I was still busy at the urinal. This was extremely strange in and of itself. But it was about to get stranger!

You have to understand, he hadn't finished his business yet, and he wanted to shake my hand. He turned to greet me, not thinking about what he was doing, and unconsciously peed on my right foot. This guy peed on me just before the fighting competition began! I couldn't believe it; some stranger just peed on my leg!

He was very embarrassed and apologetic. So much so, that he sprayed on my pants a SECOND TIME! Unbelievable! This guy peed on me, and then while he was apologizing for peeing on me, he did it again! This was unreal. Not only did this guy just pee on me, but he peed on me TWICE in the same day.

He must have been a nervous wreck! Thinking back, he must have thought that the fighting competition was going to start right there in the men's room.

Instead of going out and stretching for my first match, I headed straight to the shower and washed off my foot and pants. During the whole tournament he avoided being anywhere around me. But that is not the end of this crazy story. As luck would have it, his name was paired off with mine for the fighting competition. Sheepishly, he immediately asked the scorekeeper to be transferred to another fighting ring. That was the last I saw of the "Great Fighting Sprayer."

Sometime in 1972, things settled down a bit and we moved into our new home that we just had custom built. Both boys were transferred to a new school, which was visible from our back yard. But, only a few days into their new school year, Mark was forced off the road while riding his bike home from school. We soon found out that this was one of Rapue's guys making a statement that they still knew what school the boys were in and where to find us.

Our house now had a weapon of some sort on every level near a window just in case. For the next few weeks, I took the boys to school and picked them up after school, even if it was only a short walking distance from our home.

Malia had hidden our 911T Porsche at a friend's house, thinking that Rapue's people might attempt to put a bomb under the chassis. We had a friend, Mrs. Grimes, who was a survivor of the Holocaust. She told Malia horrible things about what happened in Germany and she started thinking that this was exactly what our lives were feeling like here in Denver.

One evening, when I was done teaching, I was followed and then passed by some of Rapue's thugs waving their sticks and knives at me out of the car window. It didn't affect me though; I had my pistol next to me and just smiled thinking to myself that these idiots are coming to a gun fight with sticks and knives. They constantly used these kinds of scare tactics on us in Denver.

Rapue's guys wanted me out of town, even when Rapue was sitting in prison. They had lost over half of their black belts to me. On top of that, I knew that Rapue was a fake, and when the instructor is a fake, that also reflects on his students. I also had information about the boys that Rapue had molested, and they wanted me to keep that information quiet.

Because of all of this, they used every tactic they could to get me out of Denver. They used scare tactics, harassed my family, and assassinated my character. I guess, when someone attempts to assassinate you and your family, you should expect anything from them. I did, and I kept a watchful eye on my family at all times. Dealing with these scumbags also taught me to always be aware, always! Always remember to expect anything from anyone; the Devil was once an angel.

It seemed that trouble found me everywhere I went in Denver. On a street near our school, was my boys' favorite hang out – McDonalds. One Friday night around 7:30, after the kids had their sparring class, they asked me to get them some food from McDonalds while they wiped down the mirrors and cleaned up the place before we closed up the shop. I drove down to Mickey-D's, and drove right into a domestic fight.

Not knowing the whole situation, I intervened because I saw this woman getting beat up by some guy. She was in the driver's seat, and he was outside of the car, punching her through the open window. I had no idea she was just caught with another man and her husband had followed her to McDonalds where she was having a rendezvous with her lover.

I came to her aid and all of a sudden I had BOTH men attacking me. I had no other choice but to lay both of them out. She got mad at me too, picked up a trash can and threw it at me. And the worst part was that I never even got the food and drinks, I had ordered at the drive through for Mark and Craig.

I left right away and drove to Kentucky Fried Chicken a block down the street. I was ordering some fried chicken, just as the police were driving into the parking lot at Micky-D's. I never really knew if I helped anyone in that mess or just added to the problem. But I knew one thing, there was not going to be any Happy Meals that night!

I learned that it is always a dangerous proposition to get involved in a domestic abuse situation. Many times, you can step in and stop the husband from beating the wife, only to have the wife attack you for hurting her husband. It is always tricky when you get involved in other people's personal lives.

Being in the martial arts business, there are people that I work with and teach, but as a rule, I don't ask questions about their personal life. I also don't go around sharing what they discuss with me in private. There is a certain amount of confidentiality that comes with our business.

They confide in me about their strengths and weaknesses, their businesses, their personal, emotional, mental, and physical needs, and financial concerns. Sometimes I just listen and when I feel I can help, I do. I understand this more now than I did when I was in my twenties and thirties.

My teachers used to tell me that you stand in life like a three legged stool. The three legs of that stool are the mental, the physical and the spiritual parts of life. All three need to be in harmony and balance. In other words, they need to be the same length or the stool will tip over. For me, that was in the old world and doesn't necessarily hold true in today's world. I think that one more leg needs to be added to that stool.

The leg of financial independence is a vital part for complete balance in today's world. It is hard to find that inner peace, that tranquil, deep spiritual and mental calm that makes you feel completely at ease, when you are stressed about your finances.

You have to have money to feed your body so your mind can stay healthy. This makes it easier to control your emotions so that you are free to be physically healthy and to perform at your highest level. This has to be a part of your overall balance.

All legs must be of equal or near equal length and strength. If they aren't, you will have a stool that is unbalanced, and an unbalanced stool will not stand the test of time. If someone is truly balanced in today's world, you know that, somewhere down the line, they have sacrificed to add that forth leg to their stool.

Me, Jim Harkins, and Dr. Robert Rapue in 1969

Working in the snow building the dog track in Loveland, CO in 1970

Mark and Craig square pose at 6 years old in 1971

Parker Turner and me in Louisiana in 1973, jumping spinning sidekick

The Denver Team in 1972
Back row left to right: Al Dacascos and Mike Radolavich
Front row left to right: Leonard Endrizzi, Fred King,
Dan Catbagan, and Rick Manenti

Chapter 7

Expanding to Europe

*Sometimes it's the journey that teaches
you a lot about your destination.*
Drake

In 1974, we moved to Germany. Five years earlier, Wun Hop Kuen Do was officially recognized as the fourth branch of the Kajukenbo system. I took Wun Hop Kuen Do to Germany and started an organization called the German Wun Hop Kuen Do Verband e.V. which grew to hundreds of thousands of students over the years.

When I first arrived in Germany, I worked under contract to teach martial arts at the Budo Club Nippon e.V. in Hamburg. Herbert Krantz, the owner, already had six established and very reputable schools throughout the city. He was also working on branching out to four other locations in Northern Germany and two other locations in Southern Germany. As far as I know, we were the first to bring Kajukenbo, in any organized fashion, to Europe.

Other individuals had come and gone, and a few military personnel held small classes while they were stationed there, but they soon left, leaving a couple of lower ranking students behind to go at it on their own. These students tried to do the best they could, but they lacked guidance.

After my arrival, Kajukenbo Wun Hop Kuen Do spread fast. This was due in part to the Kung Fu television series and Bruce Lee films like *Enter the Dragon* and *The Big Boss*. Kung Fu was very mysterious to the West, and there was a great desire to learn more about this style.

In 1972, *King Boxer*, also known as *Five Fingers of Death,* became number one in the world. It was a martial arts film directed by Chang-hwa Chung and starred Lo Lieh. Made in Hong Kong, it is one of many Kung Fu themed movies with Lo Lieh as the leading man. He appeared in many similar efforts from the 1960's, pre-dating the more internationally successful Bruce Lee.

Released in the USA by Warner Brothers, in March, 1973, the film was responsible for beginning the North American Kung Fu craze of the 1970's. It was quickly overshadowed by *Enter the Dragon*, which was released later that same year. The film has a cult following in the U.S. and was referenced in Quentin Tarantino's film, *Kill Bill*.

The summer that we moved to Hamburg was one of the hottest summers in over a decade. Herbert Kranz made the arrangements for us to have an apartment when we arrived, and we quickly made Hamburg our new home, enrolling Craig and Mark in school and settling in. Everyone we met wanted us to enjoy Germany to the fullest and proudly showed us around their city and the surrounding countryside.

Craig and Mark had a hard time adjusting to the different culture and language. On December 24, Christmas Eve, Malia took them back to California, and I was left in Germany to fulfill my teaching contract. I had signed a contract to teach in the Budo Club Nippon School for 24 months.

I have never enjoyed being alone for very long, so I looked for a roommate. I not only found a roommate, but a great translator as well. Christopher Yim became my new roommate and also helped me learn the German language.

Yim was already a popular figure in Hamburg, being an ex-singer for the Les Humphries singers, and together, we became somewhat instant celebrities. The people of Germany did not know what they were getting into making us celebrities!

After I got settled in and was comfortable with everything, Herbert Kranz set up a demonstration for me at a local Karate tournament in the sports hall. I was the center attraction, as I did my sword form breakdown and asked eight Karate black belts to assist me in my demonstration.

I had the black belts attack me in a multi-man attack. I successfully defended myself against their attacks, and at the end of the demonstration, I received a standing ovation from the crowd. The following week, the enrollment in our school reached its capacity, which is exactly what Herbert Kranz hired me for.

Since I had just started my Kung Fu classes here, I only had one student who was even capable of fighting in the intermediate class at the Hamburg Open Style Tournament – Christopher Yim. This was Christopher's first Karate tournament, and one that would make a lasting impression on him.

This was a five point tournament. Yim was three points down very quickly, and I called time out so I could talk to him. He really doubted himself, and, as so many beginners do, he was focusing too much on his defensive game. I tried to motivate him and convince him that he

could win this match, but I didn't seem to be getting through to him that he could actually win.

When I told him that he could win, he looked at me as if to say, "Are you crazy!" That's when I knew I had to snap him out of it. I slapped him across the face twice. Yim's eyes got wide, his jaw dropped, and the imprints of my hand were on both sides of his cheeks. I told him to get himself focused! I also told him that the next time it was going to be two punches to his head, instead of a couple little slaps.

That was all it took. At the end of the match, the score was 5-3 in favor of Yim. Chris had pulled it off. He went into the next three matches in the tournament with a totally different mindset than he had when he started his first match. By the end of the day, Chris had won first place in his division.

I told him that it was all a matter of attitude. I asked him if he had a change of attitude, and he replied that he was very pissed off at me, but at the same time, he didn't want to be beaten and disappoint the club. I told him to hang onto that feeling because it was exactly that feeling and attitude that would make him a winner in the other tournaments. This was the start of what would be substantial success for my students in Germany.

During this time, I also started teaching seminars on Saturdays and Sundays. For the next five to six months, I taught seminars outside of Hamburg in different cities throughout Germany. Armin Ernst, the president of the German Karate Federation, asked me to do a seminar and teach his top fighters the American way of semi-contact fighting with safety equipment.

This organization was extremely eager to learn the techniques being used in America, and I wanted them to know exactly how good the American fighters were. I brought in two of Bruce Lee's kicking bags that Linda Lee had given me the year before.

In order to totally convince them that the techniques that I was teaching really worked, I requested that the two best fighters in the federation come up and spar with me. This federation consisted of over 120 black belts from all over Germany. These guys were considered the best that Germany had to offer.

I knew that I had to back up everything I claimed that I could do and demonstrate my skills. If I couldn't back it up, my time in Germany would be very short. I sparred with each of the champions and easily beat them. After that, the American sparring techniques were eagerly adopted and were considered the best.

The interesting thing about this demonstration was that I was trying to really impress them with my skills. Therefore, I was hitting quite a bit harder than I normally would in a tournament setting or in a normal seminar. This led to an interesting development. From then on, the Karate tournaments in Germany became much rougher, with much harder contact than we had in the United States. Consequently, Germany developed many of the top fighters for future international competitions.

There was another interesting development from my first seminar in Germany as well. I became the highest paid martial arts instructor in the United States or Europe, and it all happened because of a misunderstanding.

The normal fee that I charged for seminars was $1,000 for four hours of training. Most of my peers in the U.S. were charging an average of $750 for the same type of seminar. My regular fees were high, but it was a case of supply and demand. There was no other Kung Fu practitioner doing seminars at that time, so I was in high demand.

At that time, the U.S. dollar was worth 2.50 German marks. When Ernst asked me how much my seminar would cost, I did the currency conversion and told him that it would be 2,500. To my surprise, at the end of the seminar, he came up to me and handed me this giant wad of cash and asked me to count it and make sure it was right.

I started counting it and was stunned. I counted until I reached $1,200, stopped counting, coughed, and looked up at him with a confused look on my face. I shook my head, as to say thank you, and continued counting. I counted until I got to $2,500!

Again, I looked up at him with a confused look on my face. He said, "I'm sorry. Did I shortchange you? Do you need more money?"

I just smiled and said, "No, everything is perfectly fine."

When I had told him that I charged 2,500, he had mistakenly thought that I meant $2,500. What I meant was 2,500 German marks, which equaled $1,000. But he was more than happy to pay me $2,500, and even would have paid me more if I had asked for it. Wow! I just made $2,500 for four hours of work!

From that point on, my fee was $2,500 per seminar, and I was doing six to eight seminars per month! I was ecstatic! All of a sudden, I was averaging $17,500 just for seminars, not including my $8,000 a month salary for teaching classes at Budo Nippon Schools. If this was converted into today's value, I would have been making around $50,000 per month for doing what I love.

But, like everything in life, that soon changed. Bill Wallace came to Europe soon after and only charged $750 for his seminar. If he would have asked me first, I could have helped him make a lot more money. As it was, he stopped the gravy train with his lowball price. The one thing that you can always count on is everything changes.

After Wallace's seminar, and after returning back to the USA, I did an interview for *Black Belt* magazine (1981-82), and I was asked why I charged so much more than Bill Wallace for my seminars. I jokingly answered that Bill Wallace only taught how to stretch and how to kick with one leg. I teach Kajukenbo, Kung Fu forms, semi-contact sparring, Chinese traditional weapons, variable angles of attacks, and even how to kick with your right leg. All of that is worth $2,500.

I had said this in a joking manner, but, as so many people are finding out in today's world with email and social media, sometimes jokes do not come across as they should in print form.

Well, as you might suspect, that did not go over very well with Bill Wallace; he was upset with me for over a year about that article. A couple of years later, our paths crossed in Seattle, and I profusely apologized to Bill.

The truth is that Bill Wallace could have commanded over $4,000 per seminar since he was the number one fighter in America and was extremely well known. That would have been really big money back in the 1970's! Actually, that is big money even today.

I was also starting to get many students who wanted to excel in forms, fighting and weapons competition. These students joined my classes in 1975, and a year later, they were much better. There were a lot of small tournaments in Northern Germany which gave us the opportunity to get some experience before we ventured out and started to compete all over Western Germany.

Our Kung Fu expression was well received, especially with Kung Fu getting so popular outside of China. This was the start of great things to come.

By 1976, Budo Club Nippon had put a fighting team together to fight throughout Southern Germany. Most other schools competed in the traditional white uniform, but our team wore black pants and turquoise fighting tops with turquoise fighting gear. Our unique uniforms really made us stand out and gained us extra attention.

Things were going well, that is, until this one competition in 1976. I was the last man on the team to fight. During the match, I threw a powerful, left roundhouse kick at my opponent, who lifted his right knee high to protect his lower ribs.

I heard a loud cracking sound as I fell to the ground in pain. My shin pad had shifted to the side of my calf, and my shin struck his knee full force. This was not supposed to happen! My shin was shattered and I had a compound fracture. I was not only done for that match, but for weeks afterwards.

My replacement was Christian Wulf, who took us to victory against a very strong South German team. It was a great victory, but not for me. I ended up in the hospital with a cast from my foot all the way to my hip. On the long drive back to Hamburg, I occupied the whole backseat of my 320 BMW.

This cast caused me all kinds of hassles. Malia and the boys had moved back to Germany and the bathroom in our apartment only measured three feet by six feet. Malia had to help me get in and out of the bathroom; at least most of the time she helped.

One time, she was ready to take the kids grocery shopping, and I asked her to help me to the bathroom first. She helped me to the bathroom alright, but then she forgot I was in there and went shopping. I had no idea that everyone was gone and was calling for help for what seemed like forever. They could have put me in a commercial, as I had fallen and could not get up.

I waited for three and a half hours before they got home and heard me yelling for someone to come help me get out of the bathroom. They opened the bathroom door and busted out laughing at me, the whole time, I was yelling at them. My patience had run completely dry during my three and a half hours of enjoying the softness of the floor in my temporary jail cell!

After breaking my leg, I wasn't able to teach any of my classes for a while, so Malia took over. She taught all of my classes for me, including my forms classes, my self-defense classes and my men's fighting class.

The culture in Germany, at that time, was very macho. Some of my students did not like having a woman teach them how to fight, but Malia was more than capable of teaching them. Eventually, they figured this out and things went smoothly.

It was six months before I was able to start working out again. I should have healed faster, but the bone in my leg did not heal correctly, and the doctors had to re-break it and reset it. This time they had to put a metal rod down the middle of my shinbone. I liked this because it allowed me to walk without crutches and also, the new cast did not have to go all the way up to my hip. When the cast was finally removed, my shin was stronger than it was originally. Many times, a bad situation ends up making you stronger. I guess it was a case of what does not kill me only makes me stronger.

One of my schools was in the infamous Reeperbahn Red Light District of Hamburg. This was an area of town that was notorious for drugs, prostitution and crime. Things never slowed down here; there was always something going on around the clock.

This night, I had my red BMW parked out in front of the entrance to my school. We had just finished our classes that night, and I was cleaning up the dojo, or Kwoon in Chinese, which means training hall. I was wiped out after a long day of teaching and training.

Two of my students, Christian Wulf and my son, Mark, both who were in their teens at the time, wanted to go out to my car and just drive forward and backward in the parking space. Thinking this would be harmless, I handed the keys to Christian, and told him to be careful.

About 10 minutes later, the two boys, along with two plainclothes policemen, came into the school. The cops asked me if I gave my keys to the boys and had given them permission to drive my car. I said yes, that they had permission to simply move my car back and forth in the parking spot. Christian and Mark had no license to drive and were just trying to get familiar with the interior of the car because Christian was getting ready to start driving lessons to get his driving permit.

The two policemen became irate, they told me that this was illegal and asked to see my driver's license. At that point, I let my emotions get the best of me and lost my temper. I got so angry that I stared the cops down, while, at the same time, I gave Christian and Mark a stern tongue lashing. Then, I turned and punched the wall with a full-speed punch. Everyone in the room was shocked!

I must have had a really bad day or something, because I wasn't done yet. I turned to the policemen with an attitude and said, "If you want my driver's license, come and take it from me!"

The two cops stood there dumbfounded. They were standing in my martial arts school and already knew about my reputation as the Kung Fu master. Luckily for me, they backed off and told me, "We don't want to have a problem here. Just please tell your students not to drive the car anymore until they have a legal license."

The policemen left the school rather quickly. Then I turned my anger on Christian and Mark, not realizing that my hand and knuckles were bleeding profusely. German walls are very solid and not like American drywall. My hand was bleeding all over the carpet. It seemed that still had a ways to go in learning to control my emotions and my anger.

Interesting enough, the school actually belonged to my wife, Malia. She had inherited it from Paul Winkel, who was the original owner. I was contracted to teach at six different locations in Hamburg, as Herbert Kranz's Budo Club Nippon organization was the largest martial arts organization around during this time.

He had a Karate section, a Judo section, a Jujitsu section, a semi-contact section, an aerobics and jazz dancing section, and our newly organized Kung Fu section, which I was in charge of. Malia, stepped into a major teaching role when I broke my leg, and she was also in charge of the women's classes.

Paul Winkel wanted to have his own school and made arrangements with Malia to come and teach classes at his school. Interestingly enough, his school was financed by an underground gypsy organization. I always find it fascinating to see how all the different pieces, such as this, fit together. Most people never get to know the real inside scoop and have no idea who is really behind many of the businesses that they work with.

Winkel named his school the American School of Kung fu and Karate. As I stated, this school was located right in the heart of the Reeper Bahn Red Light District, notoriously known for its shady activities. What I failed to explain before was that this school was located under a disco night club.

On one side, there was a sex shop and on the other side there was a peep show. When classes were being run during the evenings, we were always listening to the beat of the music of the discotheque upstairs.

It became so normal that when we moved back to the states, we brought the music and the same type of training back with us. During my seminars, I integrated a big boom box playing discotheque music into my training. Perhaps this was the beginning of Jazzercise and Billy Blank's Tae Bo.

Malia and Paul Winkel worked well together, at least in the beginning. Paul was teaching his Karate classes, and Malia was teaching her Kung Fu classes. But it didn't take long for the conflicts to begin. Malia's classes were growing and Paul's classes were declining. His students liked Kung Fu better than the style of Karate that he was teaching.

Paul was so disappointed and angry that one day he lost his temper and threw the keys to the school at Malia and said, "You can have this damn school!" He walked out the door and never looked back.

The next day, the Gypsy investors came into the school and made arrangements with Malia to run the school, and said that they wanted their families to train in our style of Kajukenbo Wup Hop Kuen Do Kung Fu.

Malia had inherited a turnkey business. My son Mark was helping Malia run the school. Soon after, Emanuel Bettencourt joined the school as a student. He would soon find himself being, not only an asset to our Dacascos Academy, but an international champion. It seemed that things were really going our way in Germany.

My contract with Budo Club Nippon was coming to an end, and it was time for me to renegotiate the terms. This became a turning point for us in Germany. Instead of renegotiating the contract, I handed in my resignation and joined my wife Malia's school. Once again, Malia and I were working together.

Many of the students that I trained in the other six other locations decided that they wanted to follow me to my new school and soon enrolled in our school as well. This was devastating to the Budo Club Nippon organization. I didn't mean to hurt the Budo Club Nippon organization at all; I simply wanted to be in business for myself and be my own boss.

I taught at the Budo Club Nippon schools for about 3 years before departing to join my wife. But while at Budo Club Nippon, our reputation grew. We were doing demonstrations and seminars all over Germany and Europe, and our reputation was growing by leaps and bounds.

The training in the Seilerstress school was entirely different than most training of those days. For one thing, this school had a low ceiling. We used the height of the ceiling to help students develop good jumping front kick techniques. They would leap up and do a front kick, trying to touch the ceiling. When they were successful, we put their signature and the date on the ceiling.

Most of the tall students could kick it, barely, but the shorter ones had a harder time. Out of my seven original first generation black belts, Christian Wulf, Dasos Efthadiadis, Michael Timmermann, Jorn Tiedge, Emanuel Bettencourt, Winfred Joszko, and Mark were the elite. With his extreme competiveness it was no wonder that Mark was the first to successfully kick the ceiling. He set the standard.

Dasos Efthadiadis felt the most accomplishment when out of frustration, he yelled as loud as he could, jumped with all his might, and kicked the ceiling so hard that he left an imprint of the ball of his foot on the ceiling. He yelled with excitement and utter joy, as he scrambled to find a felt pen to sign and date his accomplishment. This had been his main goal for several months and now he had achieved it and was a part of the elite kickers club. The attitude of our students always made the difference between success and failure.

Now everyone was looking at me wondering if Sifu could kick the ceiling. No one said anything about it, but they didn't have to; their eyes said it all. It took me several tries, and a couple of embarrassing moments, but I finally accomplished this feat as well. I also had the privilege of putting my signature on this special ceiling. Eventually, the whole ceiling began to look like some kind of strange, designer ceiling made up of footprints and signatures.

The Sielerstress school, as you may recall, was in the heart of the red light district of Reeperbahn. It only had one very large shower with four faucets and both males and females had to share the shower. The sauna was no different. Everything at the school was coed, and for some guys, this meant taking some long, cold showers after all the ladies had left for the night.

After class and showers, it was normal for everyone to head straight to the dry bar that we had in the school. It was kind of like a nightclub bar, but instead of serving alcoholic drinks, we served healthy drinks with no alcohol. From the outside, you would have never known that you were looking at a martial arts school. We had barstools and tables set up for relaxation and conversation. This area also served as our reception area.

Periodically, this was where we would train as well. We took our training to another level and simulated the type of confrontations that one might see in a bar. We used anything and everything within reach, as a defensive or offensive weapon.

During those training sessions, we would train in our normal street clothes to make it as real as possible. We even used cue sticks and pool balls from the pool table nearby. To make the training even more authentic, we dimmed the lights like they are in most bars. The music coming from the discotheque above us and the peep shows next door added even more reality to our training session. I have always gone to great lengths to make my training as real as possible for my students.

Two blocks away from our school was Bismarck Park, where a large statue of Otto von Bismarck, the German chancellor and prime minister, stood on a hill overlooking the red light district in St Pauli. We took full advantage of this and incorporated the park into our training as well. The park was very dirty and muddy, especially after a light rain.

The park was also positioned on an incline. Practicing our fighting techniques on a 25 degree incline helped teach my students what kicking techniques they could and could not use in this situation. Fighting in this setting was a challenge, but the students enjoyed it. This environmental training was difficult, but well worth the effort in order to prepare for a life or death confrontation. We always wore street clothes during this training because that is what we would be wearing if we ever had to defend ourselves in that situation. Good martial arts training trains students for real-life situations.

There was no way that we were going to leave those practice sessions without scratches, bruises, and looking like we had just been in a mud bath. We were fighting between trees and branches, and struggling to maintain our balance. Imagine 30 to 40 students on a hill, practicing combat training where one group of students were trying to stop the other group from reaching the flag at the top of the hill and take it back to the bottom. This was like capture the flag on steroids!

Although the fights and challenges between rival schools did not reach the level that I experienced in Denver, they did occur from time to time. Because our school was situated in the red light district, it drew a lot of attention.

One night during training, a guy from Turkey, in his mid-30's, came in with an attitude. He felt that his style of fighting was superior to American Kung Fu, and he wanted to prove it. He came in and asked for the instructor, and a couple of my students pointed to me, not knowing that this guy was looking for trouble.

When my students found out that he wanted to challenge me, several of them told him that he would have to go through them first. Although this was very honorable, I told my students to back off, sit down, and watch. This guy was wearing a brown, leather bomber jacket, which he took off and laid over by the wall, and then immediately took a fighting stance.

I was about eight feet away from him, and like you would see in an old Kung Fu movie, he bowed and immediately attacked with a powerful, spinning back kick. That was a mistake. I wasn't where he expected me to be. Instead, my trademark drop side kick landed directly in his groin and he flew past me. The whole thing was over as quickly as it started, and he hit the floor reeling from the pain. He slowly rose to his feet and limped out the door.

My students were mesmerized by what they had just seen, but for me, it was all too common. If you are in the business of teaching martial arts, expect challenges to come to your door.

The feeling in our school was one of true Ohana (family). We even spent time socializing outside of our school to keep our group close.

When we were not competing in weekend tournaments, we frequently gathered for picnics in the park and a little American football. This was an education in and of itself, as my students were used to playing soccer and instead of catching the ball, their instincts were to kick it.

At that time, everything American was being readily accepted by the younger generation. This was not necessarily true for the older Germans, as some of them still felt the wrath of World War II. This made it a little harder for us to learn the German language and teach in German; my students wanted to learn English, so my skills in the German language progressed slowly.

Many of my students knew no English at all, but within 18 months, they were very proficient with my version of English, but not so much with the British English, which was taught in school and prevalent throughout Northern Germany. And naturally, what they learned from me had a lot of Pidgin English and Hawaiian slang thrown in for good measure.

I was more laid back than Malia, at least by this time. During forms class, Malia would really lay down the law. Of course, that was the way she had learned to teach when she was my student. When I wasn't around, she would teach them how to do the traditional Chinese lion dancing and symbols, gongs, and drumming, switching the traditional rhythm to rock and roll or disco music. Imagine lion dancers doing disco and country line dancing instead of the traditional dances. It was a sight!

Back in the states, in 1978, our traveling martial arts demonstration team, Hard Knocks, was blowing everyone away. They were gaining a name as the most provocative and innovative martial arts stage act around. Hard Knocks was doing things that went way past what anyone had seen before.

The Hard Knocks team was composed of a group of hard working martial artists from Denver, Colorado with various backgrounds covering Kung Fu, Tae Kwon Do, and Judo. These young pioneers expanded the normal dimensions of self-defense and martial arts.

There were a couple of things that made Hard Knocks so different than the other teams at that time. First, the overall team concept – not only did each member have to perform well enough to hold the audience's attention with his or her individual skills, but they also had to have the ability to work with pin-point precision which required intriguing choreography.

Secondly, and perhaps more importantly from a show business point of view, the team had a knack for presenting tasteful humor in a fashion never demonstrated before by martial arts entertainers. In fact, Hard Knocks could even generate belly laughs from the old school martial artists, who previously felt that such exhibitions were beneath true martial artists.

Many of the old school martial artists did not like seeing martial arts used as entertainment. They believed that the martial arts were about self-defense and honoring the ancient arts, and that using them as entertainment was wrong.

Our troupe leader was Karyn Turner, who was both the number one fighter and forms competitor in 1976 in the United States. It is Karyn's own sense of imagination and organization that brought about the formation of the Hard Knocks to begin with. As she puts it:

> *The reason I started Hard Knocks was threefold. There was a lot of prejudice among styles, and I felt it would be a unique example if different stylists joined together in one strong demonstration team.*
>
> *Also, after I had traveled the tournament scene, I believe some of my fellow practitioners in Denver were among the best in the country."*

Hard Knocks was art in motion, a pure thing of beauty. And speaking of beauty, Karyn Turner wasn't denied her share. Many martial artists considered her the most attractive champion the sport has ever had. On stage, she took on the appearance of a professional showgirl. One thing that I can say about Karyn – she was a knock out, both in and out of the ring!

She worked together with my brother Ben, a well known sifu in the Rocky Mountain area. Ben came in with his expertise in coordinating movement to music. My brother Art, known for his dynamic empty hand form performances, was another important member. Ben's wife, Gwen, who is a good performer of the Filipino fighting arts, added spice and high energy to the troupe, which was already on cloud nine.

Gwen's petite size afforded her some comic moments in the light-hearted full contact matches, appropriately titled, "The Battle of the Sexes." Gwen battled one of the most popular members of the team, Chuck "Cookie Monster" Martinez, who was big, lovable, and occasionally menacing when he was invoking the wrath of spectators. The other members of the team were Dave Norkett, and Pete Morelas.

They were so popular that they were booked for a one week engagement at the Regency Hotel in Denver, reportedly Denver's most prestigious hotel. That, coupled with their performance at the Las Vegas Hilton, launched the troupe into stardom.

While I was in Europe, I worked with Joe Lewis on a film called, *Jaguar Lives*, which was filmed in Spain. Joe wanted me to help choreograph some of the fight scenes. I thought the film was well made, but for some reason it never caught on in the USA. Joe was an excellent actor and could cry on cue. His range of emotions was vast and impressive. I got along fine with Joe, but his career as an actor never really took off.

At that time, I thought that he would be the next martial arts superstar actor. I thought he would step into Bruce Lee's shoes. But the talk around Hollywood was that Joe was hard to work with; to what degree that is true, I don't know. What I do know from a personal perspective, Joe Lewis' ego and arrogance probably got the better of him and his chances in Hollywood faded away.

His destiny was not in Hollywood, but laid waiting for him on the East Coast, where he would build an awesome organization while doing his seminars and promoting his fighting system. Many of the top black belts would soon be adopting the Joe Lewis system. Joe's system was very good, and it was obvious that Bruce Lee had influenced Joe's fighting philosophy.

Back when I was living in Denver, somewhere around 1973, Joe held a seminar at my school. I had never fought Joe Lewis in a tournament, but we spent a lot of time sparring during the seminar.

Joe had been very successful in knocking a lot of his opponents out with his devastating sidekick. I was also a sucker for it. He and I were sparring, trying to get points on each other, when he lunged forward with a sidekick that caught me on the arm and knocked me into the wall panel of my office.

Nothing strange about that! But what was funny was that his kick revealed how frugal I was. My wall panels were stuffed with rolled up newspapers instead of the soundproofing fiberglass insulation. When Joe kicked me and I bounced off the wall, the wooden wall panel came off and all of my makeshift soundproofing flew in every direction. That was very embarrassing. I think my embarrassment hurt more than Joe's kick did.

The decade of the 1980's was really a crazy time for me. Malia and I were having marital problems that really came to a head in 1980. For about 10 years I had wanted to have another child, a child that would be Malia and my child together. We had Craig and Mark, but we did not have a child together.

In reality, I thought that having our own child would bring us closer together and solve our marital problems. Over the years, I kept asking Malia for another child, but she always gave me the same answer, "Not this year. I'm not ready."

After 10 years of this, I became more and more frustrated each time I asked. It seemed to me that her tone was getting harsher, and her attitude said it was never going to happen. She was just more interested in her career than having anymore children.

At this point, I felt that it was clear that we didn't really have a true marriage, but rather simply a marriage of convenience. Things were spiraling increasingly downhill.

I was teaching in a small town called Uelzen, about 75 miles away from Hamburg. The small town was only a stone's throw away from the border of East Germany. I drove there twice a week to teach my Kung Fu class.

It wasn't long before I met a beautiful, young woman in Uelzen, who was very intelligent. Helena was a nurse. Her parents had immigrated to Germany after World War II, walking hundreds of miles to escape communism. She became one of my Kung Fu students, and we seemed to get along really well right from the start.

During one of our conversations, I happen to open up to her about the problems in my marriage. I told her that I was ready for another child, but it had become clear that it was never going to happen with Malia.

Strangely, Helena wanted to have a child, but did not want to be married. We had a very strange and colorful conversation on this subject. By the end of our conversation, we decided to have a child together and within a few months, Helena was pregnant with my child.

During her pregnancy, we kept in close contact. Malia and I had an awkward kind of relationship, sort of like an open and closed relationship. We each knew what the other was doing, but we never really sat down and formalized what our boundaries were, or what our expectations of each other were. As I look back on our life now, I can see what a messed up couple we were! We were married and living together, but were both seeing other people.

Malia had a romantic relationship with a Japanese/German guy named Kai. Kai was a Jujitsu instructor, and he and Malia had a lot in common. Malia and I mistakenly thought that by taking some time away from each other, and exploring other options, we would somehow become closer together in the end. That didn't happen. Things quickly began to get more serious in both of our extramarital relationships.

I really needed a break from everything and an opportunity to train in Taiwan opened up for me. After giving it some thought, Mark and I decided to travel to Taiwan for some specialized training. We were planning on staying in Taiwan for several months, as we were both interested in learning different styles of Kung Fu. Mark was 15 years old at the time and was also contemplating becoming a monk and remaining in Taiwan after our training was over. Once we got settled in, Mark started teaching English to make ends meet.

But I had a change of plans. Mark was enjoying Taiwan more than I was, so I decided to fly back to Germany two weeks earlier than I had planned, while Mark stayed behind. I didn't let Malia know that I was coming home early because I wanted to surprise her and try once again to make our marriage work. As the old saying goes, absence makes the heart grow fonder.

I flew back to Germany with high hopes of getting my life straightened out and getting my marriage back on track. In my mind, it was going to be an unforgettably romantic gesture that would touch Malia's heart. But, there is another old saying that took precedence over love – The Devil smiles when we make plans. In the end, I was the one who was surprised!

I flew into the Hamburg airport, exhausted from the long trip. All I felt like doing was going home and seeing Malia. I caught a taxi home, excited to sleep in my own bed for the first time in months. But when I opened the door and headed to my bedroom, Malia came flying out, with a surprised expression on her face and asked me in a panicked voice, "What are you going here?"

Malia had a towel wrapped around her. She looked shocked and was obviously not happy to see me. That is when I heard something, or someone, in the bedroom. I asked her, in an agitated tone, "Who is in there? Is it Kai?"

Well, my guess was right. It was Kai. I stood there exhausted and now very irritated as well, as Kai hurried to gather his clothes and belongings, and ran out of the house. The visions of a romantic reunion with Malia was about to turn into more of a battlefield than a welcomed homecoming.

There was lots of screaming, yelling and accusations. Finally, I had had enough and turned to leave. I can now tell you from experience, never turn your back on an enraged woman! Suddenly, I felt a stunning blow on the top of my head. Malia had taken my prized ukulele and shattered it over my head. It was my favorite ukulele. It would be over 32 years before I ever wanted to play another ukulele again.

Instead of rekindling our love, Malia ended up leaving and moving in with her boyfriend. I did not like being alone, so I called Helena, who was soon to be the mother of my next child, for a shoulder to cry on. I asked her how she was doing and what she told me sent cold chills down my spine. She told me that she just had one of the strangest dreams that she could ever remember.

Helena dreamed that a man came to her; he was slender with black, wavy hair and approached her while she was rocking in her rocking chair. This man told her that she must name her son Benjamin Jose.

Now, this was very strange for two reasons, besides the fact that some man she had never seen told her what to name her child. First, neither Benjamin nor Jose is a common German name. And, in addition to that, Helena did not even know that the child would be a boy.

I asked Helena when she had this strange dream, and she told me that she had it on May 12, 1980. I was stunned and completely speechless. I turned pale and the hair on the back of my neck stood straight up. I just couldn't believe what I had just heard.

I had Helena come over, and I showed her a photograph of a man and asked her if, by any chance, was this the man in her dream. She looked stunned and confused, and exclaimed, "That's him! That's him exactly!"

The picture that I showed her was of my father; he had died on May 12, 1957. My dad had told me when I was young that he wanted his first grandson to be named Benjamin. At that time, I thought that this would have to be left up to my siblings because the doctor had told me that I would never have children.

About three months later, I received a phone call from Helena's sister telling me to come to the hospital immediately. Benjamin would be my second son, born on September 6, on the same day that I was born in 1942, and at almost the exact same time.

The strange thing is that none of my siblings had any male children. I feel that there must have been something strange happening because when Mark was born, I wanted to name him Benjamin, but Dolly insisted on naming him Mark instead. We settled on Mark Alan to keep the peace in the family, but I always felt that I had let my father down.

Even stranger, after my son Benjamin was born, both my brother, Artie, and my sister, Arleen, had boys of their own. It seemed that if there was some kind of jinx or curse on our family, it had been broken with the birth of Benjamin.

My marriage to Malia was now destined for divorce, but a couple more years passed before I actually filed. Malia had decided to move back to the United States. My stepson, Craig, was living in Italy, and Mark had moved back to Hawaii. I was now all alone in Germany.

Here, I must make an important point. I am in no way blaming Malia for our marriage breaking up. We were both responsible for our decisions and the direction that we allowed our marriage to go. We were both seeing other people; we just never planned on allowing our outside relationships to cause us to drift further apart. Every decision that you make in your life has consequences, and unfortunately, the consequence for our actions ended up being the end of our 18 year marriage.

While I had my extended family with Helena and Benjamin, and lots of friends in Germany, I still felt alone and missed the good ole USA. My homesickness got worse, and I made plans to move back to the states, but wasn't sure where I even wanted to go. My life seemed to be in complete disarray. My marriage was gone. My boys were living nowhere close to me, and I felt completely lost, both mentally and spiritually.

I felt like I had allowed success, money and fame to go to my head and I had lost the things in my life that really mattered. I felt, not only far from my family, but far from God. Although money and success are important, nothing in life is more important that your relationship with God, your family and your friends. It seemed that I had forgotten that and now I was paying the price for it.

I had achieved almost everything that I wanted to in Europe and then some. I turned over the Dacascos Show Team to my first generation black belts, and they kept it going strong. It is still going strong today. This kept the name of Dacascos on the forefront of the European martial arts scene. And from there, our organization and the number of our schools boomed, just like how our Dacascos fighting team began to show dominance in many of the European championships.

Hamburg had become very much a part of me and moving away was almost like cutting off my right hand. I was torn between two countries that I loved. I made sure to organize trips back to Europe twice a year for the first 10 years after I left. Later I reduced my travel to once a year during the summer. The German winters are just too brutal for a guy from Hawaii!

My departure from Germany was almost surreal. My first generation black belts were all there to see me off and gave me a picture of them, etched into a metal plate, as a memento of my time and my family in Germany. This memento is very dear to my heart to this day.

What should have been a very touching, smooth departure was made unnecessarily difficult by the German customs officers. They delayed me and took every piece of my luggage apart. They drilled me with questions to the point that I actually felt violated. They were going on and on about why I had so much film and camera gear. Funny, I never considered camera gear to be so suspicious.

The truth was that, while I was in Germany, I did not have access to my guns. Shooting had become a hobby of mine in Colorado, but I couldn't bring my guns to Germany. So I found another hobby – photography.

I loved taking action shots of martial artists and photos of landscapes and people. I even got into photo journalism for *Martial Arts Magazine* in Europe during my leisure time. I guess that if I couldn't shoot my guns, I found satisfaction in shooting other things.

Eventually, the customs officers were satisfied that I was on the up and up, but not until they had caused me to miss my flight. Although my departure didn't go as smoothly as I would have liked, when I left Germany in 1981, I am proud to say that I had reached thousands of students in Europe and would eventually reach thousands more.

I had done more than any other person at that time to spread Kung Fu throughout Europe, and I had been very successful at it. But now I felt like I was starting over again. I really didn't know where my life was going, but I was on my way. All I knew for sure was that I was meant to teach martial arts and that I had to get my spiritual life straightened out.

Spear bending in Berlin 1974

Me in a full leg cast, broken left shin bone from a fight 1976

Reeperbahn Red Light District, our school was below the sex shop

My family in Hamburg City Park in 1977
From left to right: Craig, Malia, me, and Mark

Working with Joe Lewis on his 1979 movie, Jaguar Lives, in Spain

The 1978 Hard Knocks Team, Karyn Turner in Center

The first Dacascos Show Team 1987

Chapter 8

Back on the American Rollercoaster

*To be yourself in a world that is constantly trying to
make you something else is the greatest accomplishment.
Ralph Waldo Emerson*

I left Germany and flew into New York. I wanted to drive up to
Montreal, Canada to check on one of my schools there, operated by
Sifu Leonard Endrizzi. He picked me up in New York City after I had
cleared customs, and we spent the whole day driving and catching up
on things. We had to drive through a winter storm all the way from
New York to Montreal.

Leonard was not an average driver; he was a bit heavy on the gas.
There were cars and trucks off the road the whole way, and I was
getting more than a little nervous about Leonard's driving. After
seeing so many accidents, I simply had to lay down the law with
Leonard and make him slow down. I wanted to make it back to
Hawaii, not be laid up in some Canadian hospital!

If you will remember, Leonard was my dark angel back in Denver
before I moved to Germany. I left him in charge of my Dacascos
Academies in Denver when I left, along with my brother, Benjamin.
But, as fate would have it, Leonard disappeared for a few years, and
Ben had to run my schools in Denver all alone.

Back in Denver while I was in Germany, Leonard had been shot in
the head with a 38 caliber pistol and left for dead in a back alley. His
past involvement with the Mafia had come back to haunt him. The
longer I live, the more that I am convinced that karma can never be
outrun. No matter what we do, we will eventually have to live with the
consequences of our actions. I knew that this was another reason that I
had to get right with God.

I asked Leonard what really happened, and he said that his head
was too thick and that the bullet only glazed his skull, knocking him
out. He laid there for several hours before driving himself to the
hospital. Well, I knew that there is no skull so thick that a bullet will
not penetrate it. He either got lucky or God was watching out for him.

As with most people with such backgrounds, getting more
information out of him was virtually impossible. For him, it was over

and so was his time in the mafia. He was going straight from that point on and decided to disappear to Canada to start a new life. In Canada, he met his wife, Louiselle, and started teaching the same martial arts that had saved his life many times in the past.

While I was in Montreal, I was invited to visit an old friend, Sifu Kai Sai, (his real name was Chris Casey), in Hartford, Connecticut. He wanted me to come there and open a Kajukenbo Wun Hop Kuen Do school. I first met him in Germany, and we did some training together.

In fact, Sifu Kai Sai was solely responsible for Mark and me visiting Taiwan. He had several Chinese contacts that were involved with Chiang Kai-shek Kuomintang (KMT), the Nationalist Party. He was also a close ally of Sun Yat-sen, the vicious, anti-communist group which fought against Mao Tse-tung's Communist Party during their escape from China to Formosa in 1949.

These Sifus were the best Kung Fu instructors who were able to escape to Formosa, now called Taiwan, and they had developed a large army of followers. Both Mark and I were treated very well and trained with them for several months in 1980. I trained with Sifu Lo Man Kam in Wing Chun Kung Fu, and Mark trained with Sifu Moi Shin in Black Tiger Style Kung Fu.

Christian Wulf, another one of my students, soon followed us to Taiwan and trained under Sifu Moe Shin for the summer. Sifu Lo Man Kam was a relative of Yip Man, Bruce Lee's teacher. So once again, my techniques and Bruce's techniques were weaved together.

Experiencing the winter in Montreal convinced me that Hartford was not the place for me either, even though Chris Casey offered to totally finance my martial arts school in Hartford. Chris was a finance expert who was the vice president of one of the top insurance companies in the world. His company actually insured other insurance companies.

I met him in Southern Germany as his company was operating there during the time that I lived in Germany. I later found out that he was connected to several top secret operatives and had made arrangements for me to actually be a part of the "Taiwanese Connection."

Chris had a physical condition where he was allergic to the sun. He would always wear dark glasses and would keep his entire body covered most of the time. He even had drapes that covered the windows in his car. I have to tell you, this made him seem even more mysterious and unique.

About eight months after I turned down his offer to teach in Hartford, I received a message from his wife saying that he had committed suicide; he had shot himself in the head. I have often wondered if it was really suicide or if his death had something to do with the top secret operations that he was involved in. You just never know what the truth is in such situations.

He had seemed very happy to me and knowing about the billions of dollars that passed through his hands, I had to wonder. I guess only a few people in his inner circle really know the truth. In any case, I was sorry to have lost a friend.

I left Montreal and flew to Portland, Oregon where one of my students, Fred King, was running the Academy of Kung Fu and teaching Kajukenbo Wun Hop Kuen Do. I decided to make Portland my temporary home, at least until I could move back to Hawaii. I enjoy both the weather and the people in Oregon.

But before I settled down, I decided to take a detour and visited my friend and student, Eric Lee in Los Angeles. Eric had become a celebrity in his own rights in Hollywood, and I ended up spending six months with my old student.

It was a strange environment living with Eric and his Chinese girlfriend. They didn't seem to get along very well. I stayed in their spare bedroom and one day I went into the bathroom to take a bath, and I heard a strange noise coming from under the old, claw foot bathtub. I had no idea what in the world was going on!

I discovered that Eric had a German shepherd that basically made his home under the bathtub. This dog obviously had some major issues! He only came out from under the bathtub to eat and relieve himself, and then it was right back under the tub it went. This dog was as crazy as my life had become!

Eric and I spent a lot of time together, and I became familiar with the politics of Hollywood. Hollywood is very much who you know, not what you know. We went to a lot of Hollywood parties where I felt very uncomfortable. I didn't feel that these people were genuine or sincere; it seemed that everyone wore a fake smile, but behind that smile, I knew something else was going on. I never became comfortable at those parties or with those people.

While in Los Angeles, Eric and I decided to take a road trip to Denver, to check on my Denver schools. It took us a day and a half to get there. We tried to take turns sleeping while the other person drove, but Eric's driving made me too nervous to sleep.

Eric would drive with his left knee and use his right foot to manage the gas and the brake. At the same time, he was practicing his forms without holding on to the steering wheel. How in the world was I supposed to sleep while Eric drove with his leg and practiced Chinese forms with his arms!

In those days, driving through Nevada was pretty much open road. I don't recall seeing any speed limit signs. And, of course, to us that was a license to drive as fast as we wanted. We reached speeds of around 100 mph, with Eric steering with his leg! When I did dose off, I was quickly jarred awake by any little bump in the road, thinking that my life was about to end.

Imagine a short Chinese guy, who could hardly reach the gas pedal, steering with his knee, and doing an entire form for a few hours at a time, with me sitting next to him, *pretending* to sleep, but being a nervous wreck and watching his every move. And when I did actually fall asleep, Eric would wake me up to evaluate and correct any mistakes he was making in his forms.

Eric was obsessed with perfecting his forms. The "King of Kata" would practice whenever he could. Sometimes we would stop on the side of the road, in the middle of nowhere, to take a bathroom break. There was very little traffic in the middle of nowhere, and I would look up and Eric was in the middle of the highway practicing his forms!

A couple of times he even scared me because he was so focused that he didn't even notice when a car would be approaching. I had to yell at him to get out of the road because I didn't want to clean up "chop suey" from the middle of the highway.

I was hoping that, with Eric's connections, I would be able to break into the martial arts film industry, but I did not have much luck with my attempts to get into the industry. However, I did learn a lot about how the industry worked, and I did not like it. With that, and the smog and traffic in L.A., it did not take me long to realize that Los Angeles was not the place for me, so I moved back to Portland where I was warmly welcomed.

Fred King had set up a seminar for me in Portland, and I was more than happy to get back into teaching. During the seminar, Fred auctioned off a set of one-on-one lessons with me. Ann Donica, who was Fred's student, won the lessons by recruiting the most students for the seminar.

I had already made plans to visit Hawaii, so I talked to her and made arrangements to teach the private lessons when I returned to Portland, about a month later. Her interest was not simply the physical side of Kung Fu, but the philosophical side, and she thought that I could help her with that.

My intentions were to go back to Hawaii and check on the possibility of opening up my own school there, but Hawaii had changed so much since I had been gone. When I left, there were only about 500,000 people on the islands; now there were over a million people there. The small town feelings and aloha had given way to freeways and high-rise buildings. It no longer felt like the Hawaii of my childhood.

The congestion was irritating, as I was really looking forward to getting away from the city and back to the laid back, small town beach community. After doing some research, I found that it was almost impossible to have a commercial storefront location for my school. On top of that, it seemed that Hawaii just wasn't ready to accept a commercial school.

I was extremely disappointed and made plans to relocate to Portland permanently, since I already had an established school there and many followers. Both the climate and the lifestyle in Portland were very similar to Hamburg. It had a very European feel to it.

While family and friends were looking forward to me moving back to Hawaii, I found that economically, I would have to live on the mainland, at least for a while longer. I was not willing to settle for teaching in a garage or the YMCA in Hawaii. I had become much more than that, and I still had more to do. But I knew that one day I would move back to Hawaii; I just never thought that it would take another 19 years!

I moved to Portland and the first thing I knew that I had to do was fulfill my obligation to teach private lessons to Ann Donaca. This actually worked out well because she and her husband were gracious enough to offer me a place to stay until I found a place of my own.

Living with Ann and her family and being single, but not yet legally divorced from Malia, made me question my life, as well as my morals. I started to wonder if I was really successful in life or if I was simply bouncing from one place to the other.

I had this internal desire to settle down, but I also had a driving desire to make my martial arts a success and to spread my teaching in Kajukenbo Wun Hop Kuen Do far and wide.

At the same time, living with Ann and her family opened some doors for me. I formed a company which focused on developing movie projects, and this only happened because of the contacts that Ann had with people in Portland and in Hollywood. I thought this was fantastic!

The real problem was that Ann wanted more than martial arts training. She and her husband were in an open marriage. Her husband,

Bill, had another girlfriend, and they were both very comfortable with each other playing around on the side. I, on the other hand, was not comfortable with this at all. I had already experienced firsthand what this kind of lifestyle could do to a marriage, and I wanted no part of that kind of relationship.

With me living in their home, it gave Ann an opportunity, at least in her mind, to form some kind of relationship with me other than being my manager and partner in our company. This made it hard for me to stay focused, as I was not interested in that kind of a relationship, but I did want to capitalize on the business opportunity that I had found with our partnership.

Fred King helped me quite a bit, but we had some major differences. Fred was very much involved in the Church of Scientology and tried to connect the Scientology teachings with the Academy of Kung Fu. I was not familiar with Scientology and was unable to see the connection to Kung Fu.

I was searching for a closer spiritual life with God, and he seemed very committed to his religion, so I decided to become a Scientologist in order to understand what it was all about. I even spent time in Los Angeles at their big Scientology location where Tom Cruise, Chick Carrera, John Travolta, and other high profile celebrities were members.

Well, I decided that what was good for them was not necessarily good for me, and I left the Church of Scientology. This caused complications between Fred King and me. As you may already know, the Scientologists do not take rejection very well. There were other beliefs and obligations that caused issues between us as well.

I could not see one of my academies, which was supposed to be one of the premier Wun Hop Kuen Do academies in the Northwest, being integrated with some religion that I was not totally committed to myself. My beliefs in Jesus Christ and Christianity were stronger than L. Ron Hubbard and his Scientology gibberish! I knew in my heart that it was time for me to get my spiritual life on track.

Also, Fred King and I had an arrangement that a percentage of the academy's income would come back to me as the founder of Wun Hop Kuen Do. That never happened. And in 1984, Fred King and I went our separate ways. Fred would go on to rename his expression of Kung Fu as Mu Duk Pai.

The end of my relationship with Fred King led me to build my own academy about 10 miles away from his. In doing so, many of his students left his academy and came to my school because they wanted to learn from the source. Those students became the backbone of the Dacascos Academy of Kung Fu in Beaverton, Oregon.

I had successfully removed myself from Scientology, but it seemed that the temptations that would come my way, as I searched for some spiritual peace, were not over with quite yet. I was soon contacted by one of my students from Germany, Bettina, who was visiting California for six weeks. She wanted to visit me while she was in the States, before she headed back to Germany.

Ann Donaca was a very beautiful woman, and she definitely flaunted her sexuality towards me. Her charms were very hard to resist and, as I stated, they were very distracting at times. When Bettina contacted me to visit Portland, I jumped at the chance, thinking that this would help with my little problem. I arranged for Bettina to be able to stay at Ann's house as well, but there was only one spare bedroom – she would have to stay in my room.

My resolve was already running low, and it was not long before our friendship blossomed into a romantic relationship. Bettina and I decided to move out and get our own apartment, about 15 miles away from the airstrip. This was the nudge that I needed to go ahead and finalize my divorce from Malia, who was now involved with one of my second generation black belts, George Kites, who was a student of Eric Lee.

George had visited Malia and me when we lived in Hamburg and stayed with us as a guest. To my surprise, there was more going on behind closed doors than I knew. A romantic relationship was developing right under my nose.

Soon after my divorce, I married Bettina. Although we were attracted to each other and enjoyed each other's company, this was a different kind of marriage. I had not completely gotten over Malia and our marriage of 17 years. I truly loved Malia, and we remain friends to this day.

My heart had not healed yet and because of that, this marriage was basically doomed from the start. And I have to confess, I was no angel either. Although I was searching for spiritual peace, God was not in my heart yet, as He is now. I was not the man that I should have been.

As you might imagine, my relationship with Ann was starting to deteriorate and the film project, which already had several investors and a director, was not turning out to be a positive project. The director rewrote the original script that Mark and I had written, called *Shattered Image*. It was later changed to *Thunderfoot* and was not at all what we had envisioned. We were quickly introduced to the way that Hollywood worked. It is a dog eat dog town and it was really not for me.

The complications soon caused me to break off my business relationship with Ann Donaca. It also caused Mark and I some issues, and we became distant from each other for a couple of years after that. Mark's agent didn't agree to the script or the contract, and my other partner, Tom Como, found himself in a big lawsuit with the investors. Everything fell apart! To make matters worse, the strife between Mark and I was getting much worse.

Meanwhile, my school was becoming very successful and growing by leaps and bounds. It seemed that no matter how anything else in my life went, I was always able to be successful teaching my martial arts. We were starting to develop several champions again, and I was also making many new friends. At the same time, I was becoming hated by others who became jealous of my school's success.

Jealousy is a major problem in the martial arts world. It was never supposed to be that way, as martial arts also include character training, honor, and integrity. But too many people neglect honor, respect, and integrity in the martial arts and only focus on competitiveness.

I was being featured on the covers of many martial arts magazines and had dozens of articles written about me. This led to many people, of questionable character, trying to jump on the bandwagon. It seemed that the philosophy of yin and yang continued to play out in my life, along with the good came the bad.

Within three short years, from 1984-1987, my whole life was once again in the fast lane. My life seemed to be moving at the speed of light, but I had this internal need for it to slow down, or even crash. I felt as if there had to be something more, something other than my successes in the world of martial arts. There was a void in my spirit, something missing, but I could not put my finger on what it was. All I knew was that there had to be something that I was missing.

It was at this time that I met a guy named Dan Cruz from Seattle, Washington. Dan had started a martial arts magazine for the Northwest and wanted me to be on the cover of his magazine. He came down to Portland several times to interview me for the article.

During our time together, Dan and I talked about martial arts, but we also talked a lot about God, the Bible, and religion. Whenever we weren't talking about martial arts, it seemed that religion worked its way into our conversations.

He knew a lot about the Bible and could memorize verses from the Bible, word for word. But I was soon to find out that he had a dark side which was very disturbing. Although he seemed to know the Bible, he certainly didn't internalize what he memorized.

Dan had heard that besides running my martial arts school, I was also interested in maybe getting into the security business and becoming a bodyguard. With my skill set, this seemed like a natural progression. Frankly, I was not interested in the money, but in another life experience. I also thought that this would be great for my resume and might even help me make connections in the film industry.

I had heard of a company called, ESI, Executive Security International, run by Bob Dugan from Aspen, Colorado. I had seen Bob's advertisements in the back of *Black Belt* magazine and I thought that this would be something that I could learn that would help my students too.

Dan Cruz had some contacts and told me that he could help me connect with ESI. However, at that time, I did not have the finances to spend the next several weeks in Aspen. Dan told me that he had made arrangements with his financial backers to finance my training at the academy.

He had already spoken to Bob Dugan and made arrangements for my classes to start within a week. What I didn't know at that time was that he had promised Dugan that before my training was completed, he would have the money to pay for my program. He didn't have the finances in place, as he said he did.

Within a couple of days, I had made the arrangements to fly to Aspen. When I arrived at the Denver Airport, I caught a small plane to carry me the rest of the way to Aspen. It only had eight seats, and they were all filled with guys who looked liked professional football players.

I had no idea at that time that we were all heading to the same place. I looked like a match stick compared to these guys! When the plane landed, there was a big, black limousine waiting for us. To my surprise, I was squeezed in between all of these giants, and away we went to the ESI headquarters.

The training was intense! We began the following morning at 5 a.m., had a short breakfast, and got started. Each day of training was a full 16 hours! ESI was the most successful training program of its kind in the United States.

They trained everyone from law enforcement officers to military personnel and I was not law enforcement or military. My only experience was in martial arts and a Lt. Colonel in the Reserve Officer Training Corps (ROTC) in high school.

I graduated with top honors, and was asked by Bob Dugan if I would like to join their staff as one of their self-defense instructors. I declined. He then offered me a placement in London, which I also declined. I had only been back in the United States for a short time and was tired of living in Europe. The London fog just did not sound appealing to me; I had other plans.

The money would have been great, but it wasn't my dream. I wanted to get back to Portland and implement what I learned into my training and the expression of my self-defense techniques. Nonetheless, I really enjoyed my time at ESI. The training there is the real deal.

One day we were training to quick draw and shoot fast. We didn't use blanks; everything was live ammunition. During training, a bullet whizzed by me, about an inch from my head, and hit my partner that was standing behind me square in the forehead! He was rushed to the hospital and miraculously survived.

On another day, we were learning to do reverse 180's in a car chase. We were also learning to do panic stops to take the other car out like you see in the movies. The guy that took my car out, by bumping the rear bumper, forced me onto the side of the road, going about 40 mph.

My front wheel hit the mud, and the car flipped over a couple of times. My partner was pinned upside down inside the car. I got out with only a few scratches, a small cut over my left eyebrow, and some bruises. We both had to be cut out of our seatbelts, which probably saved our lives. I was lucky; I only had minor injuries. My partner, however, ended up in the hospital for a few days with a concussion and a broken arm.

I did some undercover work for about a year after my training, but when the bullets started flying, I changed my mind. I had spent too many years learning to protect myself from attacks; I didn't like the concept of putting myself in harm's way when someone was shooting. I knew that I had a family to care for, so I decided that this was not for me. Instead, I used my training to teach individuals using my Dacascos Tactical System, DTS, a concept not fully developed and realized yet.

I had a friend in Bandon, Oregon, Mike Barnett, who was a professional painter that specialized in painting boats and aircraft. He had taken my 1982 Mitsubishi and repainted it gun-metal gray with silver accented pin stripes. I thought he did an awesome job. He was great at what he did, and he was a great sailor as well.

Mike was one of my students and a good friend. One day he invited me to come down and checkout his sailboat. It was a very nice, 40 foot boat named Storm Rider. This boat was a beauty! It was built in Holland out of concrete and reinforced steel, so it sat lower in the water.

A couple of months before, I had mentioned that I might like to buy a boat of my own. He told me that he was going to buy a bigger one and would be interested in selling me his boat. Mike was planning on using his new boat to sail to different locations around the world, so he wanted a bigger, longer boat that would keep him safer as he sailed in the open waters.

He ended up buying a bigger boat sooner than he thought. He and his wife bought a 60 foot, steel hull boat with a 120 hp Perkins marine engine. The boat was docked in Humbolt, California at the time. They had sailed their boat down the coast to purchase the new one. Unfortunately, his wife, Kathy, had broken her ankle working on the boat, and couldn't sail back to Oregon. This left them one man short for the trip back.

Mike asked if I would come and help him sail his boat, Storm Rider, back to Oregon. We were going to sail it back to Oregon, and then he was going to fly back and sail his new boat to Mexico for a much needed vacation.

I was excited at the chance to learn how to sail with an experienced sailor, who was going to teach me to sail, on what I hoped was going to be my new sailboat. I had known Mike since our days in Denver, 20 years earlier. Mike was a rare breed and one of my closest friends.

A few days before I was supposed to help Mike sail his boat up the coast, I got a call from my sister, Christine. She was frantically crying on the phone telling me that I needed to come back to O'ahu immediately.

My brother, Charlie, was very sick and in the hospital. Charlie's real name was Alan, but during the Vietnam War, his war buddies started calling him Charlie because he looked like a Vietcong and the name stuck.

Charlie was dying of multiple myeloma. It had spread quickly throughout his body, and the doctor did not discover it until it was too late. I flew in every three months to help take care of him and to spend time with the rest of my family.

It had not been very long that I had just been to Hawaii to visit my family and check on Charlie. During that visit, I had taken him to the hospital because he was complaining of a nagging pain in his lower back. This pain eventually left him in agony and walking on crutches. I dropped him off at the hospital and my sister was going to pick him up after his appointment because I had to catch a plane back to Portland.

I had just got home when my sister called and told me that I needed to come back immediately. She said that we had to make a decision about Charlie's care because the doctors said that his time was short. We had to decide whether to keep him in the hospital or to call hospice.

I called Mike and let him know that I had to fly back to Hawaii and would not be able to help him sail his boat back to Oregon. He was able to find another guy named Tom to fill in on the trip. Together, Mike and Tom sailed the sailboat from California to Oregon. But he didn't know that there had been an earthquake in Tahiti.

At 3 p.m. that afternoon, there was a tsunami off the coast of Oregon with a 32 foot rouge wave. That wave hit Mike's sailboat and damaged the vessel. Mike was down in the engine room bailing water while Tom was at the helm. The sailboat ended up going down, taking Mike with it. Later that evening, a search and rescue team found Mike's body a quarter mile from where the boat went down. Tom miraculously survived.

I got the news early the next day, and it left me stunned. I was supposed to be on that sailboat. In one instant, I lost one of my best friends. For a couple of weeks after the accident, I walked around in a daze. I knew that I had just dodged another bullet, and God was looking out for me.

Only days after the wreck, I was spending the night with my brother at the hospice in Kailua. Most everyone in the family had already come to visit, knowing that it would probably be the last time they would ever see Charlie here on earth. Around 9:30 in the evening, on January 5, 2000, Mom and Christine headed back to Honolulu for the night.

Charlie was smiling at me and seemed to be in no pain. I was sitting in a chair at the base of his bed, reading a book to him, when I heard a strange sound coming from Charlie. He appeared to be smiling at me. I thought he was just breathing hard, but then I realized that he had just passed away.

As tears rolled down my face, I knew that it was an honor for me to be there with Charlie as he went to be with God. It seemed as though he waited for Mom and Christine to leave, and for it to be just him and me, and then he passed.

I called my sister and asked her where she was and told her to turn around, that she needed to come back. She burst into tears, as she knew from the tone of my voice what had just happened.

I was not fully recovered from the passing of my dear friend and now I just witnessed the angel of death come and take my brother away. It is said that everything happens for a purpose. If Charlie's time had not come when it did, I may have gone down on the Storm Rider. In a way, Charlie's passing may have saved my life.

A few weeks after Charlie's passing, we had an elaborate celebration of life for him near Queen's Beach in Waikiki. It was held very early in the morning at sunrise. My remaining brothers, Artie and Ben, and a couple of other family members, were all dressed in traditional Hawaiian malu's, a traditional garment that wraps around the waist. We were bare chested and wore a flower crown and a flower lei.

After the morning eulogies and service, we took Charlie's ashes in a six-man outrigger canoe and paddled a half mile outside of Waikiki Beach. There we met the rest of the family, who had taken a large catamaran to the predetermined spot.

Above us was a black helicopter that released thousands of flower petals which rained down on us as we all sang Aloha Oie, a traditional farewell song. Then I opened the container holding Charlie's ashes and poured them into the center of a large Hawaiian lei in the water.

There was a light shower that day that provided us with a beautiful rainbow right at the exact same time of the ceremony. God was all around us, giving us comfort and peace. The feeling was surreal, yet humbling.

On the same day, Mike's ashes were scattered outside of the harbor where his sailboat went down off the Oregon coast. I was not able to be there because I was in Hawaii with my brother during the ceremony. Needless to say, this was a very hard couple of weeks in my life.

In 1985, a representative group of American martial artists were invited to the People's Republic of China by the Beijing Wu Shu team. This team was the most prestigious Wu Shu team in the world. In an effort to promote cultural change through the martial arts, we traveled to Beijing, Shanghai, Xian, and the Shaolin Temple in Honan Province, the original birthplace of the martial arts.

Professor Wally Jay and I were co-captains for our team. We served as emissaries of cultural exchange, performing for our hosts and observing demonstrations by the greatest masters living in China. Our American team member's disciplines included Karate, Jujitsu, Kung Fu, Tae Kwon Do, and Capoeira, the Brazilian fighting art never before seen in China.

During our trip, a one-of-a-kind documentary was produced by One Hand Productions, with my student, Bill Owens, narrating. It would be impossible to recreate this film today. We were fortunate enough to have this unique combination of circumstances that came together, at just the right point in time, to make this documentary possible. It was quite an honor to be a part of it!

The director of the Beijing Wu Shu team contacted George Xu (Xu Guo Ming) in San Francisco, to explore the possibility of assembling a group of American martial artists to visit China and to attend and do a demonstration at the First International Wu Shu Championships, to be held in the city of Xian in central China.

This would be the first time that I would actually see Jet Li perform in person. I was able to see, firsthand, his winning form and his amazing skills. This was before he even became the Kung Fu superstar and martial arts movie star that he is today.

In coordination with Brendon Lai, we began contacting martial artists of different disciplines, to assemble a team. Our intent was to organize a group that contained some of the most famous martial artists, as well as lesser known instructors, from the United States, to participate in a culture exchange with the most famous martial artists in China.

During our trip, we met with the most famous martial arts masters in China; these guys were seen as "China's Living Treasures." We were able to establish good natured dialog with these masters and we observed the positive health benefits that the martial arts had on the Chinese people as a whole.

We also had the rare honor to perform with the monks of the Shaolin Temple. At the temple, the monks performed three forms and also revealed the famous Shaolin Training Hall, where monks have practiced for over 1,000 years.

My student, Bill Owens, and I demonstrated American style sports Karate and Capoeira for them. They had never seen Capoeira before our demonstration.

The award-winning documentary of the United States Martial Arts Representative Team's journey through China was also a story of the people of China and their dedication to the beneficial health practices of the martial arts. I still view this documentary as the ultimate martial arts documentary to this day. If you ever get a chance to see it, I highly recommend that you watch it.

However, as good as it was, we were in a communist country and parts of it had to be edited for political reasons. There were parts that were never shown on Chinese television or in the documentary in the States. We had to agree to cut those parts permanently.

One of the parts that were cut was when I fought in a contest on a fortress wall, besting one of their national Chinese champions, Sifu Lee. I beat him 5-0, and could have continued to score points if the fight had not been stopped. It only ended because Professor Wally Jay told me, during a break in the fight, that we were 1,500 miles into mainland China, and if we wanted to get out of this country alive, I had better lighten up and stop embarrassing their champion.

I kind of felt that the Chinese wanted to show how their martial arts were superior to American martial arts, and I was having none of it, especially if this champion wanted to show that he was superior to me. Their national champion had no idea who I was, and thought that I was just another American coming to learn their ways.

It all worked out in the end, and after that fight, I was invited to stay longer and teach them the American version of sport Karate. That would have been a great opportunity, but since I was a part of the team, and on tour, I was obligated to stay on our schedule and return back to the United States with the team.

We returned to the U.S. and as soon as I walked off the plane, my wife, Bettina, met me at the gate and told me that she was pregnant, even before I could greet her. I have to tell you, this was a big shock! My daughter, Vanessa, was born on June 9, 1986.

During my time in China, I had made several contacts with the championship team in Beijing, and I made arrangements for them to come to Portland and do a demonstration. Sifu Brendan Lai helped me coordinate this, and the team ended up scheduled to do a tour across the United States as well as doing a second performance in Portland. We had everything set and were ready for the performance at the University, when I heard the tragic news – the space shuttle Challenger had exploded after liftoff on January 28, 1986.

All eyes and ears were focused on this tragic event. We were all stunned and shocked, as was the entire country. On top of this disaster, I was very worried that this tragedy, which had affected the entire country, would overshadow the tour that I was hosting for my Wu-Shu team that evening and that it would be a failure. This tour was a big deal and I couldn't believe what was happening.

It turned out that I was worried for no reason. We had a large crowd, and although we all had sad hearts, the performance helped to lift our spirits. The tour was an awesome success and helped to elevate the Dacascos schools to an even higher level.

Just a few months after this, our marital problems began to spin out of control. Bettina came to my school to confront me about our marriage issues. She had a key to the school, so she let herself in. At this time, our marriage was already over. I had turned one of the dressing rooms in my school into a bedroom and was actually living there.

Bettina was very upset with me, so she came in and basically destroyed my office. She took everything off of my desk and threw it all over the office in a fit of rage. Then she stomped back to where I was sleeping in the back of the school. She knocked on the door, and when I opened it, she attacked me like a wild animal!

She was throwing a barrage of kicks and punches, but the one that hurt most was the kick to the groin. Imagine getting a knock on your bedroom door at night, getting up to answer the door, and as soon as you open the door, getting kicked right in the groin! That is what happened to me, but it didn't stop there. She continued to punch and kick me in a frenzy of anger.

I did not even lift a finger to defend myself. I was astonished at what she was doing, but I knew that if I defended myself, I would be the one in trouble, so I just took it. After it was all over, I ended up with a cracked nose, bleeding all over the place, and walking a bit strangely, as my family jewels had just been used like a soccer ball!

She left the school still very angry. That is when I went to the front of the school and found my office ransacked. And, the icing on the cake was, a few minutes later, the police showed up at my door. I was shocked! I had just been assaulted, did not fight back, and now the police were at my school to arrest me.

Bettina had called the cops and told them that I had attacked her. Of course, it was pretty obvious to the cop that I was the one who had been attacked. Bettina had no marks at all on her, and here I was, covered with blood and barely able to walk. But, in true law enforcement fashion, I was handcuffed, arrested, and put into the back of a patrol car.

The cop drove about two blocks and pulled into an empty parking lot to fill out his paperwork. It was two o'clock in the morning, on a cold, wet, winter's night. Not only was I hurting, but I was chilled to the bone, as I only had on a light shirt. I have to tell you, just receiving a beating from my estranged wife, and now sitting on a cold, hard plastic seat in the back seat of a cop car, freezing my butt off, was not what I had planned for that night!

Now comes the best part of this story. The cop had short, red hair and had a very fair complexion. He was fairly tall and stocky. At first, I had assumed that he was a cop that had moved here from the Deep South. His deep, authoritative voice had a slight twang to it, as he asked me for my full name and date of birth.

I answered his questions politely, although I was feeling extremely irritated. Then he asked for my place of birth. I thought this was a strange question, but I answered calmly, "Hilo, Hawaii." I felt that maybe my calm demeanor was helping in this volatile situation.

Then, strangely, his demeanor and tone changed. He paused, turned around and looked me in the eyes. Then he spoke in Pidgin English, "Ah, bro! I come from Hilo, too. I graduated from Hilo High School."

He then looked at my face, which was now turning all kind of weird colors and swelling up nicely. Then he said, "Yeah, dat what da haole titas do." That is Pidgin English for, "Yes, that is what the white ladies do to their boyfriends when they get into a domestic fight."

I now refer to this officer as Big Red. Big Red had been on the Portland Police Department for two and a half years after relocating from Hawaii four years earlier. After we spent a few minutes reminiscing about Hilo, he got out of the car, opened the back door to let me out, and removed the handcuffs. He gave me his business card and told me to go home.

I got released and he tore up the report. His last words to me were, "You got my card; give me a call this week and you can ride around with me on patrol. There are not too many Hawaiian guys around here and it would be good to feel like I'm home again where we can talk Pidgin."

I couldn't believe it, but I felt that, even with as big of a mess as my life was in, God was still looking out for me. It was freezing cold as I walked the two blocks back to my school, but I didn't notice the cold so much anymore. As I looked at the stars, I said aloud, "Thank you, God," and slowly limped back to my school. Little did I know that this was just the beginning of a downward spiral that would last for several months.

Trust and betrayal can happen in many ways. I have been betrayed many times during my lifetime, but this one probably cost me more than all of the rest combined. This was a devastating loss for me, as my design, and intellectual property, was stolen from right under my nose, by someone I should have never trusted in the first place.

I had designed a prototype of a martial arts training dummy called the Perfect Dummy. I was very excited about the possibilities of this training tool, but it would soon turn into one of my biggest regrets and one of the biggest losses.

I first met a guy named, Edmond Silva, in my Portland, Oregon school back in 1986. He had seen my sign "Dacascos Kung Fu Academy" many times while passing by my location, and he had kept wondering if this was the same person he met some 11 years before. Curiosity got the best of him one day, and he walked into my school to find out.

Silva said that he met me for the first time in Berlin, Germany when he was in the military, back in 1974. I was on a martial arts representative team made up of the top fighters and demonstrators from America. This was a team that was put together by *Professional Karate Magazine* promoter Mike Anderson and a German promoter, George Bruckner.

Silva came into my school and introduced himself. He appeared to be a well-mannered insurance and real estate broker. We talked and became friends; at least I thought he was my friend. He told me that he was from Hawaii and was a relative of the Parkers who owned a huge ranch on the Big Island of Hawaii. He also told me that he was a relative of King Kamahamaha, the first king of Hawaii.

He was charismatic and very likable, and it seemed that we would get along like two peas in a pod. And for awhile, we did. He was a smooth talker and wined and dined me to the point that I never saw what was coming.

Silva told me that he was an investor. I needed someone to help me get my invention on the market, and he sounded like just the person that I was looking for. He said he was looking for something to invest in and could get other investors involved as well.

I was also interested in learning about his real estate business and flipping houses; it seemed as if this guy was a Godsend for me. So there I was, susceptible to his smooth talking charms and beginning to trust him, as he continued to bait me over a six month period. Silva was everything but a Godsend!

It seemed as if we had developed a good business relationship. I took him around and introduced him to a lot of martial artists on the West Coast, as he also told me that he was a black belt and had his own school up in Tacoma, Washington.

I took him at his word and never bothered to verify whether or not he was a true martial artist. But it wouldn't have mattered. He was ready, even if I had checked him out. He had a friend who was willing to verify that his successful school was Silva's and that he was just running it for him. This guy was a professional con man and had covered all his bases. He left nothing to chance, so I was quickly caught in his devious web of deceit.

As he gained my confidence, I thought we were developing a good business partnership, and I showed him some of my trade secrets and my Perfect Dummy. I needed investors and I needed to get it off the ground and start marketing it to the martial arts world. I knew it was a great idea, but I didn't have the finances to take it to the market.

One afternoon, I was supposed to go to the patent office in Portland, but I got busy teaching my private classes. For some reason, I made the terrible mistake of letting Silva take my invention down to the patent office. He was supposed to have it registered under my name, but I bet you can guess what happened next.

Instead, he registered my Perfect Dummy invention under his name, and eventually had it called the Proton Man. By the time I found out, it was too late. He had disappeared from the state of Oregon and for a couple of years straight I tried to find him. I could never pinpoint him, that is, until one day when he appeared in a Fort Collins, Colorado newspaper article.

That article stated that Edmond Silva was being held for questioning about a scam associated with a murder of a female real estate agent. The story stated that when the real estate agent found out that Silva was married and that she had been scammed out of $25,000, she demanded her money back. This eventually led to a "crime of passion."

Silva had sold partnerships for my prototype to several people who invested hundreds of thousands into his company. He had so many partners in New Mexico that it began to get hot for him and he moved to Northern Colorado. Using Fort Collins as his base, he set up an office and sold partnerships in the Perfect Dummy, or Proton Man, again.

What happened next led to multiple investigations. A couple years before he disappeared from Oregon, he had borrowed my Beretta 92 subcompact 9mm, but never returned it. According to the police, that weapon was used in the murder of this real estate agent. The pistol was then traced right back to me. I learned a valuable lesson that day – never lend your pistol to someone.

When asked about it, I said he borrowed it, never returned it and disappeared. In essence, the weapon was stolen. Edmond Silva was nearly the perfect con man, but eventually, it caught up to him. He was sentenced and served time in prison for multiple charges of swindling people, along with the murder of this real estate agent. Boy, I really don't know how I get involved with such people!

My Perfect Dummy was so unique that it would have been a very good practice apparatus, and it would have made me wealthy had it not been stolen. The Perfect Dummy stood on a platform that was designed to rotate in whatever direction an individual was attacking from. The skin was all flesh color. It could withstand blows, but was transparent enough to show the sensors of the individual target areas. It was a piece of equipment that could have been used for the military, law enforcement and martial arts.

My father once told me, "Don't tell anyone your dreams because they will get stolen." It happened twice with the same design! A few years after Edmond Silva disappeared from Oregon, I was working on a movie in Astoria, Oregon with Pat Johnson as the lead fight coordinator. Pat commissioned me to help him get martial artists for *Mutant Ninja Turtles III*.

Strange things happened while I was working on this movie in Astoria, Oregon. Our stunt crew was staying in an old house that was built in the 1850's, the kind of house that you would likely see in horror movies. And to make things even scarier, one night we actually had an experience with poltergeists!

Things started flying around in the kitchen and no one was there. These things just start moving on their own! Later we found out that there were many stories in the community about the house being haunted by ghosts. After that incident, we made a point to sleep four to five of us in each room, and with the lights on, but that did not stop the paranormal activities in the house.

On one of the shoots we had a battle scene in an open field between the Shogun's bodyguards and the samurai warriors. I was one of the Shogun's warriors. As we were charging downhill with the samurai on their horses in a heavy fog, with weapons drawn and fighting going on all over the battlefield, I got hit broadside by another horse and rider who had become disoriented in the fog and confusion.

That hit threw me into the air and I landed 15 feet away in the smoke, fog and mud. The horse panicked and started trampling me. My stunt partner was also thrown from his horse but was not hurt. I ended up in the hospital with bruises to the side of my neck, back of my head, on my thigh, forearm, and a concussion and cracked ribs to boot. My helmet and body shield were both bent. I think that the light body armor that I was wearing for the fight scene probably saved my life on that day.

After spending three days in the hospital, I was given a couple of weeks off to recuperate. I was also given a hefty compensation, basically to keep it quiet before returning to the set.

Anyway, back to my Perfect Dummy. My wife, at that time, had unknowingly explained the design in detail to the martial arts actor who played Leonardo in the movie. About five months later, there was my Perfect Dummy being advertised on national television. That relationship cost me my design, again!

I had finally gotten my design back, and I registered it the poor man's way – I put it in a package and mailed it, registered and certified, back to myself. When I received it, I put it in my file cabinet until I could raise the money that I needed to produce and market it myself.

A few months later, I had a new secretary in my office, who was sorting out my file cabinet. She saw this unopened package and did the unthinkable – she opened it, thinking she was doing me a favor and laid it all out on my desk. I could have choked her!

After all I had been through with my design, my way of proving that I owned the rights to the Perfect Dummy was just destroyed with a letter opener. Now that the package had been opened, my proof was worthless, and my dream had gone down the drain.

The sages throughout the ages have all taught us to be very careful when it comes to trusting another person. There are so few honest and honorable people in this world, that you have to be extremely careful about who you trust. Putting my trust in the wrong people not only cost me my invention, but a lot of stress and a bundle of money.

Within the next eight months, my life would spiral downward to a point where I could not handle it emotionally. I had gone through a deep depression over having my Perfect Dummy invention stolen right out from under me, and by a guy that I thought was my trusted partner. At the same time, I was getting a divorce from Bettina, who now had my daughter, who was only eight months old.

I had lost a custody battle for my daughter, Vanessa, and had some heavy child support and alimony payments to Bettina. She was not a U. S. citizen and was here on a green card from Germany. I ended up in bankruptcy because this threw my finances into a tailspin. I was so disillusioned and disgusted with my life, that one cold and dreary evening after teaching class, I sat in my office alone, closed the door, and tried to drink my sorrows away. I tried my best to figure out how I could solve my problems all by myself, but everything seemed hopeless.

Without missing a beat, I downed five cans of beer. Now, I'm not a drinker, but on this evening, I found every excuse why I should chug one can after another, to the point that I actually talked myself into taking a gun, putting it to my head, and checking out of life. What happened next is a bit blurry, as I was pretty drunk.

In haste, I pulled my 9mm out of the right, upper drawer of my desk, stuck it to the right side of my head, and pulled the trigger. I heard a loud bang and saw a flash and that is all I remember. I woke up the following morning, still lying on the floor with my face in a puddle of beer and my pistol about 2 feet away from me. The shell casing was on the chair across from my desk, and the hair on the right side of my head was burned and my hair was singed.

What was I thinking to go as far as putting a gun to my head? My guardian angel must have been with me! I know no other reason that I could have missed my target from that distance. I missed my skull by less than an inch, and the bullet lodged in my cherished *Black Belt* Hall of Fame plaque that graced the wall of my office.

I was still wobbly as I tried to stand up. I put my right hand on the bookshelf to maintain my balance and accidently knocked a book to the floor. I reached down to pick it up and put it back on the shelf and what I saw stopped me in my tracks. The book that I just knocked off the shelf, only hours after I tried to commit suicide, was none other than the Holy Bible.

I sat back down and randomly opened the Bible. It miraculously opened to a passage that talked about forgiveness. As I sat there reading a book that I had long forgotten about, stale beer all around me, and a bullet in my prized hall of fame award, I had my own epiphany.

Suddenly, I knew what it was that had been missing in my life. I had a burning desire to rekindle my lost relationship with God. I knew in my heart that it was nothing short of a miracle that I was still alive and I wanted to get my life back on track.

After all, I was not only an expert martial artist, but I had professional firearm training through Executive Security International, one of the top bodyguard training courses available. I knew how to shoot, and how to shoot well. I rarely miss my target, and I *never* miss at point blank range! To this day I know that the only reason that I am still alive is because God saved my life on that dark night.

I had gradually drifted further and further away from God until I had all but forgotten him in my life, especially after I moved to Germany. Although initially, I had tried to find a church there, I could not understand the language and in time, I faded into secularism like most Europeans had. That is when my marriage to Malia started to fall apart.

I knew in my heart that I was losing my beloved wife and family. I knew that I was drifting further and further from my God, but somehow, with my fame and success skyrocketing, I just did not slow down enough to stop my life from spiraling out of control.

I was the famous Kung Fu guy. I was on the cover of most of the English speaking martial arts magazines and my team was known throughout Europe and the United States. I had my schools and students in the United States, Europe and Canada. I felt like I had it all, but in reality, I was losing it all.

As I regained my senses, after realizing what I had attempted to do to myself just six hours earlier, I just sat there and cried like a child, begging for forgiveness. I found a church soon after that and was born again in 1987. I knew that I needed to strengthen my spiritual belief in God, but the craziness in my life did not simply disappear overnight.

My divorce from Bettina was not yet finalized at this time. I was determined to make changes in my life, but they would come slower than I would have liked. I have heard of some people who turn their life over to God and everything changes right away. It did not work that way for me.

It was about this time that I met a beautiful lady who would become my wife. Tammy had walked into the school after almost being kidnapped and thrown into a van while shopping at the supermarket. She was still shaky when she came into my school, which was just across from the supermarket. She saw my school across the street and came in for information. I was instantly taken by her beauty, as she looked like a movie star.

What started out as a student/instructor relationship turned into a different type of relationship, which according to my own professional policy, should not have happened. I now wanted to live my life for Christ, but I still had to fight the "old me." The only way out of this was for her to either quit being my student or for me to marry her.

She was a single mom; her daughter was less than a year old. In fact, she was a part of the issues that I was dealing with when I had my meltdown. I don't know if it was my state of mind at the time or something else, but she was beautiful and easy for me to fall in love with. Tammy became my fourth wife.

I wanted this marriage to be different, to actually work out and to last forever. We started going to church and became very religious. But our marriage was severely tested soon after we were married, and from the last place I would have ever worried about – our Bible teacher! You just never expect a man of God to cause problems in your marriage.

When Dan Cruz, the Bible teacher who I thought was my friend, tried to seduce Tammy into leaving me and going with him on a missionary trip to New Zealand, I was shocked. He knew the Bible from cover to cover. Our marriage was vulnerable from the start, as Tammy and I had very little in common, except for the fact that she had an interest in self-defense. The man who I trusted to teach me about God tried to have an affair with my wife!

Although my faith in God could not be shaken, my faith in preachers and the church was really on shaky ground when a preacher, who was supposed to be my friend, tried to take my wife from me. I was beginning to wonder if I could truly trust anyone. I mean, if you can't trust your wife or a man of God, who can you trust?

Tammy's main goal was to become a registered nurse, which she finally accomplished. She was a nurse, and I was a martial artist. From the very first day of our marriage, my in-laws kept saying to her that she should be with a doctor instead of a martial artist. Soon, they got their wish. She ended up falling for a doctor while working in his clinic.

I watched as yet another marriage went down the tubes. I knew that I had given my life to God and was getting my spiritual life on track, but it seemed that getting my actual physical life straightened out was going to take much longer. After seeing my fourth marriage fail, I stayed single for the next eight years.

I have always been interested in the spiritual side of life, although, at times, I put my spiritual life on the back burner. I found myself having a bit of a mid-life crisis at the age of 53. I felt kind of confused about life, and especially confused about the fact that I was having little success when it came to my personal relationships. This is when I got involved with the Virtue Project to try and help me better understand myself and learn how to better manage my personal relationships.

The Virtue Project was started by the Baha'i religion. The Baha'i faith is a religion that honors all other religions and their beliefs. I wanted to understand more about being virtuous and I wanted to integrate what I learned into my children's classes. I very much wanted to help others avoid some of the heartaches that I had been through.

After completing an extensive course, I found it very helpful and beneficial in implementing these teachings into the lessons in my schools. With the encouragement of my student and friend, Ed Ferrigan, who was also a life coach, I developed my Circle of Influence philosophy (see page viii) and it helped everything fall into place for me.

Soon after I completed this course, I received a phone call from Mark. He was excited and told me, "Dad, I'm doing this movie called, *Crying Freeman*, here in Vancouver, Canada. It has a love scene with an actress named Julie Condra. It was so real. In it, I am supposed to be in love with her, but I am actually falling in love with her and the love scene seems so real."

Wow! I had never heard my son speak of any woman like that before. I had been asking him why it was taking him so long to find the right woman, and he replied,

> *"I've seen so many things in your life, Dad, and I've lived through them with you. They have been a good lesson for me, as well as a bad lesson for me. The bad part was that I saw you suffer so much because of your relationships; the good part is that it taught me not to make the same mistakes that you did.*
>
> *With all the wives you've had, I thought that waiting for the right one to come along before I started a family would be the best thing for me, especially since I'm so busy building a career and working on films. I don't have much time to date. Since Julie is an actress, she can understand my dilemma. Dad, she's really cool and I love her."*

Those were comforting words for me to hear. I knew that he was speaking from his heart. Mark's words also encouraged me to examine my own life. I wondered to myself why our schools don't teach important things such as how to make relationships work. This would be so helpful and prevent so much heartache, broken families, and also help us to raise better kids. Our schools should be preparing kids to be adults instead of simply preparing them to pass tests.

The Circle of Influence, which I developed after spending countless hours in the Virtue Project, really helped me to understand both myself and the people in my life. That program ignited a fire in me to help others. Something needed to be done. My students looked to me for guidance and believed that I had the answers, but I didn't even have the answers for my own life.

I knew that, even though I had been a success with my martial arts, I had made a mess of my personal relationships. I found myself alone and wondering why I had not found my soulmate. Why was it taking me so long? Why did my past relationships not work out? I deduced that it was probably because I was always so busy with everything else in my life, and that I had never really focused on my own inner peace or my family.

Sometimes I find myself thinking that it must take three lifetimes for all the pieces of the puzzle of life to actually fit together. My son was making more sense than I was. He seemed to have his personal life together, where mine was a mess. This sounded completely backwards to me! But here I was, learning from my son, although he didn't know that he was teaching his dad a valuable lesson.

I had an awakening. I realized that a relationship is not based on material things, but rather, it's built on the foundation you create together; and that foundation must include God. Spending time with children is more important than spending money on children.

This was about the same time that I got a call from Wesley Snipes' manager requesting my participation in the Wesley Snipes Masters of the Martial Arts Gala, honoring the top martial artists in the world. This was a big deal and would be televised worldwide from New York.

Cynthia Rothrock and I were selected to represent the Chinese Kung Fu style. Hollywood stunt coordinator and author of several martial arts books, Douglas Ming Wong, was selected to represent the White Lotus Style of Kung Fu. Grand Master Pan Qing Fu, one of the most recognized masters in the United States was also selected to represent the art of Kung Fu.

It was awesome being in the presence of these great individuals. Not only were they honoring Kung Fu, but other disciplines as well. Chuck Norris and Don "the Dragon" Wilson were just two of the other top martial artists who participated in this event.

I was supposed to have done a demonstration at the event, and I brought along my assistant, Bill Owens, to assist me. But, by the time we got there, I was so exhausted that we opted out of the demonstration part. It was still great to be a part of such a prestigious event and to meet with so many great martial artists.

As sad as it is, jealousy was already raising its ugly head within our own Kajukenbo system. Many felt intimidated by my success and accomplishments in the martial arts. This bothered me briefly, but I knew that many of those who were criticizing me and causing issues within the Kajukenbo family were armchair black belts that did more fighting with their mouths than their martial arts. Rather than getting out there and proving what they could do or improving themselves, they opted to sit on the sidelines and criticize those of us who were on the front lines of the martial arts world. This seems to still be a problem with all styles in the martial arts world today.

Although these people did bother me briefly, I soon overcame their petty attacks on me. I knew that God was in my corner, and I thanked him for giving me the opportunity to be among the greats of the martial arts community. Also, I knew that the people who were attacking me were in the minority. The vast majority of my Kajukenbo Ohana was proud that at least one of us made it to the top.

The craziest thing about that trip actually had nothing to do with martial arts or the martial arts event in New York City. It happened between myself and a taxicab driver who drove me from my hotel to the event in Harlem.

I didn't have my glasses on when I got ready to pay the taxi driver. The driver told me that the fare was $15. I wanted to give him a $5 tip, so I pulled a $20 out of my wallet; at least I thought I did. I gave it to Bill and told him to pay the driver. Bill looked at me with a puzzled look on his face and said, "Are you sure, Sifu?"

I said, "Of course. You always want to tip your driver."

Bill, still looking very puzzled, gave the driver the money, and we exited the car. That is when I discovered that I had actually given him a $50 bill instead of a $20 bill. The taxi driver ended up with a $35 tip!

For a brief moment, I felt really stupid, but then I figured, the driver probably needed it more than I did. His foreign accent led me to believe that he may have come from Eastern Europe and driving a taxi was probably the only job he could get to feed his family. I guess it was just my day to bless someone.

It seems as if time goes by faster the older you get. For me, time seemed to be flying by so fast that I could hardly keep up with everything that was going on in my life. By the year 2000, I had been single for eight years, but soon I met the lady who would be my next wife, Julia. On the 4th of July we traveled back to Hawaii to get married on the beach in Waikiki.

Not long after that, my youngest daughter, Jadyn was born. I had not planned on having anymore children, especially at my age, but sometimes life hands us special little surprises. I was now focused on being a husband and a father again, and doing it better job this time than I had done in the past.

Julia already had two of her own children, and now we had a daughter together. I also had two of my other daughters, Jaclyn and Vanessa, living with me. All of a sudden, I had a big family again. I ended up buying a six bedroom home in a cul-de-sac surrounded by beautiful pine trees which hid our house from all the other neighbors. It had a big backyard, now filled with two big guard dogs and lots of girls. Wow, that was a big change in lifestyle for me!

For a while, things were great. I had relocated my school to a larger location across the street from where I had been for over twelve years. I felt good about everything and thought that this would be a great location and that it would be the permanent headquarters for my organization.

My mother came to stay with us for a few months. She had no one to take care of her at her home, so she spent time going from one place to the other, staying with me and each of my siblings for short periods of time. We each took responsibility for caring for her until my sister, Christine, decided to take care of her permanently, so she would not have to continue to travel so much.

During the time that my mother was living on the island of Kaua'i with Christine, she had to have regular MRI checkups for her heart. It was during one of these checkups that I lost my mother.

She was in the MRI when the nurse discovered that my mom had died during the process. I was on the road at the time, when my secretary called me and let me know. A week later, I was back in Hawaii helping my sister with the funeral arrangements. My mother died on March 6, 2002.

One month after my mom died, my older brother, George died of a brain tumor. I was on a flight returning to Portland, Oregon with one of my brothers on each side of me, but this long flight was filled with nothing but sadness, anguish, and despair. With all the success that I was having with my schools, it seemed that the other things in my life were still out of balance.

I turned to my brother Benjamin and told him that I thought it was time for me to move back to Hawaii. I had been gone for 38 years. Within four months, I made arrangements to transfer my school over to a student of mine who I knew was quite capable of running it. I made an arrangement to be paid compensation for selling the business to him. I was completing the circle of my life and moving back to Hawaii.

Charlie's memorial on Waikiki Beach

On the set of the Mutant Ninja Turtles

Cynthia Rothrock, Wesley Snipes and Al Dacascos

Chapter 9

Full Circle – Back to Hawaii

You never know what events are going to transpire to get you home.
Og Mandino

My departure from Oregon was difficult for my students. After all, I had been in Portland since 1981. This move was also hard for me, but I knew in my heart that it was time for me to complete the circle. I needed to move back to the place which has always held a special place in my heart. It was a bitter sweet move for me.

On one hand, I was excited to be going home, but on the other hand, I was really sad to leave my students and all of my new friends. My new family certainly did not have mixed feelings; they were extremely excited to move to Hawaii and start their new life in the sun and sand.

I felt that we would have plenty of money coming in from my school to last us for at least the next 10 years and to get us re-established in Hawaii without any financial difficulties. I decided to go for it! We sold everything and four and a half months later, I was back in my old stomping grounds in the Kalihi Valley of Honolulu, Hawaii. I had come full circle.

Initially, we moved into my mother's house, deep in the valley. This is where I spent my teenage years and my early twenties. We were just getting settled in when I got the news – the guy that I sold my school to, was in the hospital, dying from a brain tumor. Once again, life had thrown me a curve ball.

Brad Holt was a very capable instructor, and I had not planned on him dying. This was going to change everything! Within a month of being diagnosed with a brain tumor, he died. There was no one to run the school. All those years of building a strong school in Portland were suddenly bringing in no money. There were no other black belts or instructors who were capable or willing to take over my school, so it simply disappeared.

I had originally gone back to Hawaii to retire and live off the income that the Portland school would be bringing in. That was 80% of my income! Now, with no one to take over the Portland school, I sold all of the equipment and used whatever money we had left to purchase a restaurant in Honolulu that my wife Julia had suggested that we buy.

Julia had experience running a restaurant back in Oregon, but I hadn't even thought about the restaurant business since I was the manager at a Sizzler Steakhouse back in 1962. I panicked at the prospect of getting back into the restaurant business after being out of it for so long. But Julia was gung ho and felt that it would be exactly what we needed to compensate for the loss of my school.

Isn't it funny how life throws us unexpected curve balls, right when we think we have our life all planned out? I went from planning my retirement, with leisure time on the beautiful beaches of Hawaii, to being the owner of a barbecue restaurant called, Boomerangs.

Our restaurant primarily concentrated on the lunchtime crowd, mostly business people from the business district of Honolulu. We were successful, at least for a while. For me, after one year of working seven days a week, 14 to 16 hours a day, with no time to work out, was enough. After one year, I was ready to throw in the towel. I was simply not meant to be a restaurateur.

It was too much work with the cooking and standing behind the cash register all the time. I had no time to work out, and I was starting to gain weight. I missed my kicking and punching; I missed the martial arts.

I did meet a lot of interesting people while running the restaurant. A few of them became some of my best students. When I initially returned to Hawaii, it was supposed to be my retirement. I had no intentions of getting back into teaching martial arts. I had given the martial arts all I had, or so I thought, and I just wanted to relax and be a good father. But I ended up working harder than I ever had. At this point, I had to stick with the restaurant business because it was all we had.

It was during this time period that I was getting ready to leave for work early one Monday morning, and I heard something that sounded like someone raking my front yard. I went to the door and was shocked to see a stranger raking up the leaves on my lawn. Surprised, I asked him what he was doing.

He turned to me with his eyes wide open, rake in his hand, and fell to his knees. Then he said, "Sifu, my name is Robert. I am a friend of Vanessa's, and I want to learn Kung Fu from you."

I have to tell you, this seemed like some scene straight out of a cheesy Kung Fu movie. By this time I was thinking to myself, "What is going on here!" After I gathered my thoughts, I said to Robert,

"Don't move!" Then I went back into the house and yelled for my daughter, Vanessa, who was still in bed.

I demanded answers from her. "Vanessa," I yelled, "Who the heck is this guy? What is going on? Why is there some crazy guy out in the front yard raking leaves! He said that he was a friend of yours. You have some explaining to do!"

Julia had already gone to the restaurant a couple of hours before, and I was supposed to come in at 7:30. Vanessa, who was not quite awake yet, was just as shocked and bewildered as I was. She told me that she didn't know this would happen and that she had just met Robert on Wednesday at a job interview.

Vanessa had gone in for a job interview at the Radio Shack, and Robert was the manager there. Not being one to let any opportunity go by, Robert had asked her out for a date on Friday after the interview.

My daughter, Vanessa, is a good-looking lady. She gets more than her share of compliments, but this was really strange, so I asked her exactly what happened?

She said they went out to dinner Friday evening, and after dinner while driving on the freeway, he asked her if she wanted to go see a MMA competition. Vanessa replied that she was not really interested, and he asked why. She replied, "My whole family is involved in martial arts."

Then he asked, "Really? Who are they?"

Vanessa replied, "My brother does movies and my father is a martial arts teacher." Robert still had not made the connection yet from the last name on her job application. Vanessa continued, "My brother did a movie called *Only the Strong*, a movie about the Brazilian martial art, Capoeira. My father, Al, well, he used to have a school in Oregon."

"You mean Mark Dacascos is your brother? And Al Dacascos is your father?" Robert exclaimed.

I could just imagine how wide his Japanese eyes were as he pulled over to the side of the freeway, raised his hands in the air, looked at Vanessa, and said with a sense of urgency, "I didn't touch you, right?"

That brings us to Monday morning. After Vanessa explained everything to me, I went out in the front yard where he was still on his knees. I told him that I had retired and that I didn't teach anymore. I could see the disappointment on his face as I told him there was no need to continue to rake the leaves.

Two days later, on Wednesday morning, I heard a strange, but familiar sound. Someone was raking up my leaves again! I opened the door and there was Robert, raking my yard for the second time this week. Shocked, I asked him, "What are you doing? Didn't I make myself clear on Monday?"

Robert responded, "I want to beg you to take me on as your student. I am serious. It would be like a dream come true to have you as my teacher."

I told him to go home, and I would think about it. I could not believe that I was experiencing a scene straight out of some martial arts movie. I was starting to feel like Mr. Miyagi! I laughed under my breath as I made my way back into the house. I thought to myself, "This guy is either nuts or is really very serious about learning martial arts!"

The week went by and I had brushed the whole thing off again. Basically, I just plain forgot about it. That is, until Tuesday rolled around. This time, he was not raking leaves in my front yard; this time he came straight to my restaurant at nine o'clock in the morning and told the cashier that he wanted to speak to me.

I was in the back freezer organizing some meat products when I was called to the front of the restaurant. There stood Robert, his sorry looking eyes practically begging me to teach him, without ever saying a word. Of course, I immediately knew what he wanted, and I asked him with a smirk on my face, "You're still interested, are you?"

With a big smile on his face, he said, "Yes, Sifu!"

I told him if he was really serious, to meet me at my house at 7 o'clock on Thursday evening. And that is how Robert Tanaguchi became my first student in Hawaii. For Robert, persistence paid off, but I still had no intentions of starting a new martial arts school. Once again, more curveballs!

I was back in the restaurant a few weeks later, when I got a visit from the fire protection company. It was time for my restaurant to be inspected for fire hazards. The inspector's name was Steve. After his inspection, Steve came up to me and said that everything looked good, but that I did need to sign the papers for the inspection.

He handed me the papers and I signed my signature. I could see Steve's interest had peaked. He said that he knew the name Dacascos and that he used to see that name on a lot of martial arts magazine covers. He did not make the connection as I was wearing a cruddy uniform and certainly did not look like a famous martial artist. This was the only way he had ever seen me. I was wearing a black golf shirt, a black baseball cap, and khaki pants, with a white apron on top of everything.

Normally, my black polo shirt had the name of our restaurant on it. As luck would have it, today my normal shirt was in the wash, and I was wearing a black polo shirt with the word KAJUKENBO written on it. This caught Steve's attention.

Furthermore, being dressed like a cook instead of a martial artist, I had also put on a bit of weight since I was working too hard to find time for my work outs. In my defense, I was in my late fifties. I could see on his face that he thought maybe I might know the guy on those magazine covers. Then he asked me, "You wouldn't be related to Al Dacascos would you?"

I looked at him with a straight face and simply said, "Yes, kind of."

Then he said, "Man, I sure would like to meet him!"

I replied, "Well, wait here and I will go back and see if I can find him for you." I was already laughing on the inside. I guess now you can see where Mark got his love for joking around.

I went to the back of the restaurant, took off my white apron, my baseball cap, and black polo shirt, and put on my Aloha shirt. Then I went back out front. As soon as I approached him, I smiled and he exclaimed, "NO WAY!"

Steve was already a 4th degree black belt in Tae Kwon Do. He shook my hand with a great deal of energy and said that he had wanted to meet me for the longest time. He said that he had no idea that I lived in Hawaii and that he would really like to come train with me.

And that is how Steve Farmer became my second student, and first male black belt, in Hawaii. Steve trained from white belt all the way to 4th degree black belt with me, and all from a chance meeting.

Up until this point, I had kept a very low profile on the island. Hardly anyone knew that I had moved back to Hawaii, only close friends and family. Of course, my dear friend, Al Dela Cruz was one of the first people I told and he was very happy that I had come back home for good.

Well, people talk, as they always tend to do, and word began to spread that I had moved back to Hawaii. My class of two students was getting bigger and bigger, and my one car garage and training bag would no longer suffice. I needed a bigger place for all the students that I was starting to get.

By this time, Steve Farmer had completely remodeled his two-car garage and turned it into a training center, fully equipped with mirrors and training mats. He hadn't told me anything about remodeling his garage, but one day he invited me over to his house for a visit. He took me out to the garage and told me, "Sifu, this is for you."

Wow, what an amazing gesture. I was honored that a student would honor me in such a way. From that time on, we moved the entire class to Steve's garage and started training 4-5 days a week. The Dacascos Academy had been resurrected.

I wasn't teaching commercially, like I was on the mainland, but I was teaching nonetheless. I was mostly training and teaching to stay in shape and to keep my skills up to par. On top of that, I was enjoying having eager students, with new blood ready to be spilled on the mats. We were having fun and attracting a lot of attention.

Soon, we had a second club on the east side of O'ahu. One of my students from Portland, Sean Harflinger, had moved to Hawaii and was now running that school for me. Both the new school and our original school kept turning out local champions. The buzz about Dacascos Kajukenbo Wun Hop Kuen Do Kung Fu was alive on the island once more. What started out being two guys training in my garage had turned into a new school, turning out more champions for Dacascos Kujukenbo Wun Hop Kuen Do Kung Fu!

Steve, whose other passion was competing in MMA tournaments, was also beginning to make a name for himself locally. He was an outstanding semi-contact fighter, form competitor, and demonstrator. Zaren Mandec and Arleen Dwyer also joined the Academy and now we had an outstanding female black belt, Zaren, who was a natural. She picked things up very easily, was easy to teach, and she advanced quickly.

Her father Clyde Mandec taught her well. Zaren was already an accomplished black belt in Kajukenbo and Kempo Karate before enhancing her Kajukenbo with Wun Hop Kuen Do. She had become the first WHKD female in Hawaii to receive her 1st degree black belt from me. Soon after, Mike Walker would be my second male 1st Degree Black Belt.

I had long since had my fill of the restaurant business; Julia and I sold the restaurant. Without the income from the restaurant, our finances were taking a nose dive, and we had to find other means to keep our family afloat. I started doing seminars again throughout the United States and Europe to make ends meet, and Julia went to work at Wal-Mart.

However, that was not enough to ensure us against any unforeseen medical emergencies or other bills, so Julia decided to enlist in the Air Force Reserves and had to go to the mainland for training. All of a sudden, I was a fulltime house husband.

Enlisting in the Armed Forces was her way of helping provide for the family. We figured that she would get veteran benefits and would still be stationed in Hawaii once she got out. But then there was another curve ball. By 2004, the war in the Middle East had changed and there was a surge. Julia was reassigned to go to Afghanistan and serve on a base in Kandahar. This would change our lives forever.

Whatever happened in Afghanistan changed Julia. Her time there was so traumatic that when she came home, she suffered from PTSD, post-traumatic stress disorder. She was honorably discharged because of injuries she has received during combat. One thing led to another, and in the winter of 2005 I found myself served with divorce papers.

Again, the war against Islamic terrorists had directly affected my life. Soon after Julia returned home, I lost custodial rights to my daughter, Jadyn. Julia and Jadyn relocated to Washington, then California, and finally to Idaho. And I found myself in an all too familiar place where life was moving way too fast for me, and I had to play catch up.

The year 2006 brought many changes in my life. I had been divorced for less than a year, when fate would reconnect me with my high school sweetheart, Melveen. Melveen had been divorced for six years and was now single. So when our paths crossed, we both thought that maybe we could reignite those old sparks.

Melveen was ready to rekindle our relationship, but it was a little too soon for me, as I had just divorced Julia. We had not spent any time together for almost 38 years, so the possibility of rekindling our relationship sounded exciting for both of us. What we hadn't taken into account was how much we had each changed during that time.

This section alone could fill a book, but long story short, both of us were singers in our own singing groups back in 1961. My group was performing at her alma mater, Redford High School. Melveen and her best friend, Barbara, were in the audience because Barbara had a crush on one of the guys in my group.

Melveen had turned to Barbara and made a comment about wanting to meet me, but she didn't know how. She found out that Barbara was my cousin, so she asked her to introduce us as soon as we left the stage. Well, we were introduced, and it was basically love at first sight.

She was a stunning, cosmopolitan beauty of Eurasian ancestry. She had an awesome voice, complimented by her infectious personality. We had something in common; we both loved music and were entertainers.

But fate had different plans for us, or I should say her mother had different plans for us. She, in an effort to prevent Melveen from being pregnant in high school, sent her off to live with her grandparents on the island of Molokai.

Her mom gave birth to Melveen when she was only 17 and wanted to make sure that the same fate was not going to happen to Melveen. The move was sudden and abrupt. Her parents cut off all communication between us, including my mail to that island. Any and all letters that were sent to her were intercepted. Melveen never gave up on me, but I did not know that. I thought our relationship was over when I never received any letters back from her.

She finished high school and went to business college on Molokai to become a secretary, and I continued with my singing group and menial jobs. After I finally gave up all hope of us being together, I started dating Dolly, who of course became my first wife.

Dolly and I were married and settled into a two-bedroom apartment adjacent to my mom's house in the Valley. I was upstairs playing around on the piano when suddenly two hands came from behind me and covered my eyes. I had thought it was Dolly and told her not to mess around.

But the voice said, "Guess who?" and I was paralyzed. Melveen had returned from Molokai and was ready to continue our relationship, but she was several months too late. Dolly was eight months pregnant at that time.

Melveen was close to my mom and naturally just came up without even an invitation. My mom froze, not really knowing what to say to Melveen. Melveen was going to surprise me, but it ended up the other way around.

At about the same moment that Melveen came upstairs, Dolly came in. Here I was face to face with two women, one that I was married to and the other one that I was in love with.

Well, Melveen saw Dolly's pregnant tummy, and it wasn't hard for her to figure out what had happened. She dashed out to her car in tears! Then I got the third degree from Dolly about why she was in our apartment and whether or not I knew she was coming. I assured her that I did not know.

About 15 minutes later, Dolly and I got in the car to go to the grocery store. We drove down the street towards the store, and there, parked on the side of the road was Melveen, slumped over the steering wheel, still in tears.

My new life had begun just as Melveen's future with me was dissolving. Melveen went on to become a Hawaiian diva and won many awards for her singing. She had been through four failed marriages on her way to the top of her field. I went on to become who I am in the martial arts world and lived through five divorces. Obviously, neither of us had been successful in our personal lives.

So after 38 years of absence, both she and I had thought that our tragic lost love would finally come to fruition. We thought that we were finally going to live happily ever after, but it was not to be. We both had our share of baggage, and we ran into problems that we could have never foreseen. It just seemed that happily ever after was not in the cards for me. Our marriage would only last four years.

The love was still there, but because of Melveen's abusive relationships, she had set herself up for failure right from the beginning. The very first month of our marriage she kiddingly remarked, "If this doesn't work out, I'm going to divorce you." To me, that was a self-predicting prophecy. And over a short period of time, it became just that.

She was a very beautiful lady, and there seemed to always be men waiting right around the corner for us to break up so that they could step into my shoes. In fact, she remarried only three months after our divorce was final. Prior to our marriage, in August 2006, things looked bright and our future together looked beautiful.

I had bought her a diamond ring. One day I had it in my mouth and I kissed her, slipping it into her mouth. That was my way of asking her to marry me. I have always been a hopeless romantic, and I was really glad that she didn't swallow the ring.

Two months before our marriage in August, I had the idea of making my yearly trip to Europe to do seminars in my WHKD schools. I had taken an extra week to fly down to Yemen, where another one of my schools was located. I was hired to do some work with the security people who guarded the president of Yemen.

That trip was one that I will never forget! When I landed, I had an entourage of vehicles waiting for me, with many of the students, some armed with AK-47's. I was escorted to the station and met with some newspaper guys to do an interview which was going to be broadcasted. This was the first time I had ever gotten off a plane and been met with armed students.

During the last day of my seminar, while working with students and security personnel, I pulled my right hamstring so severely that the pop could be clearly heard throughout the gymnasium. My black belt student in WHKD, Samir Nassar, came to my aid and helped me as I limped off the floor and into the dressing room. I had another student continue the program for me.

He rushed me to the hospital where I was met by a big Russian doctor who had a syringe with a needle on it that looked like a nail. He was ready to stick that thing into me to "relieve my pain." No sir! I was going to have none of that! I told Samir to take me back to his house, where I spent the next couple of days crawling on the floor, going from the bedroom to the restroom. I taped my leg so that I could walk, and barely made it to the car. Then we went to the airport so I could catch a plane back to United States.

I returned to Hawaii, which of course, is at sea level. But being at such high altitude for over 29 hours did something to my body. I remember struggling to get from one terminal to the other in London, and finally being in an uncomfortable seat from Los Angeles back to Hawaii.

Melveen was there to meet me and take me home. The following day, I got into my car, and I blacked out behind the wheel, veered over to the side of the road, and stopped on the curbside. When I woke up, I called Melveen and told her that I couldn't move my left side, and she rushed over to take me to the hospital.

I found myself on the gurney, with tubes sticking in me, hardly able to move, and with some oxygen apparatus on me. I could not speak, move or even visually focus on anything. It was almost like I was in a coma.

Still, I could hear the doctors and nurses around me talking. Then someone asked Melveen if she was going to be responsible for having my organs donated. What! I wasn't even dead yet, and they were talking about what to do with my body parts!

Here I was, imprisoned in my own body, hearing all of these people talk, and I was not able to move, talk or even wink on my own. This sent me into panic mode, but I couldn't do anything about it. All I could do was lie there and listen…and hope they weren't going to start taking my body parts *before* I was able to snap out of it!

I found out that when I pulled that muscle there were blood clots that formed because of the high altitude in Yemen and traveling back home on the plane. Those clots moved freely throughout my body on the way to my brain. It affected me a day later, as I descended back to sea level. I was in intensive care for a couple of days and four days later, I was released to go home and rest.

Melveen and I were married twice, the first on a large yacht with my Pastor, Norman Nakanishi, doing the honors of marrying us a couple miles off Waikiki Beach in the afternoon. Later that evening, we had a Hawaiian style wedding with lavish entertainment, food, and famous personalities in attendance. It was an amazing day filled with good friends, food and great entertainment.

I was so happy to have finally found the love that was going to last a lifetime. This was it for me, no more problems, no more divorces. At least that is how our marriage began. But we were not high school kids anymore, and the flame that had burned so brightly during our early years began to slowly burn out.

We were both very dominant individuals, and I don't believe that you can have two very dominant personalities living in the same home and have a really happy, loving relationship. We never had any closure, only the signing of the divorce papers and she was gone.

After this failed relationship, my daughter, Vanessa, and I got an apartment together. The beautiful daughter that I had lost custody of back in Oregon was now my roommate. Not only did I get to live with my daughter, but with my granddaughter, Leila. I cherished the time that we were able to spend together. I was a father and a grandfather and the three of us lived peacefully together, that is until 2011.

In 2011, I had just come home from my yearly trip to Europe and was exhausted. As I walked into my apartment that I shared with Vanessa, the strangest feeling came over me. I am not even sure how to describe it.

The following morning, I was relaxing, sitting in my rocking chair, facing the front door, rocking my granddaughter. As we rocked, I was thinking about how lucky I was to have come through everything that I had been through in my life and how I am living peaceably with my daughter and granddaughter.

Rocking gently back and forth, a peaceful smile came over me, when…BAM! The Honolulu SWAT team burst into our apartment, guns pointed at me and my tiny granddaughter.

One officer signaled me, with his weapon, to raise my hands, and another signaled me to remain silent by putting his finger up to his lips. Of course, I couldn't raise my hands, as I was holding my now terrified and crying granddaughter. I had no idea what was going on, but I knew it could not be good!

They were after my daughter's ex-boyfriend, who had warrants out for his arrest. I later found out that the night before, he had taken my Colt 45 from my bed table and pointed it at my daughter's head. He was on cocaine and totally out of it. Had my daughter not talked her way out of that terrifying situation and found a way to escape from the house with Leila, I would have lost both my daughter and my granddaughter!

Vanessa had managed to escape, running out of the house barefooted with Leila. Someone called the police, but by that time, her ex-boyfriend had left. The police had Vanessa try to get him to come back to the house early that morning, but I still had no idea that there was anything unusual going on.

He had come in earlier that morning, and Vanessa had told him that they needed to talk and took him into her bedroom, which was directly behind my rocking chair. The police got their man and my daughter got out of a very bad situation.

The three of us lived together until she and my granddaughter moved to Los Angeles. Once again, I found myself single and alone. I needed to do something to bring in more money and to keep myself busy, so I got back into the workforce and worked for a private company doing investigation and security work.

Vanessa reunited with her childhood sweetheart, William Owens, and they have a nice family today. She finally met a wonderful person that would take care of her and my granddaughter.

My new job kept me occupied and also helped keep my martial arts skills sharp, as this job did present more than a few chances to use my martial arts skills on the streets again. I dealt with some ruthless criminals on the streets, and had several scrappy tests where I had to cuff people and transfer them to the police. I did this for a couple of years and it was an okay job. It sharpened my awareness because I had to deal with thugs that liked to slug it out and go to the ground fighting.

I continued to teach martial arts in my school in Hawaii, as well as to travel to my other schools and teach seminars. I also found myself working with my son, Mark, again in 2015, on his new movie, *Showdown in Manila.*

In March, I flew down to the Philippines, where the movie was being shot. Some of my best memories are when Mark and I worked together over the years. I was the fight coordinator for the movie which starred Alexander Neusky, and co-starred Casper Van Dien and Cynthia Rothrock; Sonny Sison assisted me as fight coordinator.

We had a lot of fun doing this movie and there was a great group of people who helped make the movie a success. I greatly enjoyed staying in a lavish hotel and coordinating the fight scenes. I had coordinated fight scenes for movies before, but it is always better when I get to work with Mark.

Upon wrapping up the movie in the Philippines, I visited my friends in Germany to celebrate the 40th anniversary of Wun Hop Kuen

Do, and to celebrate my son, Benjamin's, first child, my Melia. I returned to the states to continue working on my memoirs, *Legacy: Through the Eyes of the Warrior*, which you are now reading. This book was years in the making, as I had originally had a book deal with a lady from Tennessee. She was in a horrific car accident and could not continue the project with me.

I had basically given up on ever getting my memoirs published, as not only did the book deal in Tennessee go south, but I also lost much of the work that I had done on the book as well. But just when everything looked really bleak, I met another book publisher, who was also a successful, award-winning writer, Dr. Bohdi Sanders. Bohdi had successfully published a best-selling martial arts book of his own, *Modern Bushido,* and was interested in talking to me about a book deal. *Modern Bushido* was a great success and had hit number one on Amazon and had stayed in Amazon's Top 10 Bestsellers for martial arts books for 105 weeks, so I was very excited to talk to Bohdi about publishing my memoirs.

It seemed as if God was directing my path, as I met Bohdi simply by chance. We had both been asked to be on the board of a martial arts federation. Bohdi had heard that I was writing a book on Kajukenbo and contacted me one day and asked about my book.

From there, one thing led to another, and a few months later, I found myself with contracts for a two book deal, *Legacy* and *The Kajukenbo Bible*. It seemed that finally I was going to be able to tell my story to the world and share my journey through the martial arts and how God changed my life.

This was also the year that my life and contributions to the martial arts world were celebrated in a celebrity roast in Los Angeles, hosted by my student and friend, Eric Lee. Martial artists and celebrities from all over, gathered together to celebrate my accomplishments in the martial arts, and of course, to make many jokes at my expense!

Malia, my wife of 17 years, took full advantage of the situation and skewered me without mercy. She didn't hold anything back! There were many others, who had a good laugh at my expense during the night, but it was all in good fun, and I was honored that so many people came out to honor both me and my accomplishments over a lifetime as a martial arts professional.

At this roast, I saw how truly blessed I am to have so many good friends and family members who think so highly of me. When it comes right down to it, God, family, and friends are the things in life that truly matter.

While it is true that I have accomplished a lot in the world of martial arts, no legacy is built by one man alone. This book would be truly incomplete if it did not discuss the other great martial artists who are a vital part of the Dacascos legacy – Malia and Mark.

Hanging out with Buddha in Portugal in 2012

Working on LEGACY in Bohdi Sanders' dining room in 2015

Artist, Adventurer, Hall of Fame Member, Tournament Fighter, Streetfighter, Pilgrim, Student, Philosopher, see him at work and you might call Al Dacascos

A MOZART OF MOTION

by Renardo Barden

Black Belt Magazine called me "Mozart of Motion"

Headlining a Kajukenbo seminar in Kuwait City in 2014
GM Robert New, me and Prof. Alan New

Chapter 10

Malia Bernal
(Malia Dacascos)

*When one door is closed, don't you
know that many more are open.*
Bob Marley

Malia and I spent 17 years together during the heyday of my martial arts success. I first met Malia when she enrolled in my school as a student in California in 1968. I have already discussed how our relationship started and evolved, so I will not rehash that information. But no book about my life titled, *Legacy*, would be complete without a discussion of Malia's success in the martial arts world as well.

The late 1960's and early 1970's was Malia's time to shine in the United States. She later continued her work with the women's movement in martial arts in Europe until she returned to the United States in 1981. She has never retired and continues to work with women in the martial arts world today. She has developed her own champions with her unique expression of the martial arts that originates from deep in her soul.

How many women can claim the honor of being number one in both the United States and in Europe? How many can show real proof of being the top in their field internationally and having articles written about them, even deep into Asia? Malia was this kind of champion. She came along at the right time and with the right determination and attitude to become a top martial arts champion.

Let me share a little bit of martial arts history with you. John Corcoran and Emil Farkas are the authors of, *Martial Arts Tradition: History and People* and *The Complete Martial Arts Catalog: Martial Arts Title Holders and Records*. These two books, plus Bob Wall's book, *Who's Who in the Martial Arts*, are the three books which are considered to be the best when it comes to recording the history of the martial arts in America.

In *The Complete Martial Arts Catalog: Martial Arts Title Holders and Records*, there is a question asked about which American female martial artist has attained the greatest prominence in sport karate. John Corcoran and Emil Farkas wrote:

Malia Dacascos, a highly proficient Kung-fu exponent, gained national acclaim during the 1970's for consistently defeating men in kata or forms competition. She is also ranked the number one female fighter by Professional Karate Magazine. Dacascos became the only woman to be rated in the 1975 national Top Ten form ratings in the United States. She has now unofficially retired, but gives frequent demonstrations of her art along with her husband, Al Dacascos, a retired national fighter and form champion,"

In the other prestigious book, by the same authors, *Martial Arts Tradition: History and People*, The authors wrote:

Malia Dacascos, American Kung Fu Champion and Instructor, is rated the top U.S. female competitor again, by Professional Karate Magazine in 1974, and is ranked among the Top10 Women in the 1975 Black Belt Yearbook. She won 1st place in kata five times at the International Karate Championships in Long Beach, CA. and in 1969 and 1970 she won the women's sparring title in addition to kata. She won first place in kata at the 1974 U.S. Championship in Dallas. Since retiring, she concentrated her teaching to her other champion students, Cindi Petersen, Karyn Turner and Karen Shepard.

We did not go out looking to be interviewed, but because of our accomplishments, people sought out both Malia and me. Malia was starting to become well-known and appeared on several martial arts magazine covers. She had hit the big time and was known all over the world. Malia was awarded Mike Stone's Golden Fist Award, considered to be the Oscars of the Martial Arts, several times for both fighting and forms. This is a great honor for her.

Of course, being number one, or the champion, is only temporary; it is only good until the next champion comes along. But, once you have won that title, no one can take that accomplishment away from you; it is yours for life.

In an article written in *Professional Karate Magazine* in the summer edition 1974, the publisher and editor, Mike Anderson, wrote that you must give credit where credit is due. His article proves that

Malia does indeed deserve that credit. He wrote an article about the ladies who put forth at least as much effort as their male counterparts, to achieve recognition in their sport. He wrote:

Selecting the top 10 female competitors is no easy task. Their achievements have been largely overlooked and passed by as the male competitors get all the glory. This is mainly because there are 20 times as many male karate competitors and enthusiasts as there are females, so the media must cater to the greater portion of its readers.

It cannot be overlooked, however, that there are many females who fight as regularly as a man. Many of them competed more than most male competitors. Another fact rarely mentioned is that, because of their physical stature, it is much more difficult for a female to compete, in such a physically trying sport, than it is for a male. As a matter of fact, the female divisions of most big tournaments are consistently much rougher than it is for a male.

For some unexplainable reason, there is always much more uncontrolled face contact and more injuries in women's competition. Here I must say before safety equipment came in, all of us were fighting bare knuckles in competition. This leads us to ask the following questions. Is it socially proper and sportsmanlike to let this practice continue?

Should measures be taken to keep female karate competition from becoming like female wrestling or roller derby? Should women stick to form or kata competition and channel their efforts along artistic lines? Should female free sparring be eliminated altogether? Should promoters be forced to enforce stricter face contact rules at their tournaments?

A special meeting and seminar was held in July 1974 at the Top 10 Nationals Karate Championship in St. Louis to determine the future status of female competition. Only women of brown belt and higher were invited to attend, and no men were allowed in this meeting. The women had determined their own future. It was previously extremely difficult to rate the Top 10 females, as they are so scattered across the country, that it was difficult to make an accurate comparison.

So, based on the number of trophies they have won and the difficulty of the particular tournament, the Professional Karate Magazine Voting Board, which was made up of the top referees and coaches in competitive karate in the USA, put forth their efforts to come up with their most up to date findings.

By difficulty of tournaments, we mean that a female is given more credit for winning a major professional tournament than she is for a small event where she fights just a few matches against local women who are of little competition. Also taken into consideration is not how many trophies they have won, but what they were for.

For example, since it was Professional Karate Magazine's belief that karate was developed primarily as a form of fighting and secondary as an art, more credit is given to the female who wins free sparring rather than forms trophies, although the wins included free sparring, forms and weapons forms at this present time.

Also taken into consideration is the amount of travel these women do. They are given more credit for winning in areas other than just their own. MALIA DACASCOS from Denver, Colorado was classified as the big NUMBER ONE in everyone's book.

Over the past six years, this elegant lady has amassed a staggering total of 157 trophies in free sparring, forms and weapon competition, almost three times more total trophies than any other in the world. She has victories from Hawai'i to New York.

At Mike Stones Golden Fist Award Banquet, held in Hollywood in 1974, Malia was presented the Golden Fist Award in three categories: BEST FEMALE FREESTYLE, BEST FEMALE KATA, and BEST FEMALE ALL-AROUND COMPETITOR.

CINDI PETERSON of Denver, Colorado. The second most staggering amount of 70 trophies, 46 of them for first place in sparring is second only to her instructor number one rated Malia Dacascos. Cindi is a clean, versatile fighter with a wide arsenal of techniques. She has competed all over the country in the footsteps of her instructor and has built up a reputation from coast-to-coast.

Her biggest victories were first place free sparring when in the Mardi Gras Nationals and the Rocky Mountain Championships, and first place in women's forms in the Top 10 Nationals.

The following female students that Malia helped become National Champions are; Karyn Turner also from Denver, Colorado. She would be the next in line and accumulate just as many trophies as Cindi to become rated in the mid-1970's in forms and in fighting.

She would eventually be the first woman to promote Full Contact Karate for pay per view on television and getting such big sponsors like Coors Brewery in Golden, Colorado. Her stable consisted of managing some of the top rated fighters like Heavy Weight Champion Dennis Alexias and Felipe Garcia, who reigned as the featherweight champion in kickboxing or full contact karate.

Karen Shepard, also another champion in form competition, eventually pursued her acting career of which she became very successful using her martial arts skills to play various roles including the opposite of Cynthia Rothrock in a martial arts film produced in Hong Kong, which had one of the most epic fights between the two to be filmed.

At that time, Malia was a second degree black belt in Kajukenbo Wun Hop Kuen Do Kung Fu and the mother of our two boys, Mark and Craig, both competitors themselves. It is hard for any woman to accomplish what she has accomplished, but doubly hard when she also had two boys and a family to manage. The fact that she was able to accomplish all of this, while at the same time being a mother, a wife, and teaching classes, is just remarkable.

Several things contributed to Malia's success. Whenever possible, I had Malia assist me in demonstrations and seminars and this led her to be very active in the promotion of women in the martial arts. On top of this, she is driven to be the best that she can be.

She did several national TV shows hoping that women would eventually get proper recognition in the martial arts world. She was selected by *Professional Karate Association and Magazine* to escort its "Goodwill Tour" to Berlin and performed for European television with me.

I don't think Malia would be where she is today had everything not happened as it did. Our divorce in the early 1980's took a heavy toll on both of us, both mentally and emotionally. During that time, our disagreements led to her being "excommunicated" from my system and style of Kajukenbo and Wun Hop Kuen Do.

As devastating as it may have been for her, it was actually good in the long run. She was able to remold and renew herself, and it empowered her to become an even stronger force in the world of women's martial arts. Malia is not a lady who allows any obstacles to slow her down.

During the 15 or so years of being absent from the martial arts world, she worked as an assistant welder on the construction of the Trans-Alaskan Pipeline which covered over 800 miles of pipeline and 12 pumping stations. She also ended up owning her own Mexican restaurant on a small, almost desolate, island in the Caribbean.

One thing led to another and Malia ended up with her own television show, as a fitness guru and developed her own expression of Kung Fu. The plain and simple fact is, you can strip a person of their official rank, but you can never take away their knowledge or their skills.

Malia learned and attained even more knowledge during the years that she was absent from the martial arts. She used her fitness program and blended it with her new expression of Kung Fu to come up with a new identity that is truly her own.

Every coin has two sides. While our divorce and going our separate ways was hard; it made us both stronger people in the end. Also, her separation from me shielded her from any involvement with all the martial arts backstabbing and politics that was beginning to erode the integrity and credibility of Kajukenbo during this time.

It also enabled her to have time for her own personal development. She was able to develop her spiritual connection with God, something that was lost during our secular lifestyle that we lived in Europe.

Malia's personal expression of Kung Fu is called Xian Dai Kung Fu which she began to develop back in 1995. It incorporates both Northern Kung Fu and Southern Kung Fu movements. In Malia's words:

"I soon realized that I needed to work and in thinking about what I should do, I ended up putting together my first aerobic/self-defense program. Then I searched for a club that would hire me. I was way ahead of my time; I was out there doing this before Billy Blanks! My concept was to combine my martial arts moves with aerobics, and it was an instant success.

It was a hard, fast-paced program done to music. At that time, I did not teach forms, just self-defense. It was one hour of blood, sweat and tears! But my clients were getting into amazing condition, and I was happy.

People had never seen anything like it before. It was during this time that one of my students approached me and talked to me about opening a school. Of course, I was excited beyond measure.

Her plan was to open it right in the hub of Universal City. She wanted to attract the people who worked in the studios up on the hill. We scouted for a location and found a beautiful building. It was new and from the freeway, you could see my name, MALIA, in neon lights. I felt like a star!

We soon opened another school in San Francisco and I was flying back and forth, teaching my classes. It was nuts, but I did get a lot of good PR.

My style is aggressive, powerful, and awesome. I found that a lot of people cared less about the actual art and the belt. They just wanted to train and learn in the manner that I was teaching. During this period, I stayed out of traditional martial arts for almost 19 years.

At one time I was teaching 10 classes a day. It was insane! Then I was asked to teach a class called cardio kick – only two people showed up for my first class. But in less than two weeks, I had 20 students. This was the beginning of Xian Dai Kung Fu. It started with those first two students, and they are still my students to this day.

My style consisted of forms only. I found that forms, when taught correctly, and when combining both Southern and Northern moves, low stances, high *jumping kicks, and drop down stances, give you a great stretch and a workout that pushes all to a point of physical exertion. To me, this was the best of all exercises.*

I soon got back into the traditional martial arts scene, and my students were doing great. But, I was still officially ranked as a white belt. I was the white belt master, bringing my students to competition. That became a huge joke with my students.

My style has lasted and I am proud of what I have accomplished. Now, both my students and I am accepted into the martial arts world again.

Now, I teach fighting, as well as forms, cardio, and weights. I do demos and run a boot camp. I must add that without the help of my faith and belief in God, I don't know where I would be. Before, Al was my teacher in the arts, but now, God is my teacher in life."

As the articles that I quoted before stated, Malia has taught many champion martial artists, both men and women. She later spent time sharing her knowledge with the underprivileged and those with little to no martial arts experience in San Jose, California. Although she has brought her own special style and innovative form to her Kung Fu, her tradition of hard work and excellence has never wavered.

As you can clearly see, Malia carved out her own legacy as one of the best female martial artists of her time. She was invaluable in my effort to establish Wun Hop Kuen Do Kung Fu throughout the United States and Europe.

She has also played a vital role in Mark's life. She was a wonderful mother to Mark, even as she racked up so many accomplishments in the martial arts world. She successfully juggled her roles as a wife, a mother, a martial artist, and teacher, and left her own mark on the world of martial arts.

Today, Malia still teaches fitness and Kung Fu almost every single day, both at the local fitness center and in her own private gym. She is also very active in the martial arts community and has been called to serve as a board member on many different martial arts organizations. She has been honored by some of the most prestigious martial arts hall of fames and organizations.

I will end this chapter with Malia's recent comment about my contributions to the martial arts. She was gracious enough to give her insights into my contributions for my book. Even after all we have been through, we remain good friends and we always will. Here is what she said:

Al was ready to show the world what he was all about. To him, the mainland was a new beginning. He was now on his own. In the classroom, if you happened to have trained in some other style and decided to give Al's school a try, you were in for a huge awakening! Control was not a word in Al's vocabulary. Reality is what he taught. To be in his school, you had to be tough, and a little bit crazy.

There was no such thing as mats in his school. When practicing your throws, you landed on the floor. I got so used to hitting the floor that it felt natural. Pain became a way of life. His concept, of course, was correct. If you get into a street fight your body needs to be conditioned to take the fall.

He taught us kicking, punching, throwing, knives, sticks, multi-man attacks, and much more. I can still hear his famous saying, "Learn how to put it all together to suit your body. I can teach you, but you must save your own life. I can't fight for you. You're on your own. I've taught you so much; now figure it out!" His expression was unorthodox to say the least.

When he got into tournament competition, the reaction of the general public was amazing. You almost had to be there to appreciate the reaction of the fighters and the public. His fighting technique was a force to be reckoned with. His fighting stance was one which no one had ever seen before.

I can still remember one of his opponents asking the referee, "How am I supposed to fight this guy?" It was priceless!

Al left no opening for anyone to slip into. His fighting techniques were so fast that they were a blur. His back fist was so fast that he would strike his opponent in so many different places that you couldn't see them all, and his opponent could not stop them. The judges would scratch their heads and say they did not know what to call; it was just too fast!

He was also a crowd pleaser. People would gather around his ring to watch. They were in awe of this skinny Hawaiian with such speed, flashy techniques, and his wild look. He was asked to do many demos and I always loved his multi-man attacks. They were for real and truly awesome!

No one ever wanted to be his demo partner. As I said, he taught no self-control, although he did use some on occasion. He was the talk of the martial arts world. His name started to reach all parts of the United States and everyone wanted to fight him. And, at one time or another, he beat them all. The times he did lose were usually by disqualification.

His style, name, and students all made a huge impact on the changes that were to come in the world of martial arts. Al has never been forgotten and never will be.

Malia and her trophies in 1971 in Denver, Colorado

Kang Rhee, me, and Malia
We took home a car load of 1st Place
trophies and the grand championship

AL & MALIA DACASCOS

Malia and me in our fighting stances

Malia in 1974 - first woman on the cover of Black Belt Magazine

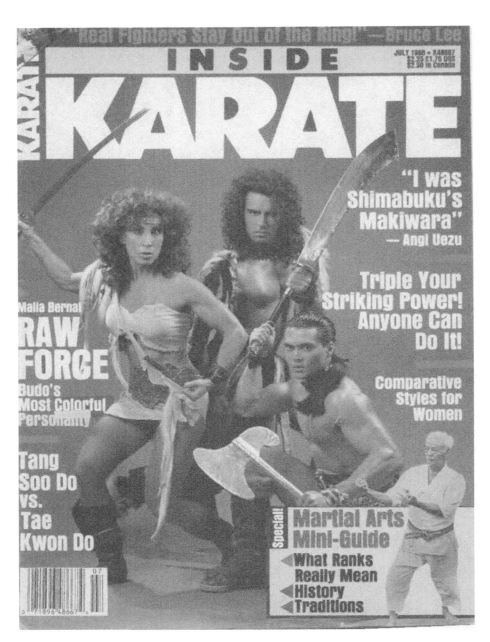

1988 cover of Inside Karate Magazine with Malia, Craig, and Mark

Winning the California State Championship in 1970

Our family in Hamburg, Germany in 1978

Chapter 11

Mark Dacascos

*The secret of health for both mind and body is not
to mourn for the past, nor to worry about the future,
but to live the present moment wisely and earnestly.*
Gautama Buddha

Just as no book about my life entitled, *Legacy*, would be complete
without talking about Malia's accomplishments, it would also not be
complete without touching on the many accomplishments of my son,
Mark.

I started training Mark around age three, and I continued to train
him until the age of 19, when he started exploring different martial arts
traditions. Mark was a successful martial artist from a young age. He
had already won numerous Karate and Kung Fu championships in the
United States and in Europe, between the ages of 7-18, before
returning to the United States in 1981. He left Europe undefeated in
his weight class.

My little Dragon came out screaming, punching and kicking on
February 26, 1964. No doubt he already had that innate martial arts
DNA twirling around in his veins. Kids emulate their parents and
sometimes it can be cute at first, but then it can get to be annoying; and
later, embarrassing.

By four years old, Mark was running around our kung fu Academy.
He would run up to potential students throwing a couple of kicks to
their shins and a few follow-up punches to their thighs. Of course,
many of my potential students thought it was cute, but when Mark
missed the thighs and hit just a little higher, and to the center, that part
was not as cute.

Fighting is a natural survival instinct, but anyone that knows
Mark, knows he is a jokester as well. He and his brother, Craig, fought
in the first official Karate tournament in Boulder, Colorado back in
1970. At age six Mark won his first first-place trophy. He won a few
more tournaments while traveling with Malia and me regionally.

One year older, Mark was ready for the big time at Ed Parker's
International Karate Championship in Long Beach. Competing in the
Pee Wee division as an orange belt, he won first place. With 15 first

and second place trophies stored away, we moved to Germany in 1974 where Mark took a little break from martial arts.

He got back into martial arts seriously at age 14. From that point on, there was no turning back! Mark blossomed into an awesome tournament and form competitor. Not only did we instill good character in both boys, Mark and Craig, but we also tried our best to teach them the self-discipline that I believe helped turn them into the successful adults they are today.

Emanuel Bettencourt was a year older than Mark when he joined the school and became Mark's best friend and training partner. They both excelled in forms and fighting competition. They also both became the finely tuned parts of the initial Dacascos Show Team in Europe and, strangely enough, they both became actors in the movies. I remember they would practice so hard on their stomach exercises that it was as if they were competing to see who would have the best six pack and who could do the best splits.

While Mark dominated the middleweight division, Emanuel Bettencourt dominated the light heavy weight division. Throughout Northern Germany, and eventually the entire country, Mark had no problems dominating his weight class and ended up being undefeated before returning back to the United States in 1981.

As ferocious as he was in competition, Mark was always humble and a perfect gentleman as he matured. He was able to avoid the trap of allowing his success to go to his head. Everyone that has met him has nothing but good things to say about him.

When fighting, Mark would never embarrass his opponent with an overwhelming barrage of techniques, but instead, he did just enough to win and come across as a good sportsman. In many of the Karate championships, not only did he compete in forms, weapons, and fighting, but he also took part in the demonstrations. This kind of load left him exhausted at the end of the evening.

Whenever we took a pit stop on our way to any tournament, Mark was in the parking lot doing his flips and butterfly kicks or practicing his form and fighting techniques. He was always mentally preparing himself. Mark's philosophy was, if you take a day off for a break, that's the day that your opponent will use to beat you.

When ring time came and Mark's name was called, there was always a hush as people gathered around to see who would be his next victim. No doubt, Mark had many who wanted to topple him from the pedestal that he dominated during this time. It was always exciting to see him fight!

There have been so many exciting fights in his career that they seem to blur into one big war. The beginning of Mark's competition as a black belt came as a surprise to him. As a matter of fact, it was a surprise to both Mark and Emanuel Bettencourt. Both had been dominating their brown belt division. At this particular tournament, which was one of the largest tournaments held in Germany, with over 2000 competitors, they had no idea what was about to happen.

They had already proven that they could really kick butt in the brown belt division. And with Malia and me as their personal instructors, we knew their every move and how they each thought. While there was no formal testing, unbeknownst to them, they were being tested throughout their years of training.

So I decided to put both of them into the black belt division. Mark was fighting as a lightweight and Emanuel Bettencourt as a middleweight. They were both very hesitant at first, until I convinced them that they had nothing to lose.

Once again, they both won their respected divisions. Continuing on, we brought our team to Italy and competed in the world championships there. This is where Mark had one of his most epic fights in his life, as he fought some of the toughest European fighters all gathered in Milan, Italy.

At the Northern European Kung Fu Karate Championship in Hamburg, Germany, the Dacascos Kung Fu Fighting Team was pitted against the Netherlands National Tae Kwon Do Team. We won that team competition with a margin of 22 to 20.

Of course the protest was coming from the Netherlanders, who said that we won because we were fighting on our home grounds in Hamburg. They put up a challenge for us to come to Holland. We went there and fought their second string team first and beat them by a margin of 24 to 17.

Then they put their first string team against us. They had expected to dominate us since it was their elite team which had won the European Championships just months before.

Instead, they faced our very hot team and lost to us 27 to 21. The anchorman that scored the most points was Mark. The Hollander's had anticipated a victory party, but no one showed up except us!

The *European Karate Magazine*, that had the exclusive rights to cover the championships between our German team and their Netherland team, never even reported this defeat of their championship team, in their magazine. It was only reported in the local newspaper. I guess the embarrassment of losing three times in a row to a Kung Fu team from Germany, when they were supposed to be the best in Europe, was too much to take.

Of course, the undertone to that is that the Netherlanders never had any kind of good rapport with Germany. This probably stemmed from the two world wars and the memories that lingered from the atrocities of those wars. Nevertheless, two members of the Holland team traveled all the way to Hamburg to train with us and try to figure out our secret to winning. The secret was simple; it was our attitude, not what we did, but how we did it.

Mark has the flexibility to perform any and all types of kicks. Burton Richardson, a Jeet Kuen Do instructor and the fight choreographer on *Kickboxer 5: Redemption*, a film that Mark starred in, said that Mark is a fight choreographers dream. Mark was simply a natural martial artist, and one with an amazing work ethic!

I began to teach him self-discipline and a humble attitude, although his streak of rascal-like behavior would get the better of him from time to time. Like any boy, his jokester side got him in his share of trouble.

You would never know that Mark was playing a joke on you, as he could keep a perfectly straight face as he did it, just like his friend Christian Wulf would. I remember both of them being in a restaurant when Christian came to visit us in the states. We were sitting in the restaurant and Christian wanted a toothpick, but he did not know the English word for toothpick. He asked Mark how to say toothpick, and Mark replied with a straight face, "Enema."

Christian stood up and went straight to the female cashier and in an innocent tone, asked her, "Can I have an enema?" Christian never understood why the whole restaurant busted out laughing.

On another occasion, we were in a Chinese restaurant and Christian was drinking a Coke. He went to the bathroom and while he was in there, Mark dumped his Coke out and replaced it with shoya sauce and mixed it with water. When Christian came back to the table, he was thirsty and took a big swallow of this concoction. He immediately sprayed it all over us as he choked on that horrible drink! It is a wonder that they are still friends after so many practical jokes.

I remember while we were living in Germany, Mark formed an exclusive club within our martial arts school. He teamed up with Emanuel Bettencourt and together they were the president and vice-president of the Doo Doo's.

They decided to wear olive green bomber jackets, blue jeans, and black combat boots to look cool. Eventually, their little club grew to 10-15 teenage "monsters" that would go around pulling practical jokes on people and terrorizing people in Hamburg. There initiation was running around the school, carrying a bag of dog crap and yelling, "The British are coming, the British are coming."

Those that passed the initiation, moved up the ranks from 1/4 Doo Doo, to 1/2 Doo Doo, to 3/4 Doo Doo, and then they were finally initiated into the honored title of full Doo Doo (full of crap) by some other hilarious and ridiculous initiation requirements.

On one particular day, Mark and Emanuel got on the subway, and just when the doors opened to get off, they threw a stink bomb into it and then ran away and watched all those inside try to get off the train as it was filled up with the smell of rotten eggs. Mark was always doing one thing or another to get a rise out of those around him.

In one class, I caught Mark doing some crazy duck walk. He did it in such a comical way that you couldn't watch him without cracking up. He later explained to me that he was just warming up but in fact, it looked like a bunch of clowns doing a drunken monkey version of Michael Jackson's moonwalk.

Naturally, with Mark and Emanuel, there was never a dull moment whether they were warming up class for me or just walking down the street. But, as a good father, I had to undo some of those bad habits. Of course, there were many other incidents that stand out in my mind, but I won't cover them all here.

As with most practical jokes, Mark and his friends took things too far at times. One day, Mark and Christian Wulf were rehearsing a sword and spear form that they were going to be performing on a German National Sports television show. While practicing, Christian was doing a 360 degree spin and extended his spear a few inches too far. He cut Mark under his eyes and my fear spun out of control. The thought of my son being blind shook me to the bone.

This same type of thing would happen a few years later, but this time when Mark was playing the Young Conan at Universal Studios in Hollywood. His partner extended his sword too far and cut Mark's face. It left a nasty gash and blood was rolling down Mark's face, but he stayed in character the whole time.

Even though blood was splattered all over the place, Mark continued the fight scene, finishing it before being rushed to the hospital. In my opinion, that was the most realistic fight scene done in front of an audience!

From those humble beginnings, Mark has become a well-known star, both in the United States and throughout Europe, Russia, and the countries in the South Pacific. I will not list all of Mark's accomplishments, but I do want to touch on just a few and give you an idea about how Mark has greatly contributed to the Dacascos legacy.

After spending years training with Malia and myself, both in the U.S. and in Germany, Mark moved back to the United States and soon entered college at Los Angeles Valley College. He joined their 1983-1984 Gymnastics Team coached by Gary Honjio, and excelled in gymnastics, which complimented his already proficient martial arts skills.

Mark is proficient in my expression of martial arts, Wun Hop Kuen Do, and has studied Muay Thai with Kru Puk, Capoeira with Mestre Amen Santo, and Wushu with coaches Eric and Debbie Chen. As a father, I think he is great in each of those styles, but Mark readily admits that he is still very much a beginner/intermediate student in those arts.

Mark got into acting and starring in many Hollywood movies. He married actress, Julie Condra, and together, they have two sons and a daughter, Makoa, Kapono, and Noelani. All of his children were born in Hawaii.

He met Julie when she was starring with him in a movie called, *Crying Freeman*, where they played a couple falling in love with each other. This role turned into more than acting for both of them. I clearly remember the day when Mark called me on the phone, after doing the love scene with Julie in Vancouver, Canada. He told me that the love scene was so real that he felt like he was falling in love with her for real. Now they live happily together and have a wonderful family. I am very happy for him.

Mark has dabbled in many different careers over his lifetime. During his last year in Germany, Mark got into fashion modeling for the *Italian Vogue Magazine*. He also performed with the Dacascos Show Team throughout Europe and on European National Television, which gave him some great exposure.

After he returned to the States, Mark was discovered by a talent agent. In 1983, Mark was walking down a street in San Francisco's Chinatown, when Chris Lee noticed him. That was the start of his acting career. Chris Lee was the assistant director for Wayne Wang's film, *Dim Sum: A Little Bit of Heart*.

Though his first scenes ended up on the cutting room floor, Mark was still very pleased with his performance. When I asked him why, he replied that he got to do a kissing scene with the famous Chinese actress, Joan Chan, on the hood of a car. It was at that point that he decided to seek an acting career.

Mark went on to establish a film and television career, primarily playing in martial arts films, although he has done parts in the television series, *General Hospital*, as well as other shows.

His martial arts expertise came into play when one of the characters on the set, who was suppose to be playing a Karate instructor, did not show up one day. Mark replaced him and began to be noticed even more. That is when his career really started to take off.

He was originally set to play the Red Ranger in a film titled, *Bio Man*, by Haim Saban. The film was never picked up but later evolved into the *Mighty Morphin Power Rangers*.

His breakout role, however, was in the 1993 film, *Only the Strong*. In this movie, Mark played Louis, a Capoeira master who takes a high school's potential failures and turns their lives around by teaching them the Brazilian martial art, Capoeira, an art based on the West African martial art. *Only the Strong* really launched Mark's career as a movie star.

After the success of *Only the Strong*, Mark found parts in *Party of Five, Double Dragon, Brotherhood of the Wolf, Crying Freeman, Cradle 2 the Grave* (with Jet Lee), and many other movies, including the movie that we just completed, *Showdown in Manila*, for which I was the fight coordinator.

He also performed in three video games, doing the voice over in *Stranglehold*, acting in *Wing Commander IV: The Price of Freedom*, and digitally recreating The Chairman in the *Iron Chef America: Supreme Cuisine* video game for Wii. Mark's career in acting has really taken off!

Mark was nominated for the Saturn Award for Best Supporting Actor in 2002 for his role in *Brotherhood of the Wolf*. He has also appeared in the television series, *The Crow: Stairway to Heaven*, which was a follow up to the 1994 film, *The Crow*.

He also participated in season nine of *Dancing with the Stars* and has landed roles on *Hawaii Five-O, Chicago P.D., Secret of the Sultan*, and currently has a reoccurring role on ABC's *Marvel's Agents of S.H.I.E.L.D.*, playing Giyera, the head of security for S.H.I.E.L.D. To date, Mark has 45 films and 26 television series roles to his name, plus an exceptional documentary on the History Channel on the life of Miyomoto Musashi.

Most people today know Mark as the Chairman on the Food Network's *Iron Chef America*. In this series, the back story is that he is the nephew of Takeshi Kaga, the original Japanese Iron Chef, although the actors have no family connection in real life.

Mark's accomplishments have amazed me, as his father. I am so proud of what Mark has done with his life and the man that he is today. He is a great husband and father and has an amazing family and career. He has put the icing on the cake of my family's martial arts legacy!

Mark at 5 years old, fighting Jim Hawkins, Jr. in Boulder, CO

Mark and me on the cover of Inside Kung Fu Magazine in 2002

Mark and me on the cover of MidWeek in 2010

Mark's first big movie roll, Only the Strong

Mark with Jet Li at the premier of Cradle to Grave

Mark on the set of Hawaii 5-0

A Fatherly kiss

Mark on the cover of COMBAT Magazine in the U.K.

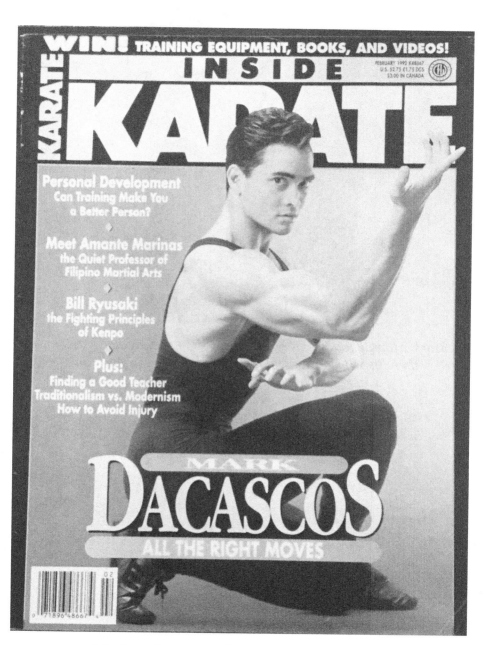

Mark on the cover of Inside Karate Magazine

*Mark's family today - in Mark's arm's is his daughter Naelani,
then his wife, Julie, and his brother Craig, in the front
row is his sons Kapono & Makoa
photo taken in 2014*

Chapter 12

History of Kajukenbo and Wun Hop Kuen Do

The secret of change is to focus all of your energy
not on fighting the old, but on building the new.
Socrates

I get so many questions from people within my own organization, as well as, from people who have nothing to do with martial arts at all. While it is impossible to address all of them in this short chapter of *LEGACY*, I will spend a little time and address some of the more important questions and give you some background about why Wun Hop Kuen Do was developed.

Many of you, who are reading this book, already know what martial arts are about, or at least you think you do. I truly don't think that any one person could answer that question precisely, in any way except to say that the martial arts mean military arts.

So I will ask, what are our military arts? Here again, we run into an abundance of questions and many different answers, all of them probably correct in some way, but lacking in others. Let's just focus on my contribution to the martial arts community, and especially my martial arts roots, which are in Kajukenbo, Tum-pai, Ch'uan fa, and Wun Hop Kuen Do. These may already present confusion to many of you.

For me, the martial arts are about discovering the truth within our very own backyard, however painful it may be. During my journey in Kajukenbo, I was led to believe and trust in what I had been told. I was told to follow, without question, what was told to me about the history, techniques, concepts, principles, etcetera, of Kajukenbo. I was even blinded at times, as I was taught that this art was *the only way*.

I find it so ironic that the martial arts world has so many people who profess that their way is the only way. This is where ego and the trait of being humble, which we are taught is a major component of the martial arts, are in conflict. As the old maxim states, there are many paths that lead to the top of the mountain. I finally realized that many will distort the truth for their own gains.

We were taught that Kajukenbo was formed by the so-called Black Belt Society, with five co-founders or contributors, in the period from 1947–1949. Strangely enough, a deeper investigation proves that only two of the five were black belts during those years, and that a third individual did not even receive his black belt until 1961. This was the same year that Al Dela Cruz earned his black belt from our instructor, Sid Asuncion, in Kempo Karate.

There is a lot of controversy about when Kajukenbo was started, how it was started, why it was started, and who the original people who were involved in it were. Because this subject is so extensive, I won't delve into it in this book, but I will be covering it in detail in my next book titled, *The Kajukenbo Bible* (working title). I will simply touch on a few things here about Kajukenbo and the martial arts as a whole.

As of the date that I am writing this, the two most credible books on Kajukenbo, and the ones most used as a source of information, are both written by John Bishop. His first book is called, *Kajukenbo: The Original Mixed Martial Arts*, published in 2006. The second book is called: *Kajukenbo: The Emperado Legacy*, published in 2011. Both of these books have very good reference materials.

The Kajukenbo system is developed with Kempo Karate at its core, which is defined by its hard style, Hung Ga, movements. For the sake of simplicity, and to avoid arguments, let's say that the main source of the hard style after 1949 was Adriano D. Emperado.

The Tum-Pai style, or branch, was an attempt by Emperado and Al Dela Cruz to incorporate more Chinese elements into the system. This happened around 1962–1963. This was considered the second style or branch of Kajukenbo, which fused Southern Style Gung Fu and hints of Tai-Chi Ch'uan movements together. Of course, this rubbed some people the wrong way and caused some conflicts. There will always be some people who are uncomfortable with change.

I was pulled into this conflict and eventually became the third person because of my previous experience with another Southern Style of Gung Fu, Choy Li Fut. This, along with my limited experience with Sil-lum Pai, meant that I was the low man on the totem pole. But I did not mind.

In the winter of 1964, I moved to the San Francisco Bay area and established my association with many of the Chinese martial artists in the area. One group, in particular, was the San Jose Chinese Physical Cultural Center. The instructor, Paul Ng, taught a Southern Style Kung Fu called Fu-Chow.

There were some noted practitioners in this small group – Kam Yuen, who was hired by David Chow to help choreograph the television series, *Kung Fu*, during the 1970's, and my classmate, Ron

Lew, of the Tai Mantis system, who eventually became a top instructor of Cacoy Canete's Doce Pares Eskrima.

The other group that I trained with was the Jing Mo Association. The focus of this group was to learn the Northern Sil-lum or Pak-Pai system from Professor Wong Jack Man. After a couple of years of training with this group and incorporating what I had learned into Emperado's Kajukenbo, Tum-Pai started to conflict with our style, as various forms were implemented, changing the core of the Tum-Pai style.

It was agreed between the three of us that we would drop the name Tum-Pai in favor of a more generic Chinese name, and that was the birth of Kajukenbo Ch'uan fa.

Little did we know, another Kajukenbo practitioner, Jon Loren, then of Kelso, Washington, had begun to resurrect Tum-Pai in 1971, incorporating Tai Chi, Southern Sil-Lum, Pak Qu, Hsing Yi, and the extensive study of Chinese herbs and medicine.

In 1974, while staying with Adriano Emperado in Hawaii, Loren demonstrated his concepts and techniques, and asked if he could call it Tum-Pai and bring the name back to life. Emperado granted permission with the acknowledgment that the original Tum-Pai followed a different path than the revised soft style.

Tum-Pai was formally recognized back into the system April 14, 1984, during a meeting in Cornelius, Oregon. In reality, the Tum-Pai section has two lives, one that was started back in Hawaii in 1963, Kajukenbo Tum-Pai, and the other, which was started in 1974, but not officially recognized until 10 years later. It came to be known as Kajukenbo Northern Tum-Pai.

Kajukenbo Ch'uan fa became the official third branch in 1966. It was at this time that major changes were taking place, as Emperado had required all schools to adopt Chinese titles to replace the Japanese titles.

He also required the new yin yang logo and emblem, which I designed for my own school, to now be the international logo and emblem for all Kajukenbo. This was implemented during the formation and incorporation of the newly formed Kajukenbo Association of America, the KAA.

The original Kajukenbo Ch'uan fa had a written system of 82 training exercises, drills, and requirements to teach the concepts and the principles of the new Kajukenbo Ch'uan fa style or branch. At the time, it was Emperado's desire to have all of the existing Kajukenbo schools convert to the new Ch'uan fa style.

Al Dela Cruz was given the assignment to teach the new Ch'uan fa to the Kajukenbo instructors in Hawaii, and I was to do the same with the instructors in California. Emperado would then be the figurehead of this new branch headed by Emperado, Dela Cruz and myself.

The conversion to this new style of Kajukenbo was met with some resistance by a number of instructors who preferred the original "hard style" kajukenbo. Emperado, being very understanding, allowed those instructors to continue to teach the original style. Some of the instructors chose to develop their own method of Ch'uan fa, and thus began the disarray of any concrete method of Ch'uan fa that exists to this very day. It was simply one of those cases of too many cooks in the kitchen.

This disarray only widened the gap between the hard style and soft style Kajukenbo practitioners within the system, causing political conflicts. Humbleness began to give way to out of control egos, which caused unity to deteriorate and also caused more misunderstandings.

For example, the system is Kajukenbo. The style, or branch, is the four officially recognized styles, Kempo Karate, Tum-Pai, Ch'uan fa, and Wun Hop Kuen Do. The methods would be the names of the instructors teaching that specific style or branch. Lastly, your expression, or interpretation of that method would be your own. The order then would be – the system, style or branch, method, and self-expression or interpretation.

The adoption of Wun Hop Kuen Do (WHKD), in 1969, would be the last officially recognized evolution change for the Kajukenbo system and was solely my brainchild. The materials in WHKD can stand alone and be totally independent, but out of respect for our roots in the Kajukenbo system, students must learn many of the hard style Kempo Karate concepts that were passed down from Emperado to Sid Asuncion and then to me.

This gave my students a more well-rounded understanding of the entire system of Kajukenbo and its different branches, of which I have been involved in all four. WHKD literally means "combination fist art style" or "self-expression way."

WHKD continues to evolve, just like the other branches and methods. While it adheres to its "Redbook" as a foundation for its tradition, it is not a fixed style. It contains a written system of techniques, training methods and philosophies.

It is important that the students understand the reasons behind what they are learning – WHY, HOW, and WHAT. These need to be understood completely to be a mature martial artist. I would like to think that WHKD accomplishes this. This process is a physical attribute, but philosophically, it can be applied to life itself. The result is a system of training methods and maneuvers that teaches one to be system-less, utilizing technical fighting principles and concepts in seven different ranges.

There are five parts of this process that I teach in WHKD:

1) Be aware
2) Be first
3) Be fast
4) Hit hard
5) Don't stop until it is over

The five phases of progress are learned as follows:

1) Primitive – everything present at this is very foreign
2) Mechanical – learning the movements
3) Technical – the how to
4) Creative – learning to think and respond independently
5) Fluidity – fluid to move from one technique to the other

Its trademark is a series of uniquely designed buzz saw drills. WHKD can be compared to jazz. It floats and flies all over the place, much like a jam session, and yet you have the distinct interpretation or self-expression of the song. Like music, it crosses over language barriers and is understood by everyone. Music is heard and is pleasant to the ears. WHKD techniques flow from one note to the other and are visual.

The attributes are there, just like the music notes. Placement and penetration (P&P) defines the result of the damage from the technique. The attitude is the emotional feeling that enhances the target placement and the degree of penetration, thus you are effective and the technique is felt emotionally.

Rhythm is another important component of WHKD. Rhythm can strike as full notes, half notes, quarter notes, and so on – high or low, soft or hard, or a low tune or loud tune. I have found that those that understand the language of music, especially jazz, tend to understand the rhythm and striking of martial arts. They understand the rhythm of life's ups and downs.

Seldom are the moves duplicated, since it is always evolving and moving; it is not fixed. It works more with kinetic and spontaneous drills rather than static traditional movements. Fighting is a higher form of playing. Watch kittens as they play. They are horning their skills for future fights and they will need those skills to survive. It is the same for armies when they play war games, as it is for you when you spar in class – Hard in Training, Easy in Battle. Train the way you fight and fight the way you train. Other hybrids would extend out of the three major branches, sometimes calling or naming their own methods or expressions, with or without any acknowledgment or official sanctioning from Emperado, Dela Cruz or myself.

While Kajukenbo has its solid foundation, it is much like a tree. The tree trunk, with its roots solidly anchored into the ground, is one, but its branches, which are many, begin to spread out, seeking the best sun light they can find in order to grow even stronger. The branches of Kajukenbo are just like the branches of the tree; they continue to search for more light, more perfection of the system, in order to bear more fruit. Those who stay in the shade wither away and perish.

In 1967, the Kajukenbo organization was going strong. At that time, it was called the Kajukenbo Association of America (KAA) and then split into another organization called the International Kajukenbo Association (IKA) in 1969-1976. The split was an attempt to strengthen Kajukenbo worldwide instead of just nationally.

Alejo Reyes was the president and chairperson until he passed on unexpectedly and the organization went into hiatus. It resurfaced to become even stronger in 1987-1995, when Adriano D. Emperado contacted me and my student, Bill Owens, to help reorganize Kajukenbo. At that time, Emperado believed that he did not have much longer to live, as he was battling a heart condition.

During this period, the IKA had the largest membership of Kajukenbo practitioners in the world. The meetings were run very professionally and were conducted in a formal manner. Coats and ties were required for all international meetings. It seemed that everyone was serious about building our organization.

The main strength of the organization was that we had a quarterly newsletter; that was before the invention of the internet. We had our own monitored Kajukenbo black belt family tree.

Three presidents served during that time – Alan Reyes, Tony Ramos, and me. We conducted quarterly seminars throughout the country and even had our yearly International Kajukenbo Association Open Championships.

Personally, I believe its demise came after I wrote an article in one of our quarterly newsletters in which I introduced "The Other Emperado." From that point on, the IKA was sabotaged, as a splinter group was formed called the Emperado Kajukenbo Association (EKA). Essentially, it was a coup d'état. After that, there was a resurgence of the Kajukenbo Self-Defense Institute (KSDI).

Like every other martial art in today's world, Kajukenbo has its share of politics that can play a part in both the organization and the life of the individuals who participate in the art.

The late Grandmaster, Joe Halbuna, once said at a board meeting, "Some individuals in Kajukenbo behave like the Hawaiian crab. Whenever there's one that is climbing out of the bucket, the others pull him back down." This seems to be a truism in martial arts today. I have seen this so many times in my personal growth, especially when "climbing out of the bucket" and thinking outside of the box.

Unfortunately, every organization will have a Judas or a Benedict Arnold in it at one time or another. It seems that no one escapes the betrayal of trust in our world. The best that we can do is to deal with those kinds of people, and the results of their malicious actions, and move on, becoming stronger than we were before. We can never let people like that make us forget our ultimate objectives.

As the fulfillment of my legacy is reaching full circle with such passion, it is giving the Kajukenbo grandmasters the visualization and honored completion of a dream come true. We have seen firsthand the evolution of Kajukenbo through students openly sharing and exchanging their knowledge across every style, system and organization, without prejudice. This has been done through the natural understanding and guidance of the Kajukenbo Ohana Association (KOA) members. The students and masters have learned from each other and the Ohana (Family) has moved beyond all prejudices.

The evolution of Kajukenbo has come full circle. KOA's *Back to the Roots* seminars have inspired masters and students alike. At The Kajukenbo United Reliance Martial Arts School in Utah in July of 2016, we fused several arts and disciplines into the Ohana. The KOA is a registered non-profit 5013c organization; as far as we know, it is one of the only active, registered Kajukenbo Mixed Martial Arts organizations. Four, eight hour days of intensive training at the school, and four nights of building Ohana at the home of GM Mike and Teresa Sandos, left me with great joy. I knew that my dreams and passion of building a better future for Kajukenbo were coming true and that the legacy of my life was on the right path.

> *Circumstances are the rulers of the weak;*
> *they are but the instruments of the wise.*
> *Samuel Lover*

Since its inception the **KAJUKENBO** *SYSTEMS* has evolved into four main *STYLES* and these styles evolving into both major and minor *METHODS*, with individual *EXPRESSIONS* of the method being taught. The chronology from the system, to the style, to the method and expressions can be defined by the evolution timeline of the styles.

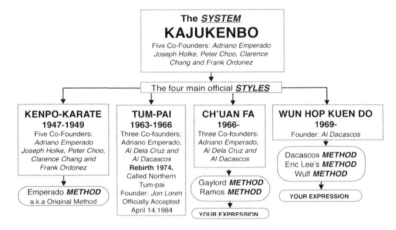

The above chart is just an example of some of the methods, and does not include all the methods and expressions.

The Kajukenbo Flowchart

Tony Ramos, Sid Asuncion, Al Dacascos, and Alejo Reyes

The original WHKD Black Belts in Germany in 2015
Winfred Josko, Dasos Efthadiadis, Michael Timmermann,
Al Dacascos, Christian Wulf, Jorn Tiedge and Emanuel Bettencourt

Me on the cover of the Spanish martial arts magazine Cinturon Negro

On the cover of Black Belt Magazine in 1976 – my first front cover!

On the cover of Black Belt Magazine in 1984

The Pacific NW Heat Seminar with Sifu Mike Mather and me
(photo compliments of Master Dan Haney)

Chapter 13

The World of Martial Arts Today

A friend tells you what you want to hear;
a best friend tells you the truth.
Marilyn Monroe

In 2007, I wrote a personal letter to Sijo Emperado sharing my opinion about the direction that I saw Kajukenbo heading. I meant no disrespect and had no intention of demonizing him, but I felt that those of us who really love the art should not stand by and do nothing when we see our beloved art heading down the wrong path.

I felt that somebody needed to step up and take responsibility and get Kajukenbo back on the right path before it was too late. I recall Master Mike Young telling me to simply do nothing and watch Kajukenbo destroy itself. Those words sent shivers down my spine!

Grand Master Ming Lum acknowledged Mike Young's conversation with me during his short visit to Hawaii. Of course, this was when both of these gentlemen were still alive; they have since passed away.

My letter to Sijo Emperado also acknowledged Master Young's conversation with me, during his short visit to Hawaii. The main purpose of the letter was to voice my concerns, as well as the concerns of many other grandmasters and black belts about the direction of Kajukenbo. Like a family, we did not always agree on everything, but we did listen to each other and respect each other's opinions. This is not true with everyone in Kajukenbo today.

I understood leadership and responsibilities. With that, I know the examples I set, whether good or bad, may be scrutinized and may be a lifelong burden to carry, perhaps even after I'm long gone. But as I expressed to Emperado, when I do speak, I call a spade a spade; there is no bull with me. I call things as I see them, with a pure heart and an open mind. I have no hidden agendas. I have to answer to God, and will not lie.

Aside from being a friend, a student, a supporter and a very active participant in the development of the other sections of Kajukenbo, Tum-Pai, Ch'uan fa and WHKD, I did, and still do, play an active role in the promotion of Kajukenbo and the name of Emperado worldwide.

But lately, I have stepped back and watched all of the chaos that now exists in Kajukenbo. And in my opinion, it has almost reached the point of premature destruction.

There is nothing truly new going on; it has been that way for the last 50 years. And during that time, I have been active and inactive, silent and vocal, frustrated and fulfilled, loved and of course, hated. I have had very loyal students and instructors and very disloyal students and instructors. I have dealt with some very honorable people and some very dishonorable people in the Kajukenbo family.

I have experienced both good and bad during my martial arts life in the Kajukenbo community. No one escapes sharing similar experiences, either in the martial arts world or in their personal life. The problems that I have seen in the Kajukenbo world are the same problems that I see in the world of martial arts as a whole.

We each leave behind our own legacy, either good or bad. Hopefully, when our eulogy is read to those few who respect us enough to honor our passing, we will be remembered as men and women of character, and those who knew us will be honored to carry on the legacy that we have created.

I hope that we are each remembered for our better accomplishments and humanitarian contributions, rather than our faults. We all have faults, and we all make mistakes. Our faults do not define us, if we are willing to acknowledge our faults and correct them. Our faults only plague us when we refuse to confront them.

With this knowledge in my heart, like Emperado, I am wiser and more experienced with my years, and I want to use this God-given wisdom to confront the challenges that lie before us all as the Kajukenbo family and as martial artists.

I loved Adriano Emperado as a father and a friend during the 1960's when Al Dela Cruz and I hung out with him in Honolulu. Back then, we were researching and developing a soft style to integrate into Kajukenbo, as I have already discussed in the last chapter. We shared the challenges that Emperado had with other Kajukenbo practitioners, at that time. We all began to understand each other's strengths and weaknesses, not only in the martial arts, but also as individuals in our everyday lives and with our families.

I don't believe that the Kajukenbo practitioners today can understand the bond that the three of us shared back then, and that Al Dela Cruz and I still share today. Our relationship was unique because of the development and growth that occurred during this time in the history of Kajukenbo.

In sorting out the confusion regarding the "Council" and the "Council of Grandmasters," all of us have been waiting for strong leadership, which in my personal opinion, has been too inconsistent and weak. Frankly, there are too many yes men and not enough people that are willing to stand up to make any constructive differences. I see this in every style of martial arts today.

I say this because we are all concerned about the integrity of Kajukenbo, which, in my opinion, has been eroding. I am seeing individuals who have no prior or credible experience in Kajukenbo, except by association. It seems that we are asked to support certain individuals, who many of us are reluctant to follow because others are much more battle tested and experienced.

I could not, in good conscience, lead my team into battle following a commander that has never been in a battle himself, but who is willing to take my whole team down with his inexperience. Am I supposed to blindly follow a leader who has less experience than those he professes to lead?

If one man on your team decides to take a risky jump off of a 20 foot cliff, does that mean that everyone on the team must make such a foolish jump along with him? A wise leader does not lead his team off a cliff. A wise leader must be experienced, must care about his team, and must listen to his advisors.

When I was President of the IKA, my son Mark knew of the problems I was dealing with and started to call me by the nickname "Pooper Scooper." What he meant by that was that he noticed that I was always cleaning up all the crap and doing damage control before things reached Emperado in a disrespectful and demeaning way.

In my opinion, Kajukenbo needs a team of damage control advisors. This would alleviate or diminish any further problems such as the ones that we seem to be continuously trying to clean up. It was Frederick Douglass that stated, "It is easier to build strong children than to repair broken men." It would be easier for us to do things correctly from the beginning, than to have to continually try to fix things through damage control.

It took twenty years, from 1984–2004, for me to go from 8th degree black belt to being awarded my 9th degree Grandmaster rank. I truly hope that this was based on my merits instead of Emperado's love for me, as some misguided individuals have claimed. I sincerely hope that all individuals are awarded rank according to their accomplishments, and merits, instead of by connections and/or financial motives. To do otherwise is to be dishonest.

I have been in meetings where I have had a grandmaster state that he did not like half of the grandmasters in the room. I believe that this man meant that half of the people in the meeting had questionable martial arts backgrounds. The falsification of martial arts rank in today's world is completely out of control.

Those who have questionable martial arts backgrounds are becoming a big problem throughout the martial arts world. It seems as if each week I hear about another so-called martial artist who has gone from a lower black belt to the rank of grandmaster almost overnight.

As I read through the list of people mentioned in the Kajukenbo Self-Defense Institute Board of Advisors, I know everyone of them. When Emperado promoted Charles Gaylord, Tony Ramos, Joe Halbuna, Alijo Reyes and myself to 5th degree black belt in Northern California in 1966, we were the very first guys from Hawaii and the mainland to be promoted to this rank by Emperado and Twinkle Kawakami, then the Chairman of the KSDI of Hawaii.

Most all of the guys on the list of advisors, with the exception of Al Dela Cruz, were still colored belts – some brown, some brown/black, and a few new black belts. I know of another first degree black belt who was accepted back into Kajukenbo, after a 20 year absence, as a 9th degree black belt! I also know of another person, who was never in Kajukenbo to start with, who was promoted to a high rank without even knowing the basics of Kajukenbo.

All of these situations only serve to lower the morale and integrity of our black belts. The *true* grandmasters of Kajukenbo have devoted many years and much effort in consistent training. Things like this cause them to question the worth and value of their own rank.

Again I ask you, with deep concern, how is it that some train consistently, with proven skills, for 45 years to get their 8th or 9th degree rank, while others, with no proven record, can manage to obtain this same rank in less than half the time? Is it that they train 24/7, 365 days a year? How is it that a student can bypass his or her own instructor's rank, which has happened more times than I care to remember in Kajukenbo?

Al Dela Cruz and I really never cared about rank; and to this day, we still don't. We knew that our own innovations, technical applications and knowledge of our history and the martial arts, as well as our worldwide contributions and recognition, meant much more than any belt rank could ever mean.

I stand on my merits alone. I dare anyone in Kajukenbo to say that they have had more credible accomplishments or have done more for

Kajukenbo than I have. I have proven my accomplishments in the martial arts world, and for me, accomplishments overrides politics.

In fact, I will go even further and say the line from Adriano Emperado to Joe Emperado, and to Sid Asuncion and then to me, has trained and cultivated more high profile name and champions for Emperado Kajukenbo than any other line in Kajukenbo. I will not list them all here, but the names and the numbers are very impressive.

In my opinion, if Kajukenbo is to survive this new millennium, it must correct its course or we will all crash. Most of the grandmasters, if they are being honest and could speak freely without fear of being reprimanded, would like to see big changes in Kajukenbo. Many are upset by what seems to be ranks which are *sold* instead of *earned*. I personally know of people who have paid up to $7,000 for rank promotion. Notice that I said, "paid," not earned.

According to Philip Galinas from Montreal, Canada, caretaker of the Kajukenbo family tree, there are over 8,400 names listed as black belts since the inception of Kajukenbo. Can you imagine that? The interesting part about this is that about 15% of the people on that list are listed twice and some are even listed three times.

Why is this being done? The answer is simply because some black belts jumped, transferred, or were promoted more than once from the various expressions of Kajukenbo and from different instructors. Still others were brought in from other styles such as Tae Kwon Do or Shotokan. These black belts were immediately promoted to the same rank or higher in Kajukenbo. Others were able to buy rank at an outrageous price or with certain "favors."

Also, this list is not complete because realistically, it would be almost impossible to record every name of every person that has ever reached the rank of black belt. Many have dropped off of the radar and others simply do not want to be listed and remain in the shadows. In addition, there are those who are on the list who merely have honorary black belts.

In my opinion, these people have no business being listed as a part of the Kajukenbo family tree. Conservatively, we could list another 1,500. All in all, if this practice continues, we could end up with a large legitimate family tree and one phony shrub. It is never an advantage to deceive yourself.

Now there is a movement to officially commit to an enforcing council so that we become more productive. Our tentative mission statement, for the Kajukenbo Ohana Association Council of Grand Masters is:

"The purpose and goal of KOA is to teach and enhance, protect and maintain the lineage, history, and reputation of the Kajukenbo martial art system in order to preserve the integrity of its founders and its foundation, under which a system of promotion, standardized techniques, training methods and certification can be established and recognized in an honorable and meaningful way."

The three section leaders, Al Dela Cruz – Chuan Fa; Jon Loren (now deceased) – Tum Pai and myself, Al Dacascos – Wun Hop Kuen Do, are committed to the true essence of Kajukenbo. The Kempo section has many great martial artists, but no strong individual stands out to me except for Don Nahulawa's group, which derives from Al Reyes's line.

Like us, there are many energetic individuals like Sam Allred, Tony Lasit, Carlos Bunda, Gary Forbach, Dann Baker, Alan Reyes, Robert New, Denise Guila, Bob Mashmier, Jay Vera and Dan Frazer, just to name a few that are genuinely serious about helping to keep Kajukenbo strong, honest, and thriving. However, there are those that use the word United or Unity, but actually divide our family instead.

And then there are those that I consider to be "parasite grandmasters." Some of these individuals, I know for a fact, have never trained any person, from white belt all the way up to a black belt, but have managed to "steal" or lure another instructor's black belt student by awarding him or her higher rank.

This has happened once too often and is not exclusive to the Kajukenbo system. I have witnessed this in other martial arts systems as well. One individual, a "grandmaster" in Hawaii, told me he had 200 Black Belts under him on the U.S. mainland. But the truth is that the only black belt he promoted on the island was a brown belt he lured to his dojo from another instructor. He hasn't trained anyone from white belt to black belt.

This same grandmaster hides behind a computer on Facebook and talks trash about others in some vain attempt to paint himself as a credible grandmaster. At the same time, he has the audacity to say that he was a WHKD black belt under my brother!

After confronting my brother, Ben, who lives in Oregon, he confirmed to me that this grandmaster was never even a black belt, or even a student under him. This is nothing short of fraud, but it happens all the time in the martial arts world. The world of martial arts is full of frauds, pretenders who are martial artists in name only. This is really not the way that martial arts were supposed to be.

The house of Kajukenbo has many rooms. While the majority of Kajukenbo practitioners are sincere and dedicated, they seem to congregate in the kitchen and in the living room. The people socialize, love to learn, and are happy, loving, beautiful people.

Then there are the few that cause all the problems and chaos. They are the few, the bad, the ugly, and the hateful that crowd themselves in the basement or into dark closets, never coming out to socialize in the light, but rather hanging out in the dark crevasses, or in the toilet, which is the appropriate place for their crap.

Unfortunately for the individuals who hang out in these confined spaces, they come out with that lingering smell that follows them everywhere they go. They hate to come out into the light, for the light shows them for exactly who and what they are. It shows their lack of honesty and integrity. Their lies are easily visible in the light, as is the fact that they are not who or what they claim to be.

These people are easily recognizable just by their egotism, their lack of respect or manners, their arrogance, their hate, and their rude demeanor. Instead of working to improve themselves, they constantly attack other martial artists. These people are con men and parasites, hypocrites, and liars. Instead of removing the plank in their own eye, they actively search for the splinter in someone else's.

These people seem to be growing in number in the martial arts world. Those of us who love the martial arts need to take control and clean up our own house! Jesus stated, "Do not give dogs what is holy; do not throw your pearls before swine. If you do, they may trample them under their feet, and then turn and tear you to pieces." This is a perfect description of this kind of person.

So where do I go from here, knowing my circle of influence? I have had many accomplishments and scores of great students, many of which help to promote martial arts in a positive manner. Then there are those few that have destroyed the trust and confidence I once had in them. These people were at one time part of my elite group. One of them, in Hamburg, Germany, jumped rank and proclaimed himself a grandmaster of Kajukenbo WHKD, a pure disappointment to the thousands of students in Germany.

Another student, who I trained from his early teenage years as a white belt all the way up to his 6th degree level professor, betrayed me when he was promoted to grandmaster by Emperado over me. Maybe it was not entirely his fault. As the old saying goes, it takes two to tango. Emperado broke his own rules and took on a student he had never trained and placed that student directly under him without any regards for me.

I am not alone, as this has happened to other black belts. Many instructors have lost their students in the same manner to Emperado. For this, I can forgive him, but I can never forget the damage it caused. Many have suffered the same fate in Kajukenbo, going back many decades.

I had one student, who was one of my best students when it came to self-defense. He had the technical skills, but he lacked the character to remain loyal to me. He accepted a higher rank than my rank, from Emperado, which was an insult to me as his teacher.

To add insult to injury, he stated that I was only his "elementary teacher." How ludicrous is that! For whatever reason, his anger with me was blistering. His satisfaction in seeing himself as a higher rank than his teacher was nothing short of blasphemy.

The story behind the veil always goes much deeper than we see on the surface and the animosities between the different camps are profound. Bill Owens, Eric Lee and Malia, all black belts of mine, were all caught off guard when Emperado called them onstage, at a tournament, and promoted all of them to a higher rank. I had another student who was also promoted at this time; he was the only one that knew that the mass promotion was to take place. If would seem that his ego got the best of him.

The other three had no idea, and even if they did accept the rank on stage, to save face for Emperado, off stage they destroyed or put the certificate away and never boasted about it as my other student did. Bill Owens, Eric Lee, and Malia gained much respect from others, as well as from me, for their loyalty and how they handled this situation.

I was betrayed and lost my respect for both my student, who I will not even honor enough to mention his name, and for Emperado. I had been betrayed by both my teacher and my student, and by both at the same time! Things from that point on would never be quite the same. While this incident was bad, it would not be the last time that I would be betrayed by someone that I trusted.

Here I must clarify another point concerning Adriano Emperado. Emperado passed away in April, 2009 in Hale Makua, Wailuku, Mau'i Hospital. The last person to see Emperado alive was his caregiver. The person given the right of power of attorney was Kalani Koa, whom Emperado appointed prior to his death.

Ayao Koa, brother of Kalani, stood in as second and Emperado's stepdaughter, Veronica Kaawa, and Dennis Kanemitsu, a captain on the Mau'i Police Department, were the only four in his room at the time of his passing. This is documented and can be proven without a shadow of a doubt.

Now, you may be wondering why I am even addressing Emperado's death. The answer has to do with another problem in the martial arts world. It has become commonplace for unscrupulous people to make untrue claims about their friendship or training with a grandmaster after his death. Unfortunately, Emperado has been the victim of such despicable actions.

I know of a certain person who claims to have been the last person to see Emperado alive. It has been proven that he has lied about this. As a matter of fact, Emperado's personal bodyguard stated that this person never even went to Hawaii for Emperado's funeral. Others, from as far away as Europe and South America, went out of their way to come to Hawaii to pay their respects to Emperado.

Two months before his passing, Sifu Mike Young (now deceased), Al Dela Cruz, and myself visited Emperado in his hospital room on Mau'i. At that time, he confided to us that he had made a lot of mistakes in Kajukenbo. He stated that one of his biggest regrets was allowing my student who betrayed me, to have Emperado's signature on the certificates that he *reluctantly* signed.

He even went on to say that the certificates which this unscrupulous guy had, would become null and void immediately after Emperado's passing. We had no idea that Emperado would even bring up such subjects with us. Unfortunately, we did not have a recorder to document what was said, but I can assure you that all parties involved know the truth.

Unscrupulous, deceitful people in the martial arts seem to go to any length to stroke their own ego and to build a house of cards that may fool many people, but there will always be those who know the truth. To use someone's death as a way to try to make yourself look important, is disgraceful. Not only is it disgraceful, but it is also dishonest and shows a lack of character. The man or woman that does such a thing has no honor.

The most recent betrayal of my trust occurred in 2015. It was such a shock to me that I could hardly believe it. This guy was the best man at my wedding in 2000. He was the godfather to my daughter and a trusted student that I endorsed to lead the Dacascos Tactical System, (DTS), but we all have our own Judases and Benedict Arnolds.

This was another example of character, honor, integrity, humility, trustworthiness, and loyalty getting superseded by egotism, arrogance, deceitfulness, conceit, and treachery. The same student, who had previously betrayed me, lured one of my students away from me by offering to promote him from 4th degree black belt to 6th degree black belt.

I was raised to forgive, and I have. But to forget would be to lose the lesson learned about the character of these two people. Always expect a snake to behave as a snake. If you forget the traits of the snake and expect it to act like a loyal dog, you will get bitten every time.

I hope that one day, all these deceitful, fraudulent, and dishonorable actions will be a thing of the past in the martial arts community and that we can be a true family. I yearn for the day that the Kajukenbo Ohana can truly be a family.

We, as leaders in the martial arts community, must lead by example. As Gandhi said, we must be the change in the world that we wish to see.

I pray that someday, martial artists will take Frank Ordonez's Kajukenbo Prayer literally, just as it was written in the 1950's. The prayer is recited at the beginning and end of each class, but apparently, it is nothing more than rote memorization for some people.

When reciting the prayer, students kneel on the right knee, with the right fist down on the floor, and left forearm resting across the left thigh. The original version was made for the United States and founded on Christian principles.

"Almighty and Eternal God, Protector of all who put their trust in Thee, accept the humble homage of our faith and love in Thee, the One True God. Bless our efforts to preserve the integrity of our United States, a nation founded on Christian principles, enlighten our rules, guide our lawmakers, protect the sanctity of our homes. Bless our efforts in these exercises whose sole purpose is to develop our bodies, to keep others mindful of Thy commandments, give us perseverance in our actions that we may use this as a means to keep closer to You, the One True God in the name of Thy beloved son, Jesus Christ our Lord. Amen"

Other Kajukenbo schools throughout the world have adopted the Kajukenbo prayer, but have modified it to their country. After reflecting on the Kajukenbo Prayer and studying the true meaning behind it, I am struck by how easy it would be to fix all of our problems if we would simply take every single word in this prayer to heart. We have forgotten that the Kajukenbo Prayer is the root of the tree that produced each of its branches. We have forgotten God.

How do we go about fixing all the problems within Kajukenbo, and the rest of the martial arts world, which has excessive numbers of grandmasters coming out of the wood work? The answer might be forming an international, a national, and a regional Council of Elders for each system.

As an example, the International Kajukenbo Council of Elders would be the overseer of Kajukenbo activities throughout the world. The National Council of Elders would oversee the Kajukenbo activities in each country, and the Regional Council of Elders would oversee smaller regions of Kajukenbo activities.

These elders would have to be over 70 years old, actively training, or teaching, and have an established record that is credible, with traceable lineage, and documentation of over 50 years in the martial arts.

There would be no more than 12 individuals on each council. Their wisdom and experience would be greatly treasured, as they would have to use their years of experience and wisdom to advise the senior grandmasters and masters down the line. Hopefully, this would be a means to help control all the loose cannons out there and try to bring legitimacy and integrity back into the martial arts.

May 28, 2016 four of my original first generation black belts were promoted to the rank of grandmaster, a title well-deserved for their personal growth and accomplishments. Christian Wulf, Dasos Efthadiadis, Michael Timmermann and Jorn Tiedge all celebrated their rank promotion in a heartfelt ceremony.

The promotion of these four Kajukenbo WHKD Grandmasters in Europe was not only warranted, but was also a good for WHKD in Europe. These four gentlemen are the *ONLY LEGITIMATE* WHKD Grandmasters in Europe.

There is another 1st generation WHKD black belt in Europe who decided to falsely promote himself to grandmaster and to erroneously place himself above his senior classmates. During belt promotions, he had a visiting grandmaster, Malia Bernal, attend the promotion event and sign everyone's certificate. This guy deviously slipped his self-promoted certificate into the batch and Malia signed it unknowingly. He had successfully conned Malia into signing his own promotion.

It's amazing how some instructors will go to any length to promote themselves. I have seen others pull this same underhanded stunt. They take a batch of certificates and rush the signer to get them all signed. Of course the master who is signing the certificates does not stop and read each one, as he or she is trusting the instructor to give her the certificates that should be signed for the promotion. I've seen this happened all too often. Even Emperado has signed certificates, thinking he had ten to sign, but a couple slipped in and he lost count.

I want to strongly emphasize that ***there are no other Kajukenbo WHKD Grandmasters in Europe besides the four gentlemen that I have mentioned***. In a couple of years, Emmanuel Bettancourt, Winfred Jozsko, and Mark Dacascos could be joining their ranks. They have the accomplishments to warrant advancement now, but lack the time. In the United States, only four other individuals holds the title of Grandmaster in Kajukenbo WHKD. Mike Sandos of Salt Lake City, Utah; Eric Lee of Los Angeles; Malia Bernal of San Jose; and Doug Jones of Oakland California.

It is high time for those of us who truly care about the future of the martial arts to step up and put an end to the chicanery in the martial arts world. We as true martial artists should be men and women of honor and integrity, not liars and conmen. We should have the highest standards. We should live a life of humility and not allow our egos to get the best of us. In my opinion, The National Council of Elders would be a giant step in the right direction.

Art Camacho, Don Wilson, Al Dacascos, Olivier Gruner

The Elite Hall of Fame in San Jose, California, October 29, 2016. (A special thank you to Master Andrew Fanelli for getting so many great martial arts masters together for one big event!)

The ONLY WHKD Grand Masters in Europe at this time:
Left to right: Michael Timmermann, Dasos Efthadiadis,
Al Dacascos, Christian Wulf, and Jorn Tiedge

Four of the original founders of Kajukenbo in 1996
From left to right: Peter Choo, Joe Holke, Frank Ordonez,
Sitting: Andriano D. Emperado

Me on the cover of Inside Kung Fu magazine in 1992

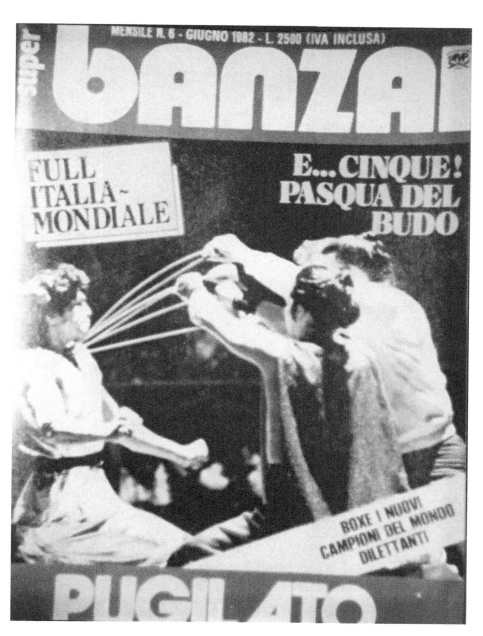

On the cover of the Italian magazine, Banzai

Mike Mathers, me and KOA president Mike Sandos

Chapter 14

Final Thoughts

*Yesterday is history, tomorrow is a mystery, today
is a gift of God, which is why we call it the present.*
Bil Keane

I often look back on my life and think about the many decades that I have taught martial arts and the thousands upon thousands of repetitions of kicks and punches that I have thrown. I still remember the names and faces of the hundreds of students, friends, and enemies who have been a part of my life. I meditate often on my mindset, the way I view the world from the perspective of a martial artist, and how the years have changed my perspectives on many subjects, in many ways.

A few nights ago, I was sitting at my desk. On the wall in front of me were pictures of my children. I began to think about what genetic traits were passed down from me to my kids, and what ideas and concepts I had nurtured in them during their childhoods.

As a martial artist, my mindset was constantly thinking about situations, coverage, angles, and the whole "smarter versus harder" concept of the martial arts. This mental practice and the magnitude of mental repetitions and visualizations changed the way that I think.

Not only did it change the way I think, but it also physically changed the way my brain works. All those years of repetition and all those neural pathways that were forged over the years were now second nature to me. I had changed my brain's circuitry over all those decades, through repetition of the mental process of martial arts discipline.

I know that it changed me physically as well. Just as the process of evolution unfolds over millions of years, that same process still works today, but on a smaller, faster level. Genetics are passed down from parent to child. The thought of this gives me a warm feeling in my heart.

I know that my efforts in the martial arts, which have spanned over a whole lifetime, have altered, not only the neurological pathways of my brain, they have also altered the sinew in my muscle, the density in my bones, and the flexibility of my tendons. All of those things come together as a genetic package, a package that I am happy to say I am extremely proud to have put together.

So I find myself sitting here at my desk, looking at the pictures of my children on the wall, and really enjoying the epiphany that I have just had about how my decision to become a martial artist, a martial arts instructor, to open various schools, and to engage the world, have changed me, and how those changes have been passed down to my kids. Thinking about this put a smile on my face as I ponder the lives of each one of the children that God has blessed me with and entrusted me to raise to become quality men and women. What trust God must have had in me to make me the father of these wonderful children!

Then I had another epiphany. If my legacy has been passed down to my children because of my decisions in life and how they have changed me, then hasn't my legacy been passed down to my students as well? Weren't their lives profoundly affected, just like mine and my children's were?

Of course! Their lives have been profoundly affected, just like mine. This is the type of legacy I can get behind! And this is the legacy that you want to leave behind as well. You want your existence to have a profound, positive effect on those around you. I humbly pursue this and hope for the best in every case, with every person that I come across. My dedication to the martial arts is a large part of my legacy and passing that legacy on is the largest reward I have ever received, other than my relationship with my Lord Jesus Christ.

I still teach a very small and dedicated group of individuals, many times in my garage, and other times in our other location in Pearl City, a suburb outside of Honolulu. Now, my first love is for God. I regularly attend the men's worship group at my church and share my testimony about how God saved me and turned my life around.

I have found that teaching the martial arts is my second love and purpose for being on this earth. I teach whenever I can, to whoever wants to learn. I think that God gives us each a special purpose and talent in this life, and my gift is the martial arts. I have met so many quality people through the martial arts and it has greatly enriched my life.

Because of my love for the martial arts, I am always teaching wherever I go. I think that I can turn anything into a martial arts lesson. There is a great example that I can recall during the process of writing this book. I flew into Denver, Colorado to meet my publisher, Bohdi Sanders, and spend some time working on *Legacy*. We made the short drive from Denver to Bohdi's house, where I was staying.

After grabbing a quick burger, Bohdi, who is also a strong martial artist and practices Shotokan Karate, showed me his small dojo. Even though we were both tired, as it was late at night, I spent a while teaching some knife and gun disarming techniques. Here we were, just before midnight, training in Bohdi's basement, and both of us willing to train throughout the night, but we knew we needed to be fresh for the next day's work.

During my stay, we spent about as much time training and talking about martial arts philosophy as we did working on the book. I feel that God is now guiding my path. He led me to Bohdi, a man who shares the same philosophy on the martial arts and on spirituality as I do.

It seems that everywhere I go I always find a way to teach those who have a desire to learn. My life in the martial arts has truly been an adventure. It has been filled with joys, victories, and lifelong friendships, in addition to disappointments, heartbreaks, and betrayals.

Martial arts have always been a defining part of my life, especially when it comes to my roots and my heritage. My dedication to the martial arts, along with my faith in God, is a large part of my legacy. Passing that legacy on is the biggest reward of my life.

As I sit here, content in my thoughts, my mind begins to turn to other endeavors. Throughout my life, there have been many opportunities for personal growth. There were opportunities I gladly accepted and learned from, and others that I did not recognize until after the fact. Our perception is constantly changing. We can all learn from the events of our lives if we will simply be mindful of that fact.

Wisdom can be found almost everywhere we look. Throughout our lives, we only need to discover the wisdom that is in front of us and apply it to our lives. As the old saying goes, God gives the sunshine to everyone; how much enters your room depends on you.

Recently I was having a discussion with a long time student and friend. We were discussing a very common narrative in the martial arts culture, one that has been repeated hundreds of times over the years.

Many times a student feels as though a higher recognition and rank is deserved, but not received. That student becomes irritated with the teacher and allows his anger and frustration to guide his actions, bringing dishonor to his teacher and his fellow students.

Sometimes the student aligns himself with another teacher where he can find the validation he seeks. And most of the time, the other teacher is an antagonist of his original teacher. This is done out of some misguided desire for a measure of revenge by the student.

During our conversation, my student presented the following question, "How do you protect yourself from these kinds of dishonorable acts?" This is the first question that comes to most students' minds.

My answer is, "You don't." In this life, we are only responsible for our own actions. We can do our best to teach our students the way of honor and integrity, but we cannot force them to develop a Godly character. We can only do our part and hope that each student internalizes the wisdom that we are trying to teach. A good teacher can only teach; the student must be willing to learn.

It has always been my wish to be of service to others. Because of my desire to be of service to others, I have given my students, friends, and family my best. For many students, my best changed their lives for the better; and for that, I am truly honored.

For other students, my best wasn't enough for them, and they pursued a different path, with different motivations. You can never protect yourself from that, but if you are truly trying to serve others, God will protect you and guide your path.

In life, you must have enough faith to take chances when they are offered to you, and pray that God will watch over you as you travel your path. Sometimes, chances pay off, and at other times, they break your heart. But, as I get older, I am still compelled to take a chance on people.

We must do our best to serve people. We can't make them accept what we have to offer, but that shouldn't matter. We must do our part. I will always do my best to serve people and to help them on their journey, knowing that some will receive what I have to offer and some will reject it. I will do my best to serve people nonetheless.

One of my greatest wishes is to have peace and reconciliation between those that I may have hurt and those who have hurt me, especially those few who have betrayed me. My other wish is that those who cross my path may see the love of God in my life today and that they may find God's peace as well.

I hope that you have enjoyed this look into the adventure which has been my life. Writing my autobiography was a memorable walk through times past for me. It brought back so many memories. It brought me laughter, smiles, regrets, and tears. I have remembered so many things that I would have liked to have done differently, but as we all know, hindsight is always 20/20.

We each have so many memories tucked away in the dark recesses of our minds which we rarely access. I have been blessed to have had the opportunity to not only access mine, but to write them down in this book for you.

Do I have any regrets? Absolutely! But I wouldn't change a thing; otherwise I would not be the man I am now. All of it, the good, the bad, and the ugly, has contributed in some way to bringing me back to my beloved Hawaii and to a closer relationship with my Lord and Savior. I sincerely hope that my memoirs have blessed your life in some way and have encouraged you to never give up, no matter how tough your life may be at this time.

You may not see it today or tomorrow, but you will look back in a few years and be absolutely perplexed and awed by how every little thing adds up and brought you somewhere wonderful or where you always wanted to be.

Please Take a Couple of Minutes and Review LEGACY!

Reader reviews are very important to authors in today's fast-paced world and I value your opinion. Reviews are the lifeblood of the author. Posting a quick review on Amazon and on Facebook, and other social media, really helps authors out.

If you have enjoyed *LEGACY: Though the Eyes of the Warrior*, please consider taking just a couple of minutes and reviewing it on Amazon and on your social media pages. Also, please tell your friends about *LEGACY*. I would sincerely appreciate it.

Also, I would appreciate your feedback on my book. You can contact me at: SifuAl@aol.com.

Mahalo nui loa kakou!
Sifu Al

Other Titles by Kaizen Quest

Other Titles by Kaizen Quest

The
WARRIOR
ETHOS

Daily Motivation for Martial Artists and Warriors

Bohdi Sanders, Ph.D.

Foreword by Sifu Al Dacascos

Other Titles by Kaizen Quest

Other Titles by Kaizen Quest

Full List of Titles by Kaizen Quest

- *Modern Bushido: Living a Life of Excellence* by Bohdi Sanders

- *The Warrior Ethos* by Bohdi Sanders

- *LEGACY: Through the Eyes of the Warrior* by Al Dacascos

- *Men of the Code: Living as a Superior Man* by Bohdi Sanders

- *WARRIOR: The Way of Warriorhood* by Bohdi Sanders

- *Occam's Razor* by Howard Upton

- *Defensive Living: The Other Side of Self-Defense* by Bohdi Sanders

- *Wisdom of the Elders: The Ultimate Quote Book* by Bohdi Sanders

- *The Warrior Lifestyle* by Bohdi Sanders

- *Of Blood and Stone* by Howard Upton

- *Warrior Wisdom* by Bohdi Sanders

- *Secrets of the Soul* by Bohdi Sanders

- *Martial Arts Wisdom: Quotes, Maxims, Stories* by Bohdi Sanders

- *As a Man Thinketh* by James Allen

- *The Mastery of Destiny* by James Allen

- *The Martial Arts Woman* by Andrea Harkins

Made in the USA
Middletown, DE
20 February 2022